STRATEGIC SPORT DEVELOPMENT

The field of sport development is becoming ever more professional, with the levels of expertise in planning and efficiency required of those working in public, voluntary and commercial sport organisations higher than they have ever been. In response to this, strategic sport development has emerged as a means of applying business strategies to the context of sport development. *Strategic Sport Development* is the first book to directly address this important new field.

The book comprehensively explains the strategic concepts and techniques that sports students and practitioners across the UK and internationally need to understand. It includes:

- national and local case studies that appraise existing strategic management practice in sport development;
- separate full introductions to sport development and business strategy;
- a range of tasks and resources that encourages the reader to develop knowledge, skills and competencies through the application of theory to practical examples;
- the application of strategic management principles to the development of sport and development through sport;
- everything the reader needs to engage meaningfully with the relevant National Occupational Standards for the sport development profession.

Strategic Sport Development is designed to help students develop the practical skills needed to contribute to development strategy in a vocational context, and give practitioners the confidence and know-how to improve the strategic development of their sport organisation. This book is essential reading for all students and practitioners of strategic sport development, and a valuable resource for students of sport management or development in general.

Stephen Robson is a Senior Lecturer in Sport Development at Leeds Metropolitan University, UK. As well as leading the Sport Development degree, he also leads the teaching of strategic management. Stephen has extensive experience of working on national-level projects related to employability and CPD in strategic sport development.

Kirstie Simpson is Deputy Head of the Department of Sport and Exercise Science at the University of Chester, UK. She began her career in local authority sport development and is now leading programmes in Sport Development and Sport Coaching. Her main research interest lies in the monitoring and evaluation of sport interventions.

Lee Tucker is a Senior Lecturer in Sport Development at Leeds Metropolitan University, UK. He is currently doing a PhD examining the transformational potential of sport. His main research interests are around the sociology of sport as well as the politics of sport.

STRATEGIC SPORT DEVELOPMENT

**EDITED BY STEPHEN ROBSON,
KIRSTIE SIMPSON AND LEE TUCKER**

Routledge
Taylor & Francis Group

LONDON AND NEW YORK

First published 2013
by Routledge
2 Park Square, Milton Park, Abingdon, Oxon OX14 4RN

Simultaneously published in the USA and Canada
by Routledge
711 Third Avenue, New York, NY 10017

*Routledge is an imprint of the Taylor & Francis Group, an
informa business*

British Library Cataloguing in Publication Data
A catalogue record for this book is available from the British
Library

Library of Congress Cataloging in Publication Data
Strategic sport development / edited by Stephen Robson,
Kirstie Simpson and Lee Tucker. -- 1st ed.
p. cm.
1. Sports--Management. 2. Sports administration. I. Robson,
Stephen. II. Simpson, Kirstie. III. Tucker, Lee.
GV713.S77 2013
796.06'9--dc23
2012032503

ISBN: 978-0-415-54400-9 (hbk)
ISBN: 978-0-415-54401-6 (pbk)
ISBN: 978-0-203-87627-5 (ebk)

Typeset in Melior
by Saxon Graphics Ltd, Derby

MIX
Paper from
responsible sources
FSC
www.fsc.org   FSC® C013604   Printed and bound by CPI Group (UK) Ltd, Croydon, CR0 4YY

CONTENTS

2　THE INTERNAL ENVIRONMENT　　25

STEPHEN ROBSON, LEE TUCKER AND ROSEMARY LEACH

3　THE EXTERNAL ENVIRONMENT　　51

LEE TUCKER AND MATT SULLIVAN

vi

4   MAKING STRATEGIC CHOICES IN SPORT DEVELOPMENT   74

JAYNE WILSON

5 STRATEGIC PERFORMANCE MANAGEMENT 1: STRATEGIC IMPLEMENTATION — 96

STEPHEN ROBSON

6 STRATEGIC PERFORMANCE MANAGEMENT 2: EVALUATING STRATEGIC SPORT DEVELOPMENT — 119

KIRSTIE SIMPSON

viii

9 STRATEGIC LEADERSHIP 197

LEE TUCKER

10 A DIFFERENT BALL GAME? IN PURSUIT OF GREATER STRATEGIC COLLABORATION BETWEEN SPORT-SPECIFIC AND COMMUNITY SPORT DEVELOPMENT 217

JANINE PARTINGTON AND STEPHEN ROBSON

X

11 TOWARDS A 'COMMUNITY PRACTICE' APPROACH 241

STEPHEN ROBSON AND JANINE PARTINGTON WITH
ROSEMARY LEACH, LEE TUCKER AND KIRSTIE SIMPSON

LIST OF CONTRIBUTORS

Rosemary Leach is a Principal Lecturer in Sport at Sheffield Hallam University.

Janine Partington is a Senior Lecturer in Sport and Recreation Development at Leeds Metropolitan University.

Matt Sullivan is a former Lecturer in Sport and Recreation Development at Leeds Metropolitan University and is now a Physical Education teacher.

Jayne Wilson is a Principal Research Fellow in the Sport Industry Research Centre at Sheffield Hallam University.

ACKNOWLEDGEMENTS

The editors would like to place on record our sincere thanks to colleagues who have influenced our thinking, provided support and ideas or helped in some other way to get this book into print. First of all we must express our gratitude to Simon Whitmore and Joshua Wells at Routledge for their patience and steadfastness during what was an unexpectedly long gestation process. Colleagues at Leeds Metropolitan University who provided help and inspiration include Jeff Abrams, Louise Derdowski and Jim McKenna. Thank you also to Val Stevenson of Sheffield Hallam University. From the University of Chester, thanks go to John Mitchell, Daniel Bloyce and Ken Green. We are also very grateful to the practitioners who provided information in support of numerous case studies and examples used in the book: Kelly Simmonds at the Football Association; Stuart Johnson at Volleyball England; Ian Duckmanton from the Cheshire and Warrington County Sport Partnership; Jackie Veal from Bury MBC; Vicky Foster-Lloyd from Badminton England; Sue Haigh at Leeds City Council and Adam Fuller of Leeds North East School Sport Partnership.

The editors are especially grateful to one of our co-contributors, Janine Partington of Leeds Metropolitan University, for her unbending support and help, particularly during those periods when the light at the end of the tunnel was seemingly beyond our reach!

Finally, special thanks go to Rosemary Leach, who was so instrumental in developing the concept of the book and getting the project off the ground, and who was with us in spirit during her Olympic adventure.

FOREWORD

The development of sport is not a new concept. Many of us have been involved in this process for decades, sometimes without being explicitly aware of it. Voluntary community sector sports clubs have been developing sporting opportunities for hundreds of years. Anyone who hails from a mining area will be fully aware that any opportunity to play sport outside school will probably have been provided directly or indirectly by the local pit or the National Coal Board. The same situation would be reflected in other areas where major employers existed. However the profession of sport development is relatively new. Particularly when compared with other professions, it is in its infancy in terms of both the length of time it has been around and how it is perceived within the wider sports world.

I believe the birth of sport development can be traced back to a number of scenarios. After the riots of the early 1980s, it was considered by the government of the day that the street leadership which had coordinated the antisocial behaviour could be converted into positive leadership using sport as the vehicle. As a result Action Sport was born. Elsewhere in the 1980s teachers' industrial action left many young people without the after-school opportunities they had enjoyed beforehand, creating a void which needed to be filled.

Whether we agree or not upon the causes of its conception, I am sure we concur that the 1980s did witness the birth of sport development. I was lucky enough to be involved at that time and I am as passionate about the profession now as I was then. No matter what position I hold I will always see myself as a sport development professional. However, because the sport development world is made up of passionate, committed individuals some of the issues we face can be attributed to this mindset. Sport development people are natural 'doers' who make things happen and provide opportunities. The crucial elements often missing from sport development practice are strategic thinking, big picture planning, evidence based decision making and political nous.

I really believe that the gaps in the literature relating to strategic sport development will begin to be plugged by this book. Subjects like strategic planning, leadership, internal and external factors and politics can be explored to help the world of sport development to expand its influence and be able to demonstrate real impact across a wide range of agendas as a result of investment.

I believe this publication will make a major contribution to support the high quality, specific sport development courses which are thankfully now available within the higher education sector. This, along with developments such as the enhanced opportunities for quality CPD and career development brought about by the creation of the Chartered Institute for the Management of Sport and Physical Activity (CIMSPA), will help to complete the jigsaw and enable sport development to gain that professional credibility is so richly deserves.

David Morby, January 2013

David Morby has been involved in sport development for over 25 years, holding various positions both in a professional and voluntary capacity with experience in the UK as well as continental Europe, in particular the former East Germany. He was a Director of the ISRM and served as National President. He is passionate about the formation of the single professional body, the Chartered Institute for the Management of Sport and Physical Activity (CIMSPA), and was part of the six-person Project Development Group which managed the process to create CIMSPA. He is currently the Head of the Active and Creative Communities Service at Kirklees Council.

From Stephen: To Sarah, Noah and Daisy, with love.
From Kirstie: For Virgil, Thea and Tom – much love.
From Lee: To Julie, Mitchell, Amelia and Josie, with love.

CHAPTER 1

INTRODUCTION

STEPHEN ROBSON, KIRSTIE SIMPSON, LEE TUCKER AND
ROSEMARY LEACH

INTRODUCTION

In response to many of the 'social ills' of society such as inner-city riots,
racism, social deprivation and youth crime, policy makers and other
powerful players within influential decision-making positions have
turned to sport for a way of overcoming these barriers to a peaceful and
prosperous society. Whether this has been due to the need for social
control or because of a more altruistic concern for the welfare of those
affected, there is no doubt that sport has been seen as a vehicle for social
change. However, despite being seen by some as a crucial tool or
intervention, sport still remains a non-statutory service within local
authorities. The resourcing of this important sector is therefore of
interest to those in strategic and operational roles within the sector, i.e.
sport development professionals/practitioners (SDPs). This imposes the
need for prudent and creative strategic management to advance the
cause within tight political and resource constraints.

Despite the importance placed on those working within sport, a paid
sport development workforce and its professionalisation are only
recent phenomena. Whereas others, such as doctors, nurses, lawyers,
teachers, have had their professions recognised as being integral to the
health, education and functioning of society, sport development
'workers' have often been perceived (or felt to be perceived) as not
worthy of this professional status. However, encouragingly, things have
changed and continue to do so through the professionalisation of the
industry via a bespoke set of National Occupational Standards

(SkillsActive 2010), honours degrees in sport development and a professional membership body, the Chartered Institute for the Management of Sport and Physical Activity (CIMSPA) amongst other developments.

Despite this burgeoning interest and progress within sport development, there is limited literature available that gives an insight into the management of the strategic processes that influence the quality and nature of the work undertaken. This book hopes to help close that gap. In beginning this journey the editors created the following vision:

> To produce a high quality resource linking strategic management and sport development, and in so doing address the paucity of academic literature in this area.

To meet the vision the book has the following aims:

- To enable students to attain a critical appreciation of the application of strategic management in sport development settings.
- To enable students to develop the practical skills necessary for contributing to strategic management in vocational settings.
- To enable sport development and related practitioners to attain the necessary knowledge, confidence and competence to enhance the strategic management of their service.

As stated, there is a lack of specific literature in this area, so in order to achieve these aims, each chapter interprets and contextualises generic strategic management literature to sport development. Reflecting the philosophical position of the authors, a major focus of the book is upon socially inclusive applications of strategic management in sport development. Development *through* sport will therefore have primacy over the development *of* sport, acknowledging that the latter will be enhanced if the former is addressed. If we accept that sport is a potential force for positive change, then those with the responsibility to facilitate sporting opportunities must be able to harness resources responsibly and effectively.

As captured in the aims, the book is targeted at both students and practitioners of sport development. It seeks to enable students to attain a critical appreciation of the application of strategic management in sport development settings, as well as enabling them to develop the practical skills necessary for contributing to strategic management in vocational settings. For practitioners it is hoped that it will enable them to reflect, challenge existing approaches and influence others' strategic thinking about sport. To help facilitate these outcomes we have added learning activities at the end of each chapter (including this one), with a twin focus on developing skills and knowledge pertinent to enhanced performance in strategic sport development. Often drawing upon the aforementioned National Occupational Standards for additional authenticity and professional relevance, these activities will enable us to positively challenge and further develop existing ways of thinking and working.

The remainder of this introduction chapter outlines the academic basis of the book as well as its philosophical underpinnings, identifying key terms, definitions and 'golden threads' before discussing approaches to strategy.

THE DEVELOPMENT OF STRATEGIC THINKING IN SPORT DEVELOPMENT

From a sport development perspective the introduction of strategy creation and strategic thinking came to the fore as a result of the introduction of Compulsory Competitive Tendering (CCT) at the end of the 1980s. Houlihan and White (2002:43) considered CCT to be detrimental to sport development in that:

> ...not only did the preparation of CCT dominate strategy discussions in the larger local authorities to the disadvantage of sports development, but the introduction of contract-based service specifications often left sports development marginalised.

One positive aspect of the CCT process was the fact that it strengthened the necessity to prepare strategic plans and develop strategic thinking, although it could be suggested that sport development objectives became irrelevant as many local authorities were unable to stipulate clear, measurable performance targets. In other words they were unable to articulate what they intended to achieve and how success would be determined. Another factor highlighted by the report was the limited number of local authorities who actually produced a sport and recreation strategy. Whilst we would all agree that merely producing a strategy does not secure success, this lack of engagement in the strategic process acted as a catalyst for Sport England to provide grant funding to support the production of local strategies and link this to on-going funding opportunities. As a direct result of this the number of local authorities producing strategies grew rapidly. In many respects, developing a strategy that is policy and investment driven rather than intrinsically motivated is questionable, however, it can be argued that this has had a significant and positive impact on the development of strategic thinking within sport development.

The current position is that all sport organisations that are in receipt of public funding must outline the strategic context of their proposals. Organisations are required to conduct a situational analysis and clearly state how their capabilities and resources match the goals they have established. They are required to indicate how they intend to both implement and evaluate their strategic proposals and to state how performance results or outcomes will be measured (Sport England 2012). Sport development practitioners must therefore be agile strategic thinkers in order to meet the demands of the profession. In this context, when using the term 'practitioner' we are referring to a wide range of sport development professionals. This includes those who work in the public sector or in national sports organisations, and also refers to those who are employed by non-sport organisations but use sport as a tool to address community or societal objectives. All practitioners must have the ability to predict, envisage, think strategically and work in partnership to initiate changes that will create sustainable sport development.

One of the factors that can impact the growth and development of strategic thinking by practitioners is the use of consultants. The 'outsourcing' of strategy development within sport is an accepted practice and over the past decade we have seen a proliferation of new, individual consultants and sport consultancy organisations who meet what can be described as a strong market demand. The use of consultants is in itself a strategic decision and can have significant implications for the organisation's approach towards strategy formulation and implementation. A sport organisation may use external consultants to determine its strategic direction for a number of reasons. It may be that they consider the research and analysis required to be too time consuming and that consultants can offer alternatives based on previous experience. It may be that they believe consultants can offer complete and objective views based upon a wide knowledge of the sector and access to specific market data and information or, alternatively, it may be there is a need to use an 'independent' source to bring certain issues to the attention of internal decision-makers. All of these reasons appear to be valid and the use of external assistance of this nature is deemed to be acceptable and appropriate. However, the impact on the organisation and the issue of ownership of the strategy needs to be fully examined. It is the task of the sport development team to determine direction, to gain acceptance and to deal with any potentially conflicting ideas and solutions. It is essential that an organisation does not abdicate responsibility for its own strategic thinking. Given the fundamental premise of any sport development body it should be attempting to foster a learning organisation and evolve its strategic thinking internally. It should be seeking to acquire and transfer knowledge, to collaborate and to create a robust core culture and this cannot be achieved by the use of external consultants. If more people within an organisation are directly involved in the strategy process, this will result in people viewing the process much more positively, feeling ownership of the strategy and acting in ways that make the implementation process more effective.

In terms of the future of strategic thinking in sport development, organisations that are willing to experiment and learn from their experiences are more successful than those who do not (Wheelen and Hunger, 2006), therefore recognition is required of the need to encourage and engender strategic thinking in all practitioners. Houlihan (2011:4) emphasises "not only the scope and diversity of sports development, but also its highly politicised character and its dynamism". It also needs to be characterised by its strategic thinking.

The professionalisation of the sport development industry has seen some real progress in recent years and the establishment of National Occupational Standards for Sports Development is a momentous step forward in developing the status of the industry alongside other professions such as medicine and law. The plethora of sport development degree courses across the UK illustrates a burgeoning interest in the sector. The new professional body, CIMPSA, should create opportunities for the continuing professional development of its members and therefore bring it in line with those professions alluded to earlier. However, the picture is not so pretty in practice.

The lack of acknowledgement of the National Occupational Standards within the practice of sport development units across the UK undermines their credibility and amounts to practitioners digging their own graves by not engaging with them. The in-fighting amongst many SDPs with colleagues in leisure and management does not help advance the cause of professionalising the image of the sector. Finally, the economic cuts that sport seems to continually absorb, alongside the 2012 increases in undergraduate student fees mean that there are likely to be fewer students studying the subject area and fewer jobs for graduates to pursue. Some of these phenomena are in the control of the practitioners themselves, such as engaging with the National Occupational Standards and sorting out differences with other professionals. Other aspects can be resisted through lobbying and uniting with others in fighting back when it appears that national policy mitigates against sport development addressing the agendas to which government apparently wants it to contribute (such as reduce crime and obesity whilst bringing success to nation through elite sport). To achieve this requires an energising workforce that possesses the skills and attributes to get the job done.

DEFINING SPORT DEVELOPMENT

Numerous definitions of sport(s) development have been attempted (e.g. Eady 1993; Hylton and Bramham 2008 to name but two). Before embarking upon a critical examination of the profession's attention to strategic management we need to be clear on what we understand by the term. This book adopts the definition utilised in the Level 3 National Occupational Standards:

> Initiate and manage a process of structural and organisational change in order to create pathways of opportunities for all individuals to achieve their potential through and in sport
> (SkillsActive 2010).

Note the use of *initiate* and *change*: join those two words into a single phrase and the role of a SDP as a negotiator and influencer (not a deliverer of opportunities) is emphasised. These words prevail throughout this book. The definition also embraces the twin (but not mutually exclusive) functions of sport development: to facilitate the development of elite performance *in* sport and – more importantly as far as this book is concerned – to enable positive change to benefit individuals and communities *through* sport.

We scrutinise strategic management processes which are undertaken to realise these outcomes and argue that an enhanced understanding of strategic sport development by all of the actors in the process is necessary to move the sector forwards. This book emphasises that this work is not exclusively the preserve of paid 'sporty types' in Sport Development Officer posts, and that colleagues in associated professions, volunteers for example, are equally instrumental in securing positive outcomes.

You will have already noticed our use of the term 'sport development' as opposed to 'sports development': it is a primary purpose of this book to challenge conventions in the interests of conceptual clarity. Much of the existing body of strategic management literature is written with less altruistic outcomes in mind than those desired by the sport development community, but we aim to show how many of the key principles can be applied to this setting with positive results. We will also offer SDPs numerous challenges to existing practice in a constructive spirit of continuous improvement.

The conscious choice of '*sport* development' in the title and throughout the book exemplifies this approach. The reader is urged to consider why this should be important: for the authors, the distinction highlights more fully the spectrum of work in the sporting arena. Whilst the term sport*s* development implicitly covers the development *of* sports (national governing body, sports-specific settings) it does not so comfortably accommodate the vast body of inclusive community development work which uses sport as its primary delivery tool. We also need to recognise the growing use of 'sport *and* development' or 'sport in development' in international settings (e.g. Coalter, 2008) so it would seem that 'sport development' is a more all-encompassing term that helps convey the essence of the book more effectively.

THE IMPORTANCE OF COMMUNITY

What will be evident throughout the book is the prevalence of the term 'community'. It is for this reason that a brief insight into what community means is proffered and how it relates to the following chapters, as its use will be frequent and important. The danger of linking the concept of

7

community to sporting provision (as well as other forms of provision) is that it can be criticised as a lazy appendage to create impression of thoughtful consideration of all citizens. As Haywood (1994) noted when discussing the term 'community recreation' it can be misused as a fashionable label without a deeper understanding of what it actually means. Tagging 'community' onto project titles can help to access funding, create images of social inclusion and frame the debate in a positive light for those using it as a means to gain popularity. However, the communities themselves ultimately judge whether a service is genuinely community orientated.

As alluded to elsewhere in this book, community can be and is interpreted in many different ways depending on how people perceive the communities they belong to (Hylton and Totten 2008). A sense of community can arise due to geographical area (e.g. the estate people live on); shared interest (e.g. the sport that they play); experience (e.g. alumni of a university and the experiences shared with others); shared virtual space (social network sites mean that people feel part of a community despite never having met others face to face); or common principles and collective action (e.g. animal rights movements and Greenpeace are examples of communities of action).

In light of this brief review it is therefore important to acknowledge the deliberate use of the term community throughout this book. Our aspiration of inclusivity in all sport development means that authentic, bottom-up, empowering approaches to addressing community needs are central to the book's discussions of community. The transformative potential of sport for communities is why we have written this book, so hopefully it will contribute to a more informed approach to identifying and meeting communities' needs. The final two chapters in particular provide a close examination of SDPs' strategic appreciation of the real meanings of community and community development.

DISTINGUISHING BETWEEN POLICY AND STRATEGY

It is also necessary to adopt a sufficiently rigorous approach to distinguishing between *policy* and *strategy*. These terms are commonly used interchangeably, often by those who 'should know better' and always to the detriment of clear thinking and shared understanding. Those who feel dismay each time a broad-brush, central government

8

document is published bearing the word 'strategy' in its title (e.g. Game Plan [DCMS/Strategy Unit 2002]) will sympathise with the authors' frustration. A clear delineation between the two terms is therefore required in order to minimise confusion and promote a sharper insight into their inextricable interrelationship. Davies (2000) helps us to clarify the distinction: "Whereas policy is a legislative function, strategy is an executive function" (2000:26). In other words, it is helpful to think of policy as long-term, visionary and representative of wider values and ideologies, with the more focused and action-oriented strategy being the means by which policy decisions are achieved. Policy, as the word implies, is created by politicians through political processes. Strategy is the response of decision-makers closer to the point of delivery to enable them to harness their finite resources effectively in pursuit of achieving the wider vision.

STRATEGY AND STRATEGIC MANAGEMENT

Strategy has been an important concept within business contexts over a substantial period of time. The majority of successful businesses embrace the idea of strategy, and think of it as a plan for governing and exploiting their resources with the objective of stimulating and safeguarding their fundamental concerns. Copious definitions of strategy exist and there is an abundant body of literature on the subject. An examination of the business strategy section in any library or bookshop reveals numerous tomes dedicated to all aspects of the strategic process and this collection expands annually. This over-abundance of material provides problems of nomenclature which are discussed at various points throughout the book.

In the spirit of critical enquiry and seeking new, more rigorous perspectives into sport development, it is useful to challenge and problematise the basic characterisations of two of the book's underpinning concepts. First, Chandler's (1962:13) classic definition of *strategy* still resonates today:

> The determination of the basic long-term goals and objectives of an enterprise, and the adoption of courses of action and the allocation of resources necessary for carrying out those goals.

Commercial strategists, as would be expected, have developed more sophisticated approaches but arguably many SDPs, as with professionals in numerous other facets of the public sector are still to evidence a subtler understanding of strategy and its applications. A more recent and outward-facing definition from Johnson, Scholes and Whittingham (2005:9) moves the debate towards more productive territory:

> ... the direction and scope of an organisation over the long term, which achieves advantage in a changing environment through its configuration of resources and competences with the aim of fulfilling stakeholder expectations.

The notion of a "changing environment" is one to which SDPs will intuitively relate. This emphasises that we cannot glibly assume that strategic thinking translates into clear strategy which is successfully implemented. It would be foolish in the extreme to suppose that the elements of strategic management can be enacted sequentially. Cole's (2003:4) definition of *strategic management* acknowledges this but debatably needs to give it further stress:

> A process, directed by top management, to determine the fundamental aims or goals of the organisation, and ensure a range of decisions which will allow for the achievement of those aims or goals in the long-term, whilst providing for adaptive responses in the short-term.

A central tenet of this book is encapsulated in Cole's phrase "providing for adaptive responses in the short-term". This idea of preparedness for 'shocks' provided by the external environment, i.e. flexibility in strategy, is introduced and developed throughout this book.

GOLDEN THREADS

This section provides an exposition of what might be termed Strategic Sport Development. A number of 'golden threads' run throughout each chapter, intended not only to bind the book into a cohesive whole but also to establish a manifesto for a more informed use of strategic management principles in socially inclusive sport development. The first of these running themes is the notion of flexible strategy.

As discussed earlier, many definitions of strategy and strategic management are predicated upon an implicit supposition that, in order for the organisation to realise its vision, strategy has to involve the long-term commitment of resources at a given point in time. Furthermore, strategic processes in sport development are often long-winded and expensive, culminating in thick, glossy documents (or pdf files!) which have questionable value shortly after publication. A number of writers (e.g. Jones 1998) are critical of strategy's power or sceptical about its legitimacy, and it has even been described as a dangerous delusion (Whittington 2001). The book therefore considers, somewhat provocatively, whether many current approaches to strategy really are little more than a comfort blanket for pressured policy makers and managers in a politicised environment.

We provide the reader with the tools to practise more agile and responsive forms of strategic management. We offer alternatives to long-term methodologies and encourage strategists to generate adaptable, bottom-up, more affordable solutions. As is discussed at length, the environment in which sport development takes place is subject to rapid and constant change, and strategists seeking the best outcomes for disenfranchised communities often need to move fast to seize upon fleeting opportunities. We argue that traditional methods of strategic management are not always appropriate in this climate, and offer constructive prescriptions for new ways of thinking to embrace this challenge.

It is appropriate at this point to consider the relevance of Checkland's (1999) notion of *layered thinking* to the sport development milieu (see Figure 1.1).

The answers to *why?*, *what?* and *how?* differ according to the perspective of the observer. This underscores the higher purpose that should be served by all sport development activity at local level. As a simple example, in many situations political will is the *why?*, government policy is the *what?* and strategy is the *how?* For instance the Sport England strategy 'Grow, Sustain, Excel' (*how?*) was for the most part a response to a central government request (*what?*) to review its approach to community sport (Sport England 2008). This was because of a political desire in Whitehall to clarify the roles of the leading sport development agencies and to seize upon the legacy opportunities of the 2012 Olympic and Paralympic Games (*why?*). From another observer's point of view

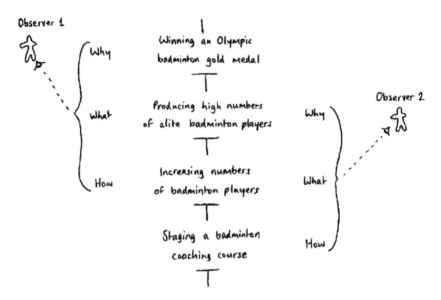

Figure 1.1 Illustration of layered thinking (adapted from Checkland 1999: p. A24)

the Sport England strategy identified a perceived need to support community sport via increased investment in national governing bodies of sport (*why?*). Thus in order to attract resources NGBs were required to produce new Whole Sport Plans (*what?*), outlining the actions to be taken to address issues such as post-16s drop-out and retaining participants (*how?*). In presenting case studies throughout this book the authors are cognisant of the presence of layering in strategic sport development.

The final, principal golden thread centres around our 4Ps model, through which we attempt to capture the essential elements of strategic sport development. The 4Ps permeate many chapters, providing a ready means of cross referencing between themes as well as a series of milestones to enable the reader to navigate safely through the strategic journey. In the interests of clarity the 4Ps are previewed here in isolation, but in recognition of their interrelatedness the authors have interpreted them according to the needs of each chapter, applying the model in a bespoke fashion to enrich and enliven the discussion. The first and arguably most important P is *people*.

Stephen Robson, Kirstie Simpson, Lee Tucker and Rosemary Leach

People

Commercial applications often involve the setting of competitive strategy by a small number of senior executives. This is then handed down to the workforce to be implemented, with the 'bottom line' of profit the all-consuming goal. Intuitively, this is unlikely to constitute a recipe for success in socially inclusive sport development, although many practitioners have felt compelled to do strategy in just this fashion. The *people* aspect of our 4Ps acknowledges the presence of many other stakeholders with crucial roles to play in determining and achieving the strategic vision. We propose some radical approaches to involving communities in strategic processes, whilst each chapter's illustrative examples recognise that understanding and engaging the full gamut of stakeholders is the way to success.

Process

The next P, inextricably linked to people, is *process*. As stated above there are numerous possible approaches to strategic sport development, differing according to variables such as timescale, methods, scope and resources. The process by which strategic decisions are made and enacted has an enormous influence over the eventual outcomes, thus it is as worthy of careful consideration as any of the other elements of strategic management. The book in effect engages in process benchmarking: each chapter highlights best practice from a range of settings, offering pressured decision-makers new perspectives on how to achieve more socially inclusive outcomes within tight resource constraints.

Product

Product is the third P. By this we refer not to trainers or televisions but to the printed word which emanates from a strategic planning cycle. The stereotypical 'glossy document' is much maligned as an expensive potential white elephant; however it is essential for strategic decisions to be disseminated to stakeholders in a clear and accessible fashion. The resulting plethora of strategy documents provides a fascinating insight into thought processes and resource allocation at all levels of sport.

Chapter 4 in particular looks at the structuring, writing and presentation of documents which inform, engage and inspire all of those with an interest in a strategy's success. The significance of clear, written communication is underscored throughout the book, drawing upon examples of live documents.

Practice

The 4Ps are completed by *practice*. Whilst process focuses minds on the conceptually-driven planning stages of strategic management, practice is a more action-focused term. It is immensely important to understand *why* we are doing something, but once the rationale has been established there is much doing to be done! This part of our model is addressed in all chapters, but has particular prominence within chapters on implementation and performance measurement.

The 4Ps illustrate the underpinning theme of the book that strategy as a *product* is a means to an (socially inclusive) end and not an end in itself. Excellence in strategic management, in which appropriate *processes* and *practices* are designed and enacted by the appropriate *people*, is the key.

Each chapter contains exercises that provide an engaging and useful opportunity for readers to synthesise the key concepts covered within the chapter to their own contextual situations. The use of the National Occupational Standards provides a backdrop for many of these exercises as the authors feel it is important that both practitioners and students utilise these more consistently in the workplace or in their studies.

APPROACHES TO STRATEGY

This section plays a pivotal role in charting the conceptual territory surrounding notions of flexibility in strategy and approaches to strategy which are utilised throughout this text. Porter (1980:xvi) describes strategy as "a broad formula for how a business is going to compete". This definition was developed further by Porter and linked with Henderson's (1989) concept of "competitive advantage". Competitive advantage can be described as a function of strategy that enables a business to establish itself in a stronger position than its competitors.

14

Strategy, therefore, is the pursuit of a purposeful plan of action that can improve a business's competitive advantage and expand it further. Competitive advantage, however, is an interesting term to use in the context of sport development, given that the concept of competitors seems more relevant to what is happening on the field of play rather than off it. It is also problematic to identify competitive advantage alongside the inclusive, community-oriented sport development referred to throughout this book.

We draw upon the substantial body of work which confirms that organisations who engage in strategic planning and development frequently perform better that those who do not. Developing a strategy provides an organisation with a lucid sense of strategic vision, gives incisive clarity to what is strategically significant and can provide a better understanding of the fast shifting environment. Strategy within a sport development context is highly regarded by the organisations that fund and direct activity as a method of measuring success. However, as we have already argued there is a lack of understanding as to the difference between policy and strategy and what determines successful, long-term, sustainable outcomes.

In sport development an effective strategy needs to be many things to many people. It is required to communicate a persuasive rationale to all stakeholders as well as determining the organisation's specific strengths and how these can be utilised to seize upon opportunities. It should enable interested parties to determine current success whilst investigating new potential and accessing new resources. Overall, a strategy for sport development should direct and channel new activity and be flexible enough to respond to new circumstances and challenges that arise over time. Given the weight of expectation on the shoulders of any strategy for sport development, the choice of approach taken to determining the strategic direction of an organisation is crucial as it can be a multifaceted and lengthy process that requires stamina and exceptional commitment.

According to Mintzberg and Waters (1998) strategy is best characterised as a series of decisions made over a period of time which can only be detected retrospectively. 'Strategic planning' within sport development has long been considered to be of significant importance due to the fact that it demonstrates organisational logic to the range of stakeholders involved. It can be argued that strategic planning reveals how realistic and contemporary an organisation's thinking is. Within sport development settings what is of interest is the process by which strategies are actually formed. The use of consultants in this regard has already been discussed, but the idea of flexible strategy is crucial here if SDPs are to respond appropriately, and more importantly, quickly to changes within the industry.

Mintzberg and Waters (1998) provide a framework of the types of strategy-making structure and suggest a continuum with planned strategy (where intentions are clearly formulated) at one end and less prescriptively set out, more movable strategy at the other. These positions are defined as deliberate and emergent approaches to strategy. Deliberate strategies are fairly straightforward, carefully articulated and communicated widely throughout the organisation before being implemented with specific outcomes in mind. Emergent strategy is where an outcome is realised despite, or in the absence of intentions. The crucial distinction between the two types of strategy rests on the purpose that underpins them: deliberate strategy is precise and preordained, but an emergent strategy lacks specific intent. An emergent approach to strategy does not mean the organisation is out of control but that it is open, adaptable and receptive, in other words willing to learn. This stance is particularly significant when the operating environment is multifaceted or insecure to grasp or too commanding to disregard. Acceptance of emergent strategy indicates that management are able to act before all aspects are fully understood, in other words to be "… responding to an evolving reality rather than having to focus on a stable fantasy" (Mintzberg and Waters 1998:271).

It can be argued that the majority of public sector strategy is deliberate as the public purse demands this transparency and perceived stability, however despite this intent it is not always clear whether outcomes have been achieved. The contribution of Mintzberg and Waters (1998) highlights that some strategies are in fact deficient in intent. They advise that few strategies are solely deliberate or exclusively emergent, but instead are likely to include a mix of both tendencies. A number of strategy types are outlined by Mintzberg and Waters indicate which the variety of approaches that may be taken to the strategy process, and these are discussed below.

16

Planned strategy

'Planned strategy' is characterised by formal planning with explicit objectives. The strategy is communicated widely by senior executives and is carefully implemented. This is a deliberate strategy, and in this approach strategy is tightly controlled. Examples of planned strategy within a sport development context can be seen within the Whole Sport Plan process, whereby national governing bodies have been provided with a specific framework and if they are to achieve funding through this mechanism then they must fulfil criteria established by Sport England.

Entrepreneurial strategy

'Entrepreneurial strategy' is where an 'entrepreneur' formulates the strategic vision. It has express intentions and a vision for the future (although it is prone to being changed or halted depending on the entrepreneur's whim). This is a broadly deliberate strategy and is tightly controlled by the entrepreneur. From a sport development perspective entrepreneurial strategies exist in terms of a number of the smaller NGBs (who are not part of the Whole Sport Plan process) and to a certain extent in a number of local authority sport development units, where an individual SDP leads the strategic process.

Ideological strategy

'Ideological strategy' is often seen in ideological organisations (such as political/lobby organisations), who often have a strong culture which organises group members into pledging to a specific set of targets. These targets are often inspirational and motivating to members of the organisation. Ideological strategy is generally deliberate and often determines methods as well as objectives. It could be argued that the Youth Sport Trust has developed an ideological strategy based on its innate commitment to developing opportunities for young people.

Umbrella strategy

An 'Umbrella strategy' can often be seen where an organisation consists of a range of different interest groups and exists in an environment of uncertainty. Senior strategists will define broad boundaries, allowing others discretion to adopt strategies within these boundaries. An umbrella strategy is in one sense deliberate, setting broad goals, and in another sense emergent, allowing flexibility to realise these goals. County Sport Partnership strategies can be considered umbrella strategies as they are centrally driven but allow local flexibility to meet varying needs and utilise available resources.

Process strategy

In a 'Process strategy' the central leadership of the organisation controls the process through which the strategy is formulated and the people charged with making the strategy. The content of the strategy is, however, at the discretion of those making it. An example of this might be in a multi-divisional organisation where individual sub-units are allowed to formulate their own strategies (although they use the established process to arrive at this strategy). Sport England previously developed strategy in this manner, allowing each regional organisation to formulate its own strategic direction. To a certain extent this autonomy has been withdrawn due to the fact the organisation has become more centralised and the regional focus diminished.

Unconnected strategy

'Unconnected strategy' is where part of an organisation with considerable autonomy is able to develop its own strategy. From the vantage point of the group making the strategy it could be considered deliberate or emergent but from perspective of the organisation this type of strategy-making is always emergent. It could be argued that the 'Big Four' NGBs (the Football Association, English Cricket Board, the Lawn Tennis Association and Rugby Football Union) have the finance and therefore resources to remain somewhat autonomous and develop a relatively independent strategic direction.

Consensus strategy

'Consensus strategy', meanwhile, is generally emergent with consensus emanating from discussions between the different interest groups within an organisation. This would normally entail negotiation and the organisation having a 'feel' for a particular issue. One would anticipate that the vast majority of sport development strategies are consensus-based and involve the range of stakeholders who will be involved in implementation. However, as we will see in subsequent chapters this is not always the case.

Imposed strategy

'Imposed strategy' is when a powerful group or an event from outside the organisation determines strategy for the organisation. An example of this is national government levying cuts on a sport organisation (e.g. the Youth Sport Trust and the cuts to school sport announced in 2010). From the government's perspective the imposed strategy would be emergent by nature, although it might become the subject of deliberate intent by the organisation.

These eight approaches are not exhaustive but they can be used to demonstrate the difference between deliberate and emergent strategy. We can infer from this typology that deliberate strategy is focused on pursuing a particular direction and tightly controlling the implementation of a strategy. Emergent strategy is more concerned with adaptation to circumstances and strategic learning.

As Mintzberg and Waters (1998) state, the majority of strategies are likely to combine both deliberate and emergent features and whilst some such as planned strategy are more obviously deliberate, others such as unconnected strategy are essentially emergent. As sport development, by its nature, is subject to a range of factors that impinge on its strategic direction, in terms of approaching strategy a first step must be the identification of possible opportunities and threats in the external environment and strengths and weaknesses in the internal environment. A sport development organisation should attempt to avoid unexpected pitfalls and to ensure long-term strength of the strategic direction by identifying external environmental variables. It should be noted that the shared environment includes general forces (factors such as economics and politics, discussed in more detail in Chapter 3) that do not directly impinge on the short-term activities of the organisation but can influence its long-term decisions.

Any organisation's working environment includes those groups who directly impact on it and are affected by it (i.e. stakeholders such as local communities, special-interest groups – typically the industry in which the sport organisation operates). It is almost impossible to successfully examine all external factors. Choices must be made in terms of which factors are important and which are not. Personal values and experiences as well as the impact of existing strategies are likely to bias an individual's perception of what is important to monitor and their interpretations of what they perceive. The willingness to reject unfamiliar as well as negative information has been referred to by Ansoff (1991) as 'strategic myopia'. In many respects it can be argued that sport development suffers from this, in that there appears to be short-sightedness in terms of SDPs being strategically ambitious or seeking new and innovative paths.

Given the competing factors sport development faces, we should consider following a dual strategy approach. Huff *et al.* (2009) define a dual strategy as one that attempts to optimise current performance whilst preparing at the same time for likely future challenges. Thinking in terms of dual strategies becomes central if the expected future is radically different from the current position. As sport development mainly operates within such a setting it appears obvious to follow the dual strategy path and pursue two strategic models. The first and more certain approach should match the contemporary, competitive environment and correspond with present resources and existing 'customer' desires and appeal. The second approach is less certain and predicts how the competitive environment is likely to progress, how 'customer' desires might change, which new/potential 'customers' may become available and how the resources of the sport organisation will have to alter to meet the new position.

Hamel and Prahalad (1995) refer to the second approach as 'competing for the future' and argue that strategists should not 'crystal ball gaze', but instead they should strive to create their own desired future state. Huff *et al.* (2009) suggest that this requires a significant change of mindset for strategists, as they must overlook existing recipes for success and be prepared to tolerate major adjustment within the organisation as

Stephen Robson, Kirstie Simpson, Lee Tucker and Rosemary Leach

former associations and methods are dispersed. This, of course, can be considered risky as it is impossible to predict accurately in sport terms how things will evolve or if the organisation can acclimatise to the new situation. Tushman and O'Reilly (1996:8) argue that if this is managed well then it can be deemed an "ambidextrous organization" and suggest that:

> ...ambidextrous organizations manage the inconsistent demands of supporting current businesses while developing new entrepreneurial opportunities.

Sport development would benefit significantly from being ambidextrous and having a full, critical awareness of successful strategic practice in alternative environments. There have been a number of conscious decisions to appoint people with strategic experience outside the sport sector to senior positions in a range of sport organisations. Cross cutting themes such as regeneration, health, community safety and lifelong learning are complex and require flexibility and adaptability. As such a multi-agency approach is required to deal with such themes, therefore the ability to think strategically and plan effectively is essential. Sport England's original intention for County Sport Partnerships was that their key focus should be strategic planning and performance measurement (Sport England 2004), and this was reinforced in the 2008–2011 strategy (Sport England 2008). Subsequent changes reduced core funding, which required a durable strategic approach aligned with rich strategic thinking, underpinned by a need for exceptional strategic leadership.

SUMMARY

This chapter has attempted to outline the concepts that underpin each chapter – in other words each 'golden thread' – including our 4Ps model. We have critiqued definitions of sport development, strategic management and strategy and adopted a somewhat politicised stance regarding the definition and nature of sport development, asserting that effective sport development professionals need to be agents of organisational, bureaucratic and societal change. In so doing we have set the scene for the less orthodox nature of some of the book's key discussions. The notion of 'bottom-up' strategic management as a means of achieving more meaningful outcomes at community level has been trailed.

We hope that practitioners and students alike can derive favourable outcomes from the book. We have shown how working methodically through the chapters and engaging with the examples and exercises will enable to you critically evaluate your own and others' strategic practice and identify improvements. The first such opportunity for you to take a fresh look at strategic sport development commences in Chapter 2. The authors wish you well as you embark upon the strategic journey we have set out for you. We hope that your copy of *Strategic Sport Development* will serve as a valued resource for years to come.

LEARNING ACTIVITIES

As stated above, the learning activities throughout the book focus on key skills and knowledge relevant to strategic sport development. Prior to embarking on these exercises it will be useful for you to study the Level 3 National Occupational Standards for Sports Development (SkillsActive 2010).

Developing skills

Before reading the rest of the book, use the National Occupational Standards as a reference point to help you identify what you consider to be the most important skills for success in strategic sport development. Conduct a review of your current strengths and weaknesses in these areas, highlighting the most urgent and important areas in which you need to develop.

Developing knowledge

As discussed in this Introduction a key theme of this book is the role of strategic **thinking** in sport development. We have already provided some hints as to the authors' views on what this means, but what about you? Record your answers to the following questions:

Stephen Robson, Kirstie Simpson, Lee Tucker and Rosemary Leach

1   What do you consider to be the essential distinctions between the terms 'strategic thinking' and 'strategic planning'?
2   What kind of strategic thinker are you? In your academic and professional practice to what extent are you focused on the *product* in terms of the strategy document versus the *process* of thinking strategically about every situation and how it relates to the wider picture? To what extent does it matter?
3   What influence are you hoping this book will have on your strategic thinking in sport development?

REFERENCES

Ansoff, I. (1991) 'Critique of Henry Mintzberg's The Design School: reconsidering the basic premises of strategic management'. *Strategic Management Journal.* Vol. 12, pp. 449–461.

Chandler, A. (1962) *Strategy And Structure: Chapters in the History of the American Industrial Enterprise.* Cambridge, MIT Press.

Checkland, P. (1999) *Soft Systems Methodology: A 30-year Retrospective.* Chichester, John Wiley & Sons.

Coalter, F. (2008) 'Sport-in-Development: a monitoring and evaluation manual'. UK Sport. Available at <http://www.sportanddev.org/toolkit/?uNewsID=17>.

Cole, G.A. (2003) *Strategic Management.* 2nd ed. London, Thomson Learning.

Davies, W. (2000) 'Understanding Strategy'. In *Strategy and Leadership.* 28/5, pp. 25–30.

DCMS/Strategy Unit (2002) *Game Plan: a strategy for delivering government's sport and physical activity objectives.* London, The Strategy Unit.

Eady, J. (1993) *Practical Sports Development.* Reading, ILAM, Longman.

Hamel, G. and Prahalad, C. (1995) *Competing for the Future.* Harvard, Harvard Business Press.

Haywood, L. ed. (1994) *Community Leisure & Recreation: Theory and Practice.* Oxford, Butterworth Heinemann.

Henderson, B. (1989) 'The Origin of Strategy'. *Harvard Business Review.* Nov–Dec. pp. 139–143.

Houlihan, B. (2011) 'Introduction'. In Houlihan, B. and Green, M. eds. *Routledge Handbook of Sports Development.* Abingdon, Routledge. pp. 5–8.

Houlihan, B. and White, A. (2002) *The Politics of Sports Development.* London, Routledge.

Huff, A., Floyd, S., Sherman, H. and Terjesen, S. (2009) *Strategic Management: Logic and Action.* Hoboken, NJ, Wiley.

Hylton, K. and Bramham, P. eds. (2008) *Sports Development: Policy, Process and Practice.* 2nd ed. Abingdon, Routledge.

Hylton, K. and Totten, M. (2008) 'Community Sports Development'. In Hylton, K. and Bramham, P. eds. (2008) *Sports Development: Policy, Process and Practice.* 2nd ed. Abingdon, Routledge. pp. 77–117.

Johnson, G., Scholes, K. and Whittington, R. (2005) *Exploring Corporate Strategy: Text and Cases.* 7th ed. London, Pearson Education.

Jones, G. (1998) 'Perspectives on Strategy'. In Segal-Horn, S. ed. *The Strategy Reader.* Oxford, Blackwell, pp. 409–429.

Mintzberg, H. and Waters, J. (1998) 'Of Strategies, Deliberate and Emergent'. In Segal-Horn, S. ed. *The Strategy Reader.* Oxford, Blackwell, pp. 20–34.

Porter, M. (1980) *Competitive Strategy: Techniques for Analysing Industries and Competitors.* New York, The Free Press.

SkillsActive (2010) 'NOS: sports development'. Available at http://www.skillsactive.com/skillsactive/national-occupational-standards/level-3/item/3260/3260.

Sport England (2004) *The Framework for Sport in England.* London, Sport England.

Sport England (2008) *Grow, Sustain, Excel: Sport England Strategy 2008–2011.* London, Sport England.

Sport England (2012) 'Investing in National Governing Bodies'. Available at http://www.sportengland.org/funding/ngb_investment.aspx.

Tushman, M. and O'Reilly, C. (1996) 'Ambidextrous Organizations: managing evolutionary and revolutionary change'. *California Management Review.* 38/4 Summer, pp. 5–19.

Wheelen, T. and Hunger, D. (2006) *Essentials of Strategic Management.* 4th ed. London, Prentice Hall.

Whittington R (2001) *What is Strategy and Does it Matter?* 2nd ed. London, Thomson Education.

Stephen Robson, Kirstie Simpson, Lee Tucker and Rosemary Leach

CHAPTER 2

THE INTERNAL ENVIRONMENT

STEPHEN ROBSON, LEE TUCKER AND ROSEMARY LEACH

INTRODUCTION

The following three chapters examine the processes required to determine the current position of the sport development organisation with regard to its internal and external environments, prior to making the strategic choices which give direction to its work. As with everything else covered in the book these activities should not be thought of as taking place at a fixed point in time: we have already discussed the limitations of long-term strategy which is launched on the back of a period of analysis that is not returned to for some time. Assessing the organisation's capabilities and place in the wider sport development environment should be an ongoing endeavour in order to maintain the currency and relevance of the organisation's work. A product of these processes should be the successful alignment of the outcomes with the organisation's sense of purpose in order to ensure strategic fit. This is captured effectively in the 'E-V-R congruence' model (Thompson 2001), where E stands for environment, V for values and R for resources. This is represented diagrammatically by Thompson in a deceptively simple Venn diagram, but the task of achieving true congruence is anything but straightforward.

The four models of incongruent organisation are of particular interest as several of them are familiar in sport development settings. The 'consciously incompetent' organisation is aware of what is required for success in its field but is unable to achieve the standards of quality and service required. Given that conscious incompetence is often attributable to resource shortages, in austere times this description can be applied to legions of sport development organisations! Congruency is only assured via a constant 'fire fight', resolving stakeholder issues and attending to the demands of the ever-changing external environment. Following the 2010 budget cuts, even the more agile School Sport Partnerships learned that this reactive approach cannot be sustained in perpetuity.

Whilst access to resources is often competitive and not entirely within the control of the strategic leader, it is entirely possible for the sport development organisation to avoid becoming 'unconsciously competent'. This is another unsustainable position. Initially, on a superficial level the sport development organisation appears to be performing effectively (sometimes, according to Thompson (2001) more due to luck than judgement) but the non-alignment of V with E and R means that over time performance will decline and the organisation will fail to achieve in areas relevant to its core values. From a sport development viewpoint, for instance, 'quick wins' can be obtained by directing resources towards soft targets, i.e. short-term participation increases can be achieved by aiming programmes at those with the predisposition to take up a particular activity. However, the underlying goal of addressing inequalities will not be met and increasingly E and R will become misaligned.

The other route to becoming a 'lost organisation' is via strategic drift. This term has entered into common parlance in recent times and refers to the organisation becoming disconnected from the demands of the external environment. Whilst a focus is maintained upon the organisation's core values and resources are aligned accordingly, its increasing separation from external realities leads to its work having diminishing relevance. This is typical of the many sport development organisations that have attempted to plan decisively and rigidly for inappropriately long periods; so that resources tied to less relevant initiatives and opportunities, such as technological developments or surges in the popularity of particular activities, cannot be seized upon. These brief examples stress the importance of E-V-R congruence and, more importantly, they stress the need for strategic leaders to attend to it. If not, sport development organisations might therefore be resigning themselves to an existence that is at best consciously incompetent. This chapter aims to add some clarity to this process with an examination of the processes involved in analysing the internal environment, including the V and R elements of the model.

We are often exhorted to 'put our houses in order', in other words to take greater care of those aspects of our private and professional lives over which we have the most control. Relating this notion to strategic sport development this chapter examines the influence of the internal environment in relation to performance, survival and service. Visible evidence of strategic thinking in sport development most often appears in the form of published strategy documents. As we are usually unable to personally immerse ourselves in sport development organisations, such documents provide us with possibly our only glimpse of life within the organisation and an indication of the attention which has been paid to assessing the internal environment prior to making strategic choices. Many writers (e.g. Clegg, Kornberger and Pitsis 2005) remind us of the complexity of organisations and trumpet the need to manage their design and structure as well as human behaviour within them.

As the E-V-R congruence discussion illustrates, sport development professionals need to appreciate the range of internal variables that should be considered in conjunction with external factors (see Chapter 3) in order for effective strategic development to be achieved (Wolsey and Abrams 2001). For example Handy (1993) provides a useful framework of key factors that may be considered, including important aspects of internal organisational dynamics such as leadership, group relations, systems and structures, individual behaviour and motivation. It is therefore perhaps surprising that so many of the aforementioned strategy documents offer little evidence that rigorous analysis of the internal environment preceded the strategic decision-making process, the setting out of the organisation's strategic direction and the accompanying commitment of precious resources.

We should not hastily conclude from this that internal analysis is routinely neglected in sport development, but it would not be unreasonable to expect the outcomes of these processes to be more explicitly shared with stakeholders. This chapter will therefore seek to provide sport development practitioners with tools to enable them to address internal analysis with renewed confidence and enable all interested parties to be better informed of the outcomes. Organisational culture will be given particular prominence in this chapter, and the marked cultural differences between disparate organisations such as local authorities and national governing bodies will be covered.

It is useful at this stage to define what we mean by the term 'organisation'. Sports organisations have similar characteristics to those in other industries. Slack and Parent (2006:5) offer a broad definition of a sport organisation, which they characterise as:

> … a social entity involved in the sport industry; it is goal-directed, with a consciously structured activity system and relatively identifiable boundaries.

The term 'social entity' implies it is composed of people interacting to achieve organisational goals. As we will see the uniqueness of each sport organisation is largely a product of its constituent workforce. Involvement in the 'sport industry' usually refers to those organisations where sport is the central focus, so we may adapt this for the purposes of this book to specify an involvement in strategic sport development as the primary role of the organisation. The presence of a 'goal-directed' focus suggests that sport development organisations have a guiding purpose for their existence in the form of an intrinsic and/or extrinsic mission supported by strategic aims. One of the reasons for conducting internal and external analysis in sport development organisations is to test the currency and validity of such aims. A 'consciously structured activity' system involves the main functions being broken down into tasks or groups of tasks. The structuring of a sport development organisation is a crucial aspect of resource allocation which can be a 'deal breaker' in determining whether it achieves its aims. An 'identifiable boundary' distinguishes members from non-members ('members' in this sense usually refers to the workforce and not subscribers, such as those who pay fees to a national governing body of sport). Members have an agreement to receive money, status etc. for their involvement in the organisation's activities. Organisational boundaries may change over time as priorities shift in response to internal and external drivers, for example, as the availability of resources changes, a common phenomenon in sport development.

We have already established that sport development is thought about, discussed, practised and evaluated in a myriad of settings with no prospect of a 'one size fits all' approach. As highlighted by many writers including Clegg, Kornberger and Pitsis (2005), the German sociologist Max Weber, around a century ago, was instrumental in pointing out the bureaucratic design of many organisations. Weber was interested in

Stephen Robson, Lee Tucker and Rosemary Leach

why people respond to authority and how bureaucratic organisation forms were designed to reinforce power relations. Blau and Scott (1963, cited in Clegg, Kornberger and Pitsis 2005) focused on who benefits from the existence of an organisation, ranging from the members themselves (e.g. a volunteer-led sports club) to "public-beneficent" organisations which attempt to serve the whole community (e.g. local authority sport development units with a perhaps less strategically focused approach). This suggests something which is borne out in practice, that an almost limitless range of organisational forms is evident across sport development in the public, voluntary and commercial sectors. Many of the specific sites of sport development activity are sub-units of much larger entities (e.g. sport development units within leisure departments within local authorities). This adds several layers of complexity to the challenge faced by strategic leaders in defining precisely what it is that needs to be subjected to analysis. As argued by Tovstiga (2010) and many others the emphasis needs to shift away from a strategic *planning* approach per se to one of strategic *thinking*. A manager in sport development who acts as a strategic thinker rather than strategic planner is better equipped to deal with complexity in a conceptual sense and therefore to lead a context-specific, practical process of capturing the identity and form of the 'organisation' which needs to be analysed. This will lead to better questions being asked and better-informed strategic decisions down the road. A strategic thinker is more advantageously positioned to encourage and enable organisational members to challenge the purpose and values to which they tacitly subscribe through their work, an essential aspect of strategic sport development in an ever-changing environment.

ORGANISATIONS

The purpose and values of an organisation (or sub-unit with a specific responsibility for sport development) are self-evidently key drivers in determining the strategic direction to be taken at any given time. They are a product of human interactions and reflect the stated needs and wants of internal and external stakeholders. In a dynamic world the organisational purpose and values are not necessarily permanent, but they should provide long-term guidance and should be specific enough to illustrate that the organisation is distinct from all others. Harquail (2011) defines organisational purpose as "how the organization aims to contribute to the larger world, in a qualitative way". In other words it is necessary to identify the deeper, underlying reasons behind the existence of an organisation and the collective work in which its members engage. For Harquail this gives meaning to the organisation's distinctiveness beyond its headline goals. For example, a local authority sport development team may state "increasing participation in sport in marginalised communities" as its overriding purpose, but it is perhaps more meaningful to look at the qualitative reasons *why* it wishes to achieve this: for instance, increasing life chances for under-represented groups, addressing health inequalities, reducing anti-social behaviour.

Identifying the organisation's distinctiveness helps to answer the question 'why us?' (Harquail 2011) and contributes greatly to enhancing direction, teamwork, leadership and responsibility. Often organisations within sport development will more or less have their broad purpose set out for them by some political entity that requires them to meet necessary targets, etc. to gain the required resources that keep people in jobs. How this purpose manifests itself into something desirable and appetising to those throughout the organisation is controlled by internal forces and therefore a process can occur that allows all stakeholders to influence how this takes shape. Inevitably this process will be influenced by the prevailing culture of the organisation, so it is essential that strategic leaders are equipped with the means to analyse it and make use of the outcomes.

The culture of an organisation has a fundamental impact on its ability to operate successfully in its relevant field. In part, this is due to external impressions and their influence upon prospective partners/customers/ service users. However, a more crucial role of culture is how it determines the internal workings of the organisation and whether or not this climate is conducive to encouraging the buy in of all stakeholders. It is representative of how those people involved in the organisation actually portray their place of work and whether or not this is positive or negative, therefore having an impact on various factors such as motivation and trust. This is what Mintzberg, Ahlstrand and Lampel (2005:265) refer to as collective cognition:

> It becomes the 'organisation's mind,' if you like, the shared beliefs that are reflected in traditions and habits as well as more tangible manifestations-stories, symbols, even buildings and products.

30

Schein (2010) offers an insightful analysis of the many different factors that impinge upon culture, listing factors such as group norms, espoused values, shared meanings, structural stability, depth and breadth amongst others. The embedded culture permeates all facets of the organisation and becomes normalised through the various communication networks, decisions, processes, and interactions of individuals and departments. As alluded to above, culture is a stable feature of many organisations, and although this can be challenged it is often the case that culture outlasts individuals and is therefore influenced by tradition and even folklore. Whetton and Godfrey (1998) state that an organisation's identity follows a similar process to that of an individual. It is socialised through its various networks, partnerships, political climate, comparisons to others in the industry and tasks that they engage in. Individuals and organisations can also have multiple identities depending on context and audience. This complements the thinking of Schein and his categorisation of different levels of culture (see Table 2.1).

As can be seen from Table 2.1 it is possible to have microcultures within an organisational culture, which will not be surprising to those working in larger organisations. However, despite this potential for a fragmented workforce (not necessarily a negative phenomenon) there is still a link between the departments that make up an organisation and how it is perceived within its own walls as well as in the external environment. It is often the role of a leader to present and convey the culture of the organisation, but this is not as straightforward as it seems.

Table 2.1 Adaptation of Schein's (2010) 'categories of culture'

Culture	Category
Macroculture	Nations, ethnic and religious groups, occupations that exist globally: FIFA, IOC
Organisational culture	Private, public, non-profit, government organisations: Sport England, NGBs
Subcultures	Occupational groups within organisations: sport development professionals, school sport partnerships within education
Microcultures	Microsystems within or outside organisations: tennis development team within a wider sport development unit

LEADING OR BEING LED BY CULTURE IN SPORT DEVELOPMENT

Leaders strive to ensure that their organisations' staff are customer friendly: service users are supposed to have a good experience when accessing whatever is on offer and this is done by creating a climate of customer-centeredness. Increasingly organisations recognise the need to be staff-centred and therefore create an environment that secures loyalty and ownership. These are factors that may impact upon culture but they are only factors and not culture per se. Such factors are controlled by managers or leaders and can be influenced by organisational policy and disciplinary procedures, etc. However, it is not always easy to prescribe the culture of the organisation despite attempts to do so. This is because, as noted above, it is the case that there is a presiding culture that greets new organisational leaders which can be difficult (and sometimes harmful) to radically change. This is neatly summarised by Schein (2010:3):

> The connection between culture and leadership is clearest in organizational cultures and microcultures. What we end up calling a culture in such systems is usually the result of the embedding of what a founder or leader has imposed on a group that has worked out. In this sense, culture is ultimately created, embedded, evolved, and ultimately manipulated by leaders. At the same time, with group maturity, culture comes to constrain, stabilize, and provide structure and meaning to group members even to the point of ultimately specifying what kind of leadership will be acceptable in the future.

Different organisations will relate differently to this situation and may well display a convergence of the two (i.e. a charismatic leader comes in and shakes things up in a very traditional organisation without jettisoning the historical importance and core values embedded within it). There are many examples of this dynamic within the world of elite, professional sport (how often do we see managers assuming leadership of sporting teams bring their own backroom staff and style of play?). There are also instances where we can see this kind of influence within NGBs: think about the relative professionalisation of many NGBs compared to their previous incarnations. This has sometimes been driven by external influences such as goal setting and funding dictated by governmental influence and the National Lottery. To drive these

32

changes we see more people coming from outside of sport to bring a different perspective and new methods in producing results, as can be seen in the examples of Jennie Price at Sport England (trained as a barrister and held posts in various fields before coming to sport) and Adam Crozier, formerly of the FA (background in advertising with Saatchi and Saatchi). Crozier in particular brought significant changes to the FA (thought of as a very traditional organisation) through his commercial activity, structural changes and the first ever foreign manager of the men's national team. These were not always met with appreciation by those affected by the change. There are doubtless examples of this kind of change within many different sport development units throughout the UK. Whether or not they are bought into or not will be dependent on many factors: what the actual changes are, how receptive existing members of the organisation are to any change, how these changes affect working conditions (more or less responsibility, freedom or constraint), the personalities of the various protagonists, etc. This is why there are many books now written on change management as it is seen as a critical aspect of developing organisations to be more productive.

ORGANISATIONAL CULTURE SHOULD BE FIT FOR PURPOSE

We have highlighted above the importance of having a clear notion of the organisation's purpose and developing culture accordingly (the issue of how to ensure people within the organisation feel empowered and can influence culture is covered in a more practical way in Chapters 5 and 7). There are numerous models of the prevailing cultures to be found in organisations, including the model popularised by Handy (1993) that connects culture to the structure of the organisation. As stated above these organisational forms may arise 'organically' or be deliberately instigated, particularly if a conscious link is made to structure.

One of Handy's culture types is the *power culture*. This is exhibited in organisations where power is concentrated among a small number of people and radiates outwards like a web. In this situation, the state of one's individual relationship with the central leader figure(s) may be more important than position in the hierarchy. In theory this approach should be rare or non-existent in inclusive, strategic sport development settings. However, there are examples, such as that of the Youth Sport Trust, in which charismatic individuals have established power cultures. This has not necessarily been to the detriment of the service as clear direction can be given by the charismatic leader, but a balancing act must be performed to maintain the engagement and support of the workforce and external stakeholders. A *role culture* is instinctively more familiar to sport development practitioners, particularly those in local authorities. Here, roles are very clearly defined, the organisation is structured hierarchically and line management is given prominence.

The bureaucratic nature of such organisations can mean that individuals without 'position power' can find themselves marginalised or undermined regardless of their expertise. A typical local authority sport development unit is embedded within a wider department or directorate, and its level of strategic autonomy is largely dependent upon the preferences of more senior colleagues. A *task culture*, conversely, can be a much more motivating environment, in which small teams are formed to address particular challenges. Power is conferred upon individuals as a consequence of expertise rather than position in the hierarchy. Imaginative, flexible structures are deployed in order to obtain solutions. Larger sport organisations such as some national governing bodies of sport are particularly well placed to take advantage of this approach.

The England and Wales Cricket Board (ECB), for instance, has over 100 development staff across England and Wales, many of whom are specialised, for example, women's and girls' development. Bringing together this regionalised expertise benefits women's and girls' cricket in a myriad of ways and provides the professionals concerned with a fulfilling experience. Finally, Handy highlights a *person culture*, which exists when the organisation is seen as subordinate to the individuals working there. This is a relatively unfamiliar scenario in strategic sport development, which is just as well since the goals around which the organisation was formed may be undermined by those of key individuals. Most organisational structures in sport development mitigate against this type of culture, although it may be witnessed in some of the smaller consultancy firms which provide services to sport development organisations.

In reality, were we to analyse a typical sport organisation we would find a potentially bewildering cocktail of charismatic individuals, productive working groups, stifling bureaucracy, abuses of position/power etc. In financially straitened times such as those of the post-'credit crunch' era, redundancies and other effects of budget cuts can have a demoralising effect on the culture of a sport organisation. Added to this is inclusive sport development's need for bottom-up decision-making, which requires meaningful engagement with customers. The strategic leader in sport development therefore needs to be cognisant of the inextricable relationship between culture and structure, and must work with staff, partners and service users at all levels to manage these and find the right blend in accordance with the organisation's purpose.

It is crucial that this insight into the organisational culture is recognised so that the resulting findings can be used to benefit the organisation. Organisational vision should incorporate the values of the organisation and therefore reflect the prevailing culture. Taking this a step further, it should be encouraged that your organisation's culture (presuming it is a positive force) is promoted in the external environment. This will hopefully foster positive relationships with stakeholders who have shared values. (Chapter 5 explores the analysis of culture in more depth with particular relevance to strategic implementation.)

ANALYSING CAPABILITIES: INTERNAL ASPECTS OF A SWOT ANALYSIS

A SWOT (Strengths, Weaknesses, Opportunities and Threats) analysis is the starting point for the development of strategic options (Lynch 2000) as it is the tool which encourages organisations to look at the current status of the organisation:

> The major attraction of SWOT analysis is that it is familiar and easily understandable by users, and it provides a good structuring device for sorting out ideas about the future and a company's ability to exploit that future. However, in practice the use of this tool has generally become sloppy and unfocused
>
> (Piercy 2001:539)

Strengths and weaknesses are identified from an internal, resource-based analysis of the organisation. Opportunities and threats are analysed by scanning the external environment (discussed in the next chapter). SWOT analysis can be undertaken at a number of levels from corporate down to team or project level. A key issue when using SWOT as a tool is to ensure that it is not so broad that the results become difficult to interpret. Doing SWOT analyses for different services may generate a range of strategic options for different areas of sport development work in the same organisation. Here we will consider the 'SW' of SWOT in the context of a wider analysis of internal capabilities.

First steps

Before analysing the organisation's strengths and weaknesses consider the following guidelines which will help generate better quality analysis:

- Keep it brief: pages of analysis are not necessary.
- Focus on the **key** strengths and weaknesses.
- Relate strengths and weakness to critical success factors for your area of work.
- Describe strengths and weaknesses in relation to the competition, expected standards or in terms of customer feedback; do not simply state that you are good or weak at something!
- Be specific: explain **why** something is a strength or weakness.
- Be realistic about your strengths and weaknesses. The analysis should distinguish between where you are now and where you want to be. Put yourself in the shoes of your customers, partners and stakeholders. If you think you can record something as both a strength and a weakness you have not analysed it well enough.

At all costs avoid meaningless statements. Here are a few examples (see Table 2.2) from actual experience of strategy planning workshops in sport development settings. These are classic examples of what Piercy (2001) would describe as 'motherhood' statements.

Table 2.2 Examples of statements from strategy planning workshops

Strengths	Hidden meaning?
'Breadth of service'	Jack-of-all-trades, master of none.
'Latent creativity'	We have some great ideas but we don't give ourselves time to develop them.
'Realistic delivery'	Customers don't expect a lot!

Stephen Robson, Lee Tucker and Rosemary Leach

In terms of the process involved in completing a SWOT analysis there are various key factors that should be addressed. Firstly, there is a need to decide who should be involved within the SWOT identification process. There are obvious factors to consider here, such as time commitment and members' roles/stake in the process, which need to be aligned with the ownership that this process offers. Getting the balance right between commitment and empowerment, whilst still making sure daily routines are not adversely affected is something of which leaders of this process need to be aware. It is impossible to state here who these participants should be as it will vary from organisation to organisation. However, be mindful that the outcomes which emerge should reflect the feelings and thoughts of all stakeholders and not just those privileged to be responsible for the end product.

Once the make up of the team who will conduct the SWOT is finalised the process itself needs to be figured out. One of the problems that can sometimes hinder the process is a lack of creativity in determining what the actual strengths and weaknesses are within an organisation. Staff may feel stifled by their discomfort in criticising others, or alternatively may feel a lack of confidence in stating what they are good at. As stated previously, unlocking the group's creativity is extremely useful to enable innovative changes to be made. Sloane (2006) explains that innovation is the implementation of creative ideas. There are many different methods available to help with this process. For instance, two problem-solving methods suggested by Parker and Stone (2003) are *helicopter vision* and *synectics*:

- **Helicopter vision**: this involves taking a dispassionate view to analysis rather than getting caught up emotionally. This could be achieved by getting someone from outside the immediate team to help objectively analyse your organisation's strengths and weaknesses (obviously this will be dependent on the availability of resources).
- **Synectics**: this method involves using analogies/metaphors to distort the problem (such as identifying weaknesses within the team/organisation). The distortion is then analysed and the results applied to the real problem. An example of this could be a hypothetical rival organisation or a sporting team.

As stated above it is not feasible to get all stakeholders around a table to facilitate this process but care must be taken to give them all an opportunity to comment upon the outcomes, including a chance to influence the final product. This needs to be built into the strategic process that the SWOT entails. The process may take on a timeline such as is this:

Step one: selection of SWOT identification steering group.

Step two: each member of group conducts mini-focus groups with those from their immediate areas/units.

Step three: identification of analytical tools to be used to aid process.

Step four: staging of initial SWOT meeting.

Step five: dissemination of initial outcomes of SWOT to all stakeholders, inviting feedback.

Step six: reconvening of steering group to consider feedback and amend SWOT where appropriate.

Step seven: dissemination of final outcomes including determination of how SWOT is to be used in strategic planning process.

Obviously this potentially lengthy process may not be necessary if the SWOT is purely for a small team rather than a sizeable organisation. However, what is important is adherence to the principles of inclusion, creativity and productivity in a strategic framework that helps with the effectiveness and efficiency of the organisation.

Table 2.3 below illustrates the strengths and weaknesses elements of a fictional SWOT for a district council's sport development service, undertaken as part of the process for developing a new sport strategy. Developing the SWOT in this format is only the first step. The next step is to generate strategic options by analysing the internal strengths and weaknesses and matching them with the opportunities and threats identified in the external environment (see next two chapters).

Table 2.3 SWOT example: the strengths and weaknesses of Cavendish Borough Council Sport Development Team

Strengths	Weaknesses
■ Experienced team with collective commitment to the strategic vision.	■ Lack of knowledge of disability sport within the team.
■ John sits on several project teams across the council, eg workplace health initiative.	■ Poor links with socio-economically disadvantaged communities in Fairfax and Priestley wards.
■ Jenny chairs the Cavendish Community Sports Network.	■ Limited knowledge within team of the principles of community development.
■ Often approached by County Sports Partnership to be the pilot authority for new projects.	■ A number of community-based sport development projects about to run out of funding (3 year projects).
■ Improved links with regional NGB teams in football, swimming and cricket. Now joint planning and good talent identification pathways developed.	■ Team has access to a number of qualified coaches/instructors to support activities, but mainly football, cricket and athletics and not in sufficient numbers.
■ Long history of school holiday sports coaching courses.	■ No expertise in outdoor adventurous activity.
■ Sport development team has achieved Quest Quality Award for Sports Development (82%).	■ Poor links with private sport clubs – (identified as an issue in Quest assessment).
■ Imran has lots of experience of attracting funding from sporting and other funding pots.	■ No team member able to use British Sign Language.
■ Core budget has been protected despite wider cuts so we still have money to spend!	■ Too much staff time expended on meeting in-house, bureaucratic requirements.
■ Team has protected, daytime access to leisure facilities.	■ Limited autonomy of sport development team to make strategic decisions.
■ Good range of sports coaching activities provided by the team at leisure centres for young people, but in mostly traditional sports.	■ The current 'Leisure Card' scheme has been declining in popularity and needs reworking, further diminishing the team's ability to support deprived communities.
■ Strong club development networks for traditional sports with many of these clubs in receipt of Clubmark or equivalent.	■ Current restrictions on recruitment of new staff due to budget cuts.
■ Good links with further and higher education establishments in Cavendish which has led to the development of a number of participation and volunteering programmes.	■ Lack of presence on Cavendish Metropolitan Borough Council website, and limited knowledge of, and use of social media technologies.
■ Sport Development Team has access to a large supply of good quality sports equipment.	
■ Sport Development Team has good links to local professional sports clubs who are happy to send players to support sports events across the borough.	

IMPLICATIONS OF THE STRENGTHS AND WEAKNESSES EXERCISE

Identifying the strengths and weaknesses that exist with your team is not the end of the process. Once the main headlines have been agreed there is then the need to analyse the implications of this, followed by generating necessary actions to build upon the strengths and diminish the weaknesses. Two examples of this are given below.

Example one

Strength: good range of sports coaching activities provided by team for young people, but mostly in traditional sports.

Implication: lots of income is generated via this provision and this is linked to strategic plans that have been written in partnership with NGBs and local clubs. This work can be used as a base to work more strategically in other sports and with other 'target groups'.

Action: develop a steering group of existing partners and new partners interested in developing minority sports and provision for other target groups.

Desired outcome: broader strategic planning and provision for more people to engage in more sports in the future.

Target: steering group to develop strategies for three different sports not currently part of the team's provision and for consultation with local community leaders to determine where provision is most needed and for whom.

Example two

Weakness: lack of knowledge within team regarding disability sport (links to current lack of provision).

Implication: if awareness and knowledge of disability sport are not increased we are neglecting a significant group of people within the community.

Action: training course to be delivered by Disability Sport Development Officer to all staff members. Team leader to organise by August 2014.

40

Desired outcome: development of knowledge and skills can increase opportunities to work with disabled participants.

Target: 20% increase in participation within first year.

The specific outcomes of the exercise will obviously differ for each organisation and team dependent on current provision, geographical location, resources, etc. but the principles remain the same for all. How you format and disseminate this plan will be dependent on the contextual specifics of who is conducting it. What is given above and what is offered in the next chapter in the section on 'How to do structure an external environment scan' are indicative examples. The most important thing is that the exercise creates awareness of what you are good at and what you need to improve upon, therefore making sure you move forward in a strategic manner, supported with evidence (being pro-active) rather than waiting until something becomes a crisis and dealing with it (being reactive). This is not to be confused with the principles of migration management covered in Chapter 5, as that model concerns the overall strategic direction of an organisation and how it is impacted upon by major shifts in the environment. Instead this SWOT exercise examines the short- to mid-term possibilities that you have to consider based on the resources at your disposal.

SKILLS AND ATTRIBUTES AUDIT

In order to develop a complete picture it is necessary to identify the skills and attributes required by the organisation and to cross-reference these with the actual position. In other words, it is important to be cognisant of your core purpose, what culture is preferred and accepted, what roles are necessary to deliver the activities that contribute to the successful achievement of the core purpose and thus the skills, knowledge and attributes that each person needs to enable them to contribute to this big picture. Clearly there will be processes in place to ensure this happens to a certain degree such as job descriptions, person specifications and performance appraisals. However, proactively interacting with the external environment and all the challenges it presents necessitates consistent monitoring and evaluation of what you have, what you need and what you do not need if you are to maintain a team capable of achieving success. This is particularly important for sport development organisations that wish to avoid becoming consciously incompetent, where resources (in this case, the all-important human variety) are out of alignment with the organisation's values and the work it wishes to undertake in the external environment.

The National Occupational Standards for Sport Development (SkillsActive 2010) provide a ready guide to the generic expectations of the industry in terms of what constitutes a sport development professional, but as discussed in the Introduction they have been woefully underused by the very profession they were developed to support. If the process of skills auditing begins with the task of assessing requirements for success in the external environment (Cognology 2011) then an external reference source such as the Standards is an invaluable start point. For instance, one of the themes of this book is inclusivity and the serving of communities in an authentic way. Standard D61, "Facilitate community-based sport and physical activity" emphasises that this requires sport development professionals to communicate effectively (listening skills are vital here), negotiate with people and empathise with others (SkillsActive 2010). In each specific situation, engagement with communities is necessary in order to identify the precise expression of these skills required for success.

The identification of any skills gaps is then achieved through a process of assessing or appraising team members' current levels of skills and knowledge. Evidence to support this activity can be generated through reviewing preceding personal development plans, assessing feedback from clients, colleagues and partners and perhaps most importantly, through personal reflection. An honest picture can thus be painted of each individual's stage of development relevant to the demands of the external environment. Wolsey and Whitrod Brown (2012) stress that this should be a consensual, bottom-up and *exciting* process which is aspirational and developmental. As with all other strategic processes covered in this book it should not be presumed that this is a 'once every few years' task; instead strategic leaders should facilitate skills auditing on an ongoing, incremental basis in line with all other aspects of flexible strategic management.

New personal development plans can subsequently be developed to ensure that teams are capable of meeting (primarily) the needs of the community they work with and (secondly) the professional standards they should be pursuing (discussed further in Chapter 5). As Wooden and Jamison (2005:46) note:

The best leaders understand that to successfully compete at any level requires continuous learning and improvement. Unless the leader communicates this up and down the line and puts mechanisms in place to ensure it gets done your team will not be at 100 percent in its performance level.

The key message is therefore that a commitment to the development of staff is essential if they and their organisation are to realise their potential. The beauty of engaging meaningfully with this process is the added bonus of people feeling valued and better motivated to bring success to the organisation.

ASSESSING MOTIVATION

Having knowledge of the various skills of the workforce is self-evidently important in identifying organisational strengths and weaknesses. However, just as important, if not more so, is a workforce whose members are motivated to do the tasks necessary for success within an organisation. This relates to sport teams: some have a team of stars and others have a star team. Having the most skilled people within your team does not always guarantee results and in fact, these teams often achieve less than those 'less skilled' but more harmonious teams whose members want to do well for each other. Assessing commitment to the team can be difficult as it may be hard to interpret the outward signs given by someone sitting at a desk. This can be achieved through the adoption of an organisational culture that promotes trust and honesty, and therefore enables people to *problematise* their lack of motivation. Supportive colleagues can work with that person to find the missing ingredient that restores the necessary enthusiasm we presume they had when first applying for the job.

Henry and Lee's (2004) seven principles of transparency, accountability, democracy, responsibility, equity, efficiency and effectiveness can be adopted by those responsible for improving governance. Furthermore Ellen *et al.* (2006) discuss how managers, by embracing social exchange theory, can impact upon motivation by creating relationships of trust between employers and employees. This does not happen overnight and requires employees to want to stay with an organisation for a period of time, but the resulting delegation of responsibilities and provision of social support should engender a trustful relationship and therefore a more positively motivated employee. Having this kind of culture is probably the most effective way of being able to engage with workers regarding their motivational levels in an honest way via conversations, team meetings and appraisals.

LEADERS, FOLLOWERS AND TEAMS

Reference to team meetings points us towards another important aspect of analysing the capabilities of an organisation. Having an awareness of the strengths and weaknesses of individuals (leaders and followers) as well as whole teams is critical to establish the potentiality of the organisation. The power of self-analysis should not be underestimated: giving individuals and teams the opportunity to identify their own strengths and areas for improvement will increase their prospects of contributing to the overall goals of the organisation as well as their own personal development. However, this form of navel gazing is sometimes resisted by individuals who may well feel uncomfortable shedding light on the insecurities they feel regarding their ability to perform their role effectively. Therefore, having somebody from outside the team come in to provide objective but sensitive opinions on how the team operates can add new perspective and unearth nuances of the team's work that they have not been aware of themselves. (This is explored further in Chapter 9 in a discussion of the Johari window process.)

ANALYSING RESOURCES

Examining business strategy formulation is an action that would be of significant benefit in sport development. Porter (1985) proposes that there are two broad competitive strategies for outperforming other organisations in a specific industry or sector. 'Lower cost strategy' is the capability of an organisation to design, produce and market a similar product more resourcefully and efficiently than its rivals. In sport development terms this could be a governing body developing a new programme and having a superior ability to devise, generate and promote it than any of its close adversaries. 'Differentiation strategy' is the capability to provide exclusive and enhanced merit/value to the buyer in terms of product quality, special features and after sales services.

44

From a sport development perspective this differentiation is about providing a new activity/initiative that varies significantly from others, has something unique about it and provides opportunities for future engagement and advancement.

Developing this theme further, Porter suggests that an organisation's competitive advantage is determined by its 'competitive scope': the extent of the organisation's target market. Before deciding to use one of the two broad competitive strategies the organisation must decide on the product varieties, the distribution channels, the type of customer it will serve, the geographical area into which it will aim the product and who or what they will be competing against. Sport development strategists should therefore be aware that they can choose a wide target audience or concentrate on a narrow audience (aiming at a specific niche).

Carrying out this level of detailed analysis of the external environment alone is not sufficient to provide an organisation with a competitive advantage. It is also essential to look inside the organisation and detect internal strategic aspects: the critical power and limitations that are potential barriers to whether or not an organisation can take full advantage of opportunities and avoids threats. In any sport development organisation entering a strategy development process it is crucial to determine and develop the resources available to them. Wheelen and Hunger (2009) suggest that a resource is a strength controlled by an organisation if it leads to competitive advantage. They also state that a resource is a weakness if it is something the organisation does badly or does not have the competence to do correctly.

Barney and Hesterly (2009) provide the VRIO framework for analysis (value, rareness, imitability, and organisation) and recommend four questions to appraise an organisation's key resource:

1   Does it offer competitive advantage (value)?
2   Is it unique to our organisation (rareness)?
3   Would it be costly/difficult for others to copy it (imitability)?
4   Is the organisation able to enhance and develop the resource (organisation)?

If it is possible to say yes to these questions for a specific resource then that resource can be deemed a distinguishing force and a unique proficiency. Once the importance of these resources has been assessed it is then possible to determine how the organisation will be able to establish and sustain a competitive advantage. A sport development organisation should examine its distinctive competencies and select the strategy that best makes the most of them. At the same time it should identify resource gaps and invest in any perceived weaknesses.

In many aspects sport development in the UK operates entirely in a competitive environment. What we have is a set of organisations offering interconnected products, services or experiences. It is a competitive situation in which sports organisations can imitate success almost immediately due to the fact that development information is freely available. This is a direct result of collaboration being a founding principle of sport development (Robson 2008). Information on successful programmes, products and initiatives is frequently made available at conferences, seminars and in meetings. As there are no opportunities for establishing 'price wars', there is no need to be covert or vague and everyone appears to give generously their ideas and materials. Essentially, although sport development organisations function within a 'hypercompetitive' environment (in that there are numerous players, there are only temporary opportunities to sustain advantage and there will always be some winners and losers in terms of the level of success linked to participation) they do not seek competitive advantage to the detriment of others and continue to collaborate and develop strategic alliances.

THE RELATIONSHIP BETWEEN RESOURCES AND ORGANISATIONAL PURPOSE

It can be argued that resource allocation is a crucial aspect of strategic planning and implementation. In many situations resource allocation occurs towards the end of the process, but in a more continuous or emergent planning process resources are provided then reallocated throughout the year, depending upon current conditions and the viability of projects. However, a guiding principle here is that resource allocation should be driven by, and in line with, the overall purpose of the organisation. Hopefully it is obvious that the SWOT process discussed above (as well as the external analysis discussed in the next chapter) should help determine what opportunities can be exploited for

Stephen Robson, Lee Tucker and Rosemary Leach

the betterment of the organisation and its goals. It should also unveil any weaknesses that can impact on the organisation's purpose and therefore help to develop solutions to remedy such problems. It is also important that the organisation's purpose is realistic bearing in mind the resources it has or can potentially tap into. So, if the key purpose of your organisation is to deliver affordable, introductory tennis sessions as a means to bring young people together then there is no need to purchase top of the range equipment and hire out private courts. Money would be much better spent on a development officer who has a good grasp of the issues faced by the participants and understands the local area.

SUMMARY

The focus of this chapter has been to stress the influence of internal factors upon organisational performance. It therefore aimed to encourage sport development professionals to consider the measures that they can put in place to give the organisation the best possible chance to fulfil its potential. Controlling the 'controllable' factors is one thing that you do have power over within an otherwise uncertain social and economic climate. Ensuring that those in positions of influence actively and effectively listen to those delivering the services of the organisation is key to building an organisation based on trust and respect. This principle is developed in the Strategic Leadership chapter later in the book. Taking steps to understand your organisation and the decisions necessary for improvement in its core areas of work should be done via a SWOT analysis, but equally important is to foster a positive culture.

This integral process of critical self-analysis paves the way for better strategic thinking. Alongside this is the need to ensure that people work within resource constraints. Being cognisant of the skills possessed by those within the organisation is critical in being able to meet the demands and expectations the organisation lays out in its purpose. This matching of the organisational values with resources is a key aspect of the E-V-R congruence model. Once this has been established the organisation should be in a stronger position to deal with the demands of the external environment, discussed in Chapter 3.

LEARNING ACTIVITIES

Developing skills

National Occupational Standard A12, "Contribute to strategic development in sport and active leisure" identifies the need for professionals to be able to "Monitor the internal environment, to assess organisational capability and identify key issues relevant to your area of responsibility and those of your colleagues". (SkillsActive 2010). To advance your development, conduct an analysis of strengths and weaknesses in a team, unit or department in which you operate. This analysis should be focused upon the ability of the team, unit or department to achieve an agreed outcome (e.g. delivering an event or project; helping a sport club to increase participation amongst under-represented groups, etc.). You should seek to lead the analysis according to the principles of *helicopter vision* and *synectics* set out earlier in the chapter, using the seven-step process as a guide. For each strength and weakness you identify remember to assess its implication and generate at least one action, one desired outcome and one target in order to capitalise upon the analysis.

As well as making best use of the outcomes of the analysis you should ask your colleagues for feedback to enable you to perform even more effectively next time. You can cross-reference the analysis of your performance to the principles set out in the leadership chapter (Chapter 9).

Developing knowledge

Conduct an analysis of a team, unit or department in which you operate to identify which combination of Handy's (1993) four culture types is in evidence. (This may entail conversations, observations or formal interviews so please ensure this is not done covertly but with the full knowledge and consent of colleagues.) Consider the implications of your findings, for example:

1 Is the current situation the most beneficial in terms of the team, unit or department achieving its vision?
2 What combination of culture types would be more beneficial?

48

3   What steps are needed to achieve the preferred situation (CPD, structural changes etc.)?

REFERENCES

Barney, J. and Hesterly, W. (2009) *Strategic Management and Competitive Advantage*. 3rd ed. Harlow, Pearson Education.

Blau, P. and Scott, W. (1963) 'Formal Organizations: A Comparative Approach'. London, Routledge and Kegan Paul. In Clegg, S., Kornberger, M. and Pitsis, T. (2005) *Managing and Organizations: An Introduction to Theory and Practice*. London, Sage.

Clegg, S., Kornberger, M. and Pitsis, T. (2005) *Managing and Organizations: An introduction to theory and practice*. London, Sage.

Cognology (2011) 'Competency Assessment'. Available at http://www.cognology.co.uk/cbawhatis.htm.

Ellen, P., Webb, D. and Mohr, L. (2006) 'Building Corporate Associations: consumer attributions for corporate socially responsible programs'. *Journal of the Academy of Marketing Science*, 34 (2), 147–57.

Handy, C. (1993) *Understanding Organizations*. 4th ed. London, Penguin.

Harquail, C. (2011) 'Make Distinctiveness Matter by Linking it to Organizational Purpose'. USA, Authentic Organisations. Available at http://authenticorgan izations.com/harquail/2011/06/14/make-distinctiveness-matter-by-linking-it-to-organizational-purpose/.

Haywood, L. (1994) *Community Leisure and Recreation*. Oxford, Butterworth Heinemann.

Henry, I. and Lee, P. (2004) 'Governance and Ethics in Sport'. In Beech, J. and Chadwick, S. eds. *The Business of Sport Management*. Harlow, Pearson Education, pp. 25–43.

Jackson, P. and Delhanty, H. (2006) *Sacred Hoops: Spiritual Lessons of a Hardwood Warrior*. New York, Hyperion.

Lynch, R. (2000) *Corporate Strategy*. 2nd ed. Harlow, Pearson Education.

Mintzberg, H., Ahlstrand, B. and Lampel, J. (2005) *Strategy Bites Back: It is a lot More, and Less, than You Ever Imagined*. Harlow, Prentice Hall.

Parker, C. and Stone, B. (2003) *Developing Management Skills for Leadership*. Essex, Pearson Education.

Piercy, N. (2001) *Market-Led Strategic Change*. GB, Butterworth Heinemann.

Porter, M. (1985) *Competitive Advantage*. New York, The Free Press.

Robson, S. (2008) 'Partnerships in Sport'. In Hylton, K. and Bramham, P. eds. *Sports Development: Policy, Process and Practice*. 2nd ed. Abingdon, Routledge, pp. 118–142.

Schein, E. (2010) *Organizational Culture and Leadership*. 4th ed. San Francisco, Jossey Bass.

SkillsActive (2010) 'NOS: sports development'. Available at http://www.skillsactive.com/skillsactive/national-occupational-standards/level-3/item/3260/3260.

Slack, T. and Parent, M. (2006) *Understanding Sport Organizations.* 2nd ed. Champaign, Human Kinetics.

Sloane, P. (2006) *The Leaders Guide to Lateral Thinking Skills.* 2nd ed. London, Kogan Page.

Thompson, J. (2001) *Understanding Corporate Strategy.* London, Thomson Learning.

Tovstiga, G. (2010) *Strategy in Practice: a Practitioner's Guide to Strategic Thinking.* Chichester, Wiley.

Wheelen, T. and Hunger, D. (2009) *Concepts in Strategic Management and Business Policy.* NJ, Pearson Prentice Hall.

Whetton, D. and Godfrey, P. (1998) *Identity in Organizations: Building Theory Through Conversations.* London, Sage.

Wolsey, C. and Abrams, J. (2001) *Understanding the Leisure and Sport Industry.* Harlow, Longman.

Wolsey C. and Whitrod Brown, H. (2012) 'Human Resource Management & the Business of Sport'. In Trenbirth, L. and Hassan, D. eds. *Managing Sport Business: An Introduction.* London, Routledge, pp. 146–168.

Wooden, J. and Jamison, S. (2005) *Wooden on Leadership.* New York, McGraw-Hill.

CHAPTER 3

THE EXTERNAL ENVIRONMENT

LEE TUCKER AND MATT SULLIVAN

INTRODUCTION

Achieving a strategy that meets the challenges and demands of the external environment is probably the most difficult and complex aspect of the strategic process. The dynamic nature of all that is external to the organisation creates barriers, problems and issues that need to be addressed through the use of a combination of forward thinking (some would say clairvoyance), meticulous research and in-depth knowledge of the social structures and processes that impact upon the services provided by sport development professionals (SDPs). Mintzberg, Ahlstrand and Lamped (1998:287) state how "leadership as well as organisation becomes subordinate to the external environment", recognising the importance of scanning the environment within which sport development professionals operate. They also discuss how 'the environmental school' draws upon contingency theory as opposed to classical management theory due to the diversity of factors organisations such as sport development units need to be aware of when operating within a complex environment.

The dynamic, complex, diversified and hostile environment (Mintzberg 1979: 268–269 in Mintzberg, Ahlstrand and Lamped 1998) that SDPs have to negotiate makes this one of the most challenging professions. The impact of governmental change upon funding is an example of the dynamic nature of sport development. It is complex due to trends and tastes that emerge and have to be exploited; it is diversified due to the nature of the very different individuals and communities with whom

SDPs will be expected to work; and it is hostile due to the competition and sedentary temptations that are part of modern day society, such as computer games, cheap alcohol, etc.

DEFINING THE EXTERNAL ENVIRONMENT

"The external environment is literally the big wide world in which organisations operate" (Capon 2008:30). Factors that can affect an organisation's strategy can range from localised, parochial issues to the global markets that impact on entire industries and economies. Activities ranging from recruiting volunteers in a local setting to tapping into national funding streams can be enhanced through scanning the external environment. The external environment within which each organisation/ agency is located is unique, ranging from sport specific units looking to increase participation in small rural areas to large sport development units delivering a diverse range of activities and projects across major cities. The scope of issues aligned to the external environment creates a number of challenges as well as opportunities.

PROBLEMS, BENEFITS AND CONSEQUENCES OF SCANNING THE EXTERNAL ENVIRONMENT

The time to do an effective external environment scan is something very few sport development professionals possess, yet without it they are delivering blindly to customers without the necessary evidence to support their programmes and overall strategy. Sufficient time must therefore be given to this process as without it the whole strategic vision is built on weak foundations. The danger of this is that it leads to tokenistic delivery plans that have no long term benefit for the communities they espouse to serve. Ultimately a recycled 'vision' or 'plan' will be rolled out every few years to tackle the same problems with the same ideas but with different coloured equipment and the latest 'sport accessory'. The underlying purpose behind strategy must be thought through in detail before commencing analysis of the external environment.

Another complication is provided by partnership working, a fundamental requirement of contemporary sport development (Robson 2008) (see

52

Chapter 7). Partner organisations have different priorities, resources and cultures, so the scanning of the external environment on behalf of a partnership initiative needs to be the subject of negotiation alongside all other aspects of joint working. This is an important responsibility. Expedient lip service which ticks boxes such as 'consultation with stakeholders' via a few questionnaires must be avoided. Meaningful engagement in external scanning by all stakeholders results in a purposeful, shared vision.

A key benefit of taking the time and effort to conduct a thorough external environment scan is that greater credibility is afforded to headline targets and key performance indicators (KPIs). Space can be given in the strategy document to an exposition of the reasons for specific targets via the accrued evidence, a good example of which can be seen in the Sport Leeds 'Taking the Lead' strategy (Sport Leeds 2006). A genuine knowledge of the socio-political environment within which the SDP works is crucial in determining what these targets should be.

DATA GATHERING

As has been stated elsewhere the fact that sport development is developing into a graduate profession means that more and more people will be entering the industry having had formal tuition on the benefits and processes of data gathering. Adopting appropriate methodologies to help understand patterns of behaviour as well as demands and desires of stakeholders needs to be strategically planned and facilitated, to ensure useful information is made available from which to make effective and efficient decisions. Leaving a pile of questionnaires on a table in the hope that people will complete them, or having a comments box will not suffice (although this is not to say these methods will not be used). Instead, careful consideration needs to be given to the methodological process, including forethought on how the data will be analysed once gained; what kind of sampling process will be adopted (random, purposive, stratified, etc.); and what the size of the sample should be to ensure the data generated is valid and representative. All of these questions, and others, are instrumental in the following sections where each factor relating to the external environment is analysed using the STEEPLE model. There are pockets of readily available data, such as those generated by the Active People Survey (Sport England 2011a) but often you will be faced with the challenge of getting the information you need yourself. If you are not familiar with this process and how it can be improved, then there are plenty of research methods texts available to aid you (e.g. Long 2007).

INTRODUCING THE STEEPLE MODEL

We now turn our attention in detail to the principal factors that should be taken into consideration when doing an external scan. For practitioners it will hopefully encourage you and your colleagues to afford the deserved consideration and resources necessary to do an effective external environment scan, and consequently improve relationships and practice within the communities you serve.

Although there are various models that can be applied to do this we have selected the STEEPLE (social, technological, economic, environment, political, legal and ethical) model for two key reasons. First, we believe that this model covers the most essential areas of the external scanning process within a sport development context and second, more pragmatically the seven areas can be covered in sufficient detail within the space available to us! Each of these will be taken in turn, starting with social factors.

Social factors

The social element of the STEEPLE model encompasses factors such as the demographics of an area served by the sport development team and the specific cultural needs of various communities. An assessment of the actual needs and desires of those people for whom services are created is a crucial step in the process of ensuring that provision is both effective and efficient. Sociology of sport, 'the study of sport and society', raises many issues in terms of how sections of society are either prevented or discouraged from participating in certain sports (and physical activity in general). Many factors impinge upon the sport and physical activity experiences and perceptions of individuals and groups within society which will influence their participation in the opportunities created and presented by sport development teams.

Gendered approaches to sport and physical activity often mean that females have had less encouragement and less opportunity to participate in the wide range of activities to which males have privileged access. This can stem from family influences in deterring girls from playing 'rough games' to the gendered approach often evident within school PE provision. 'Racial' stereotyping is another disabling influence that can result in such issues as 'stacking', by which people with one ethnicity will be presumed to have greater strengths than somebody of another ethnicity, based purely on skin colour (Coakley and Donnelly 1998). This can then become a self-fulfilling prophecy that prevents individuals trying other activities or even other positions within some sports. Due to medical breakthroughs and greater awareness of healthier lifestyles it is also important to recognise that people are living longer. SDPs need to recognise that this brings with it a need to provide bespoke provision as much for older people as they do for other target groups.

There are also issues around class and sport. The cost of equipment is often influential in determining whether a sport is offered as an option to people within certain schools or communities. The cultural markers of certain sports can also influence participation decisions based on whether individuals believe they have the cultural capital to negotiate certain cultural fields. Complex factors such as clothes, accent, terminology and brand of equipment can all highlight differences in people and can result in exclusion from groups and the sports they play. Disability is another social factor that can be exclusive and cause drop out for those feeling either devalued or simply not catered for. This can range from something as simple as being treated with respect to not being able to participate due to access issues with facilities and activities.

It is not possible here to give an in-depth analysis of all these individual and structural barriers that prevent people from participating in sport and physical activity but there is plenty of literature that performs this task. Coakley's tenth edition of 'Sport in Society' (2010) or Cashmore's fourth edition of 'Making Sense of Sport' (2005) are good starting points for closer scrutiny of these issues. SDPs need to be aware of this and support other 'sport development practitioners' such as teachers, coaches, parents, etc. to be aware of the role they have when providing opportunities for target groups.

The Sport England (2011b) market segmentation tool offers a profile of what is referred to as 'dominant segments' within specific geographical locations. The nineteen different segments have distinctive profiles such as 'male recent graduates, with a work-hard, play-hard attitude' and offer a back-story to that person's life including ethnicity, interests, etc. Although a diverse range of profiles is given, the model is open to criticism due to the boxes into which it tries to put people. The ability to classify people within the same segments is therefore fraught with problems of identity and homogeneity. However, despite these flaws it may provide SDPs with prompts towards lines of enquiry they need to follow to ensure their work is socially inclusive.

An empathy of these issues is only the starting point towards providing a robust programme of activities that will be bought into. As noted earlier, without consulting local individuals and communities we are left with a top-down, exclusive approach to programming rather than a bottom-up, inclusive model of practice. Bramham (1994) discusses how this leads to an attempt at the 'democratisation of culture', which tries to assimilate people into a pre-determined plan of delivery and culture. More preferable is an inclusive, cultural democracy approach, which empowers people to take ownership of their own leisure time, and therefore promises a much more integrative approach to sport and physical activity engagement.

A good example of how this consultation process can work is highlighted in 'Kevin McCloud's Big Town Plan', a Channel 4 (2008) documentary on the social and economic regeneration of Castleford in West Yorkshire. The documentary followed four major projects within the Castleford area aimed at engaging communities and improving the social and economic conditions of the area through engineering. Rather than just transporting 'experts of design' into the area and 'giving the local communities their medicine', the communities had a genuine voice in what was to be implemented via the representation of local champions – people who actually lived and worked within the affected areas. They were responsible for deciding which engineers got the work and they monitored the project throughout. There is no reason why this process cannot be rolled out into the sport development sector. For instance, the use of local sport alliances in Leeds is one way in which we are aware that local voices can influence wider strategic decisions.

Technological factors

Rapid technological advances within the UK and the rest of the Western world can prove to be both frightening and exciting for SDPs. Software packages, social networking and mobile devices can be intimidating. However, those more 'techie' individuals who embrace this new age of media technology and communication are presented with a raft of opportunities for them to tap into and potentially interact with more people more efficiently.

However, one of the key issues to consider – and why the external scan is so important – is that it is necessary to know what technology your stakeholders have access to, and are comfortable with before deciding on your choice of communication method. Email and the Internet may be commonplace, but in many of the communities served by SDPs such technology is a relative luxury so it is important for the environmental scan to identify the prevailing methods of communication in settings of interest. Good old fashioned leaflets and posters in community venues as well as interpersonal communication with individuals and groups may seem archaic to some but they are still valid approaches! Interaction with people is still considered a key part of the SDP's armoury.

The situation will differ from person-to-person and community-to-community, so the external environment scan must identify what works best in each and every area of interest. How you collate this information is context specific, but small scale surveys and questionnaires directed at strategic places and times should create the data you need to help plan your future communication and practice. Once you have relevant information then keeping a record on a database should help you to keep track of trends as they emerge over time and how technological advances are being adopted or jettisoned by the stakeholders that are important to you. Keeping databases for different aspects of your work can also be helpful to avoid duplication and develop co-ordination between your unit and others who may be targeting the same communities for different purposes, leading to more efficient and effective working practices for you and working relationships with others.

A relatively new technique for the evaluation of your working relations and methods is social network analysis. This method allows you to distinguish what interactions are taking place, what information is being shared (or not) and who are the integral individuals who receive and share the most information. This can help to highlight the key players in the relationships, as well as those individuals who may be more prone to stress due to the sheer amount of information and responsibility they are obliged to manage/process. This method can also be helpful in terms of identifying leaders within target communities, therefore influencing the communication 'hierarchy' and methods that you pursue. For more practical and theoretical information on social network analysis see Scott (2000) and Cross and Parker (2004).

The final technological aspect of the external environment to be covered here is the role and use of the media within sport development. A range of media can be used to keep track of other services and products available to communities, ensuring you are aware of service gaps as well as opportunities to form alliances with similarly motivated agencies. Identifying the most appropriate medium for each message you want to send is also important. Whether it is for grand opening events or the marketing of a weekly aerobic class, the use of relevant, local media to help 'get the word out' is vital.

Economic factors

The financial events of 2008–09 and the subsequent recession meant that significant changes took place in the lifestyles of many individuals and the practices (or even existence) of many organisations within the UK. This challenge is likely to demand more creative and expedient ways of delivering sport development. The 'sports industry' contributes to the economy through a plethora of factors such as the manufacturing of sport equipment, sportswear, facility hire, sport events, spectatorship, etc. Despite the economy of sport often being associated with professional and elite competition, many of the above factors are affected by the day to day engagement of ordinary people and the choices they make. It is a SDP's responsibility to ensure they have a balance of affordable and accessible provision whilst ensuring they act within budget constraints. Sourcing external funding support is a now daily consideration for many in sport development.

Financial constraints and opportunities that arise

Something that many SDPs are accustomed to is the need to do more work with fewer resources. Having worked in a sport development unit where cuts appeared to be an annual inevitability but where output needed to be maintained or improved/increased, we can confirm that

Lee Tucker and Matt Sullivan

this presents a test of SDPs' mettle to remain upbeat and positive about the work they do. However, this is often what spurs these same professionals to be creative and enduring people that are able to make the best out of constrained parameters. In fact these circumstances can actually lead to more inclusive and bottom-up provision, due to their ability to negate certain resource by the empowerment and ownership of local people 'doing it for themselves'. Ledwith (2005), Hylton and Totten (2008) and others discuss the importance of this type of provision where people are given the opportunity to act for themselves rather than being dependent on 'the professionals' being parachuted in to give others the 'benefit of their expertise'.

Funding/grants

One way in which SDPs are crucial in supporting the empowerment process is through their cultural capital, which allows them to navigate the confusing terrain that accompanies funding and grant applications. Indeed, some organisations employ people (whether paid or unpaid) whose sole responsibility is to deal with these issues, current examples being British Cycling (voluntary) and Oxfam (paid). Being aware of opportunities to receive funding can be crucial in the survival of many local sport clubs. The Community Amateur Sports Club scheme is something that many clubs may not be aware of, as it is estimated that sports clubs are losing £60 million per year by not registering with it (Community Amateur Sports Club 2010). SDPs should be aware of such schemes and pass this knowledge on to others to help fund sport provision within communities.

Strategic approach to managing the 'economy' of sport development

The above issues highlight the need for SDPs to strategically plan their route through the financial landscape that impacts upon practice and provision. Being aware of funding and grant opportunities can be extremely beneficial in aiding sport development work, but alongside this is the need to pool resources through the use of strategic partnerships and therefore avoid duplication (see Chapter 7). The shifting political, cultural and social context that SDPs have to negotiate means that their flexibility when it comes dealing with economic issues as they arise is key to their chances of success.

Environmental factors

This section refers to 'the environment' in terms of the physical world we inhabit. Growing government interest in environmental policy has encouraged many organisations from the public, voluntary and commercial sectors to make similar considerations when creating and developing their own strategic plans (Carter 2006). The emphasis on modern living being environmentally conscious is an important aspect of most policy movements (Moisander and Pesonen 2002), which often start at a global level and permeate into national government policy; regional fora and partnerships; local authority alliances; and the lives of individuals within society. It is not this chapter's intention to examine these policies or political movements in any detail; rather it looks to raise awareness of them in a sport development context. Important, global, political movements have shaped green policy and include: Brundtland Commission Report 1987; the 1992 United Nations Conference on Environment and Development; the 2002 World Summit on Sustainable Development; the Climate Change Act 2008; the 2009 Copenhagen Climate Change Conference, although it was criticised by the media for accepting weak agreements for global policy (Vidal, Stratton and Goldenberg 2009); and the London Olympics and Paralympics 'One Planet Olympics' theme.

The relevance of global, environmental debates to sport development should be evaluated as part of the STEEPLE analysis. Traditionally, any sport organisation's examination of its immediate and broader 'environment' through STEEPLE (or similar models) would be related to physical objects such as an urbanised or rural landscape, the number of football pitches and other green spaces, and the number of existing sports organisations that might pose a potential threat or be an ally (Torkildsen 2005). Yet while these aspects may still appear in an environmental analysis, the previously discussed 'green policy' should feature in any future investigation. With the 2012 London Olympic Games finding its way into most sport development organisations' discourse, it is hard to imagine that such an event, whether held in a positive or negative light by people, would not influence sport and recreation activities. So many policy agendas of this sort meander or crash into sport and recreation initiatives and programmes, and the SDPs need to respond accordingly. It is this issue that should make the assertive and mindful SDP consider how their activities, events, and

60

programmes affect the environment and how the environment impacts upon their strategic planning. Examples of this include Youth Games; sports clubs; school sport festivals; and adult health activities, such as organised walks and charity runs. These all project the same environmental concerns as those of London 2012 (although on a smaller scale). For example, participants and supporters travelling to and from these events provide an interesting issue, with government policy focusing on promoting greater use of a more efficient, green and effective public transport system (House of Commons Library 2011). The use of green spaces for sport and recreation at the possible expense of wildlife reserves can create many interesting debates too. The preservation of green spaces, which are often lost to housing developments, is another perhaps unexpected policy space into which SDPs are being drawn.

Political factors

It has become essential for modern day SDPs to grasp political awareness and any sport development organisation must have the ability to assess the current and potential political power that will ultimately govern their existence in the field (Coalter 2007). Not only does the organisation need to account for the political ideology of the government of the day, but they also need to look towards European and even global political activities to grasp a complete political picture (Hylton and Totten 2008). The synergy between sport and politics has been strengthened significantly over the last two decades as key sporting figures have become more effective lobbyists. UK Prime Ministers Major, Blair and Brown also saw sport as a crucial social tool within the UK and promoted its benefits through increased investment.

SDPs should consider their own programmes and activities, and the role they can play in safeguarding sport development's future. Strategic thinking should begin with an understanding of the national government's ideology (more on this can be seen in Chapter 8) and how sport development organisations can exist alongside it (Houlihan and White 2002). To keep this potentially unwieldy area in some order, this section of the STEEPLE analysis should be subdivided into three categories: macro, which focuses on national policy issues; meso, which examines regional policy issues; and micro, which discusses local policy delivery and evaluation (Houlihan 2000).

Macro

As suggested earlier a good understanding at a macro level of politics will help the sport development organisation establish why and how policies exist, and formulate their response to them (Bramham 2008). When analysing the political forces which shape policy, the sports development organisation should be prepared to look beyond UK shorelines. A focus on United Nations and the European Union movements may prove interesting (Houlihan and White 2002 and Heywood 2007).

When New Labour came to power in 1997 the 'social inclusion policy movement' was probably the most dominant of its core ideologies (Houlihan and White 2002). Yet support for elite sports was prominent through initiatives such as the World Class programme and the governmental backing for the 2012 bid. It is interesting to consider the impact of this movement upon localised sports planning. Some recent examples include the sport and development approach used to tackle humanitarian and conflict crisis (International Platform on Sport and Development 2012); Sports Action Zones; Active Sports; sports facilities development often through the Private Funding Initiative (PFI); the PE and Sport Strategy for Young People (PESSYP); Sports Unlimited; and the Community Amateur Sports Club Scheme. This list includes many casualties of governmental change and cutbacks, illustrating that it is not only essential for SDPs to be aware of existing opportunities, but also to be able to anticipate future developments. Minimising dependence upon central policy moves makes an important contribution to future-proofing the service.

Meso

Many sports policies will permeate from the national arena to a meso level, which allows a more localised perspective to be applied (Houlihan and White 2002 and Bramham 2008). Various consultation activities, sports fora, boards and groups will assemble at this level of planning and help create a more recognisable form of programme, which is almost ready for delivery (Bramham 2008). Some examples of meso policy activities (past and present) include Sport England regional fora; Regional Sports Boards; Active Sports; County Sport Partnerships (although they do deliver at a sub-regional level); Sports Unlimited; the Community Sports Coaches scheme (where policy planning takes place); and NGB fora. There is perhaps more of an opportunity for the well-informed and future-focused SDP to influence the outputs of bodies at this level.

Micro

The micro or local stage of policy is where the delivery of policy actually occurs most often in the form of sport and recreation schemes, programmes and initiatives. These services should exhibit a strong local flavour relative to the crude, national policy (Houlihan and White 2002). They will most commonly happen in schools, sports clubs, leisure centres, community halls, fitness centres and youth centres. The organisation should now have a clear picture of what activities exist and where the gaps are.

The origins of these activities provide the sport development organisation with a history from crude policy to activity on the ground. Following this process will allow the organisation to shape itself into a strong and pragmatic resource for the future in an increasingly politically volatile world. Examples of policy delivery (past and present) include: TOP Sport programmes; Champion Coaching; Active Sports activities; Youth Games; SSP Festival; Coaching for Teachers; Activemark and Sportsmark accreditation schemes; Sportivate; Sport Makers; district and borough sports fora; outreach holiday activity schemes; swimming lessons; and GP referral walking schemes.

It is by following the levels from macro to micro, and appreciating the wider sports policy universe that sport development organisations can establish where they exist in a global and local context, and the impact of policies upon them (Bramham 2008). The organisation can then manoeuvre itself through the rough waters of politics, to safer and more productive areas. Yet this is not just about the survival of sport development; for concentrating solely upon this would not constitute a strategic approach. Whilst it is acknowledged that project funding for sport development is always an issue, understanding of the political environment should be used to create direction for the organisation's own beliefs and values, rather than solely as a means for political survival.

While undertaking this section of the STEEPLE analysis, it would be prudent for the organisation to be aware of the issues affecting the political arena. As illustrated earlier, wider global and national political movements impact upon local delivery and that very point still applies here. The question needs to be asked: what are the current issues and needs relating to our service users? This answer will probably be that their issues and needs are diverse (Hylton and Totten 2008). Some examples of the issues include cultural diversity; economic status; social class; gender barriers; racism; violence and political mistrust (some of which we covered earlier in the section on social factors). With sport reflecting society this means the two are entwined and the same issues exist in both. Therefore, consideration of the wider issues in society is a crucial aspect of sport development organisations' strategic thinking (Hylton and Totten 2008).

A final point for sport development organisations to reflect upon is whether they can incorporate more radical ideologies into their thinking. It has long been argued that the ideologies of three main UK political parties are very similar, with some suggesting an end to ideology at this level (Henry 2001). The ability of the Conservatives and Liberal Democrats to form a coalition government in 2010 illustrates the lack of diversity at the top of UK political structure. Therefore, the use of other beliefs, values and perspectives could provide a refreshing and creative platform for political action for organisations (Bramham 2008). An additional advantage to this approach would be the encouragement of SDPs to work more effectively with harder to reach communities through a keener cultural understanding of people's viewpoints (Coalter 2007 and Hylton and Totten 2008). Through a thorough STEEPLE analysis the relevant ideologies should become apparent, allowing the astute SDP to align service provision to users' needs and creating a proactive, pragmatic feel to programmes. This reinforces the earlier point that sport and recreation development should be much more about the growth of sport and recreation, rather than just survival.

Legal factors

Legal responsibility is a term which is common in current discourse in everyday life, be it through newspapers, television adverts, or in general discussion between people in a formal or informal setting. It often brings with it a sense of fear and dread for those responsible for its implementation and upholding. Yet it is crucial that sport development organisations investigate the legal context that surrounds and exists within their administration (Hartley 2001). The following areas should be considered by the sport development organisation when conducting this section of the STEEPLE analysis.

The Health and Safety Executive (HSE) is an independent national organisation that is responsible for monitoring and evaluating health and safety at work and to reduce work-related ill health, death and serious injury (Health and Safety Executive 2012). It also has the authority to prosecute those employers who are failing in their health and safety duties towards their employees. It would be appropriate for any sport organisation to consult the HSE website (www.hse.gov.uk) for further advice and guidance when conducting this analysis as it provides useful support and direction for anyone seeking a deeper understanding of workers' responsibilities health and safety at work.

There are a number of areas that employers need to consider under the category of workers' responsibilities. A brief summary of some of these include controlling risks to health and safety; workers being provided with personal protective and safety equipment free of charge; workers' ability to express health and safety concerns to their employer and working time regulations. Sport development organisations should consider these areas through their management's responsibility towards its workers; the sports coaches, leaders and other relevant staff within its wider activities; and the safeguarding of the user groups. As discussed further in Chapter 6 the 'workforce' for sport development often extends far beyond paid employees so it is necessary to account for legislation affecting these stakeholders. This element of the STEEPLE analysis should therefore be regularly updated.

Corporate social responsibility is an approach which allows organisations to self regulate their own business aims in relation to ethical, moral, legal and international standards (Smith and Westerbeek 2007). Ultimately corporate social responsibility will actively encourage people to have an input into the organisation's policy and strategy, which will have a strong emphasis on society, the environment, and the business profit of the organisation (Doane 2004). It is conceivable that a large number of sport development organisations from all three sectors may not adhere strictly to the characteristics highlighted above, but some similarities will exist in relation to social sensitivity and responsibility.

Elsewhere the Criminal Records Bureau police file checks (Directgov 2012) and further inspections through the Independent Safeguarding Authority (2012) have become an integral part of sport development organisations' employment of staff working with vulnerable people. Whilst this system is time consuming, it is an essential form of safeguarding the service users from potential harm and most, if not all, sports leaders and coaches go through this checking procedure as part of their sport development employment.

The right of workers and service users not to encounter discrimination is an area of the legal landscape that has become high on most management team's agendas. With the Equality Act 2010 integrated into contemporary society, allegations of discriminatory practices attract much more media attention, raising awareness of the legalities amongst the general public. Such practices often relate to gender; religion; belief; disability; sexual orientation; age; and 'race' (Home Office 2012), all of which are areas commonly addressed by sport development.

Sport development organisations are not exempt from this legislation, and the organisation should use the STEEPLE analysis to undertake a thorough examination of current legal regulation. Acts of Parliament such as the Equality Act 2010 and the Freedom of Information Act 2000 have led sport development organisations to consider accessibility as well as the data kept on personnel and others (Hylton and Totten 2008). Sport development organisations are often amongst the most astute and effective promoters and practitioners of equal rights, but they can only maintain this status by staying up-to-date in this sometimes overlooked corner of the STEEPLE analysis.

Ethical factors

A major ethical issue relating to practice in the sports sector is sponsorship. Through media coverage, sponsorship could be morally and ethically questionable and certain sponsors may not be appropriate to sport, recreation and the promotion of physical activity (Torkildsen 2005). Sponsors such as fast-food chains, chocolate, crisp and sugary drinks manufacturers have been deemed by some as inappropriate for sport and recreation activities. There are obvious health concerns related to the sponsors' products and whether sport should be promoting products which are in contrast to its health benefits. As well as considering external, ethical factors, at this stage of the STEEPLE analysis the sport development organisation therefore needs to engage in a process of reflection regarding the ethical position it is taking on such issues.

A starting point when assessing ethical factors is to consider the public and the organisation's staff. This would include a scan of people's beliefs, values and cultures (Robson 2008). Questions to be asked from this initial scan are: does the organisation's mission statement and aims have synergy with that of its workers and ultimately those of the service users? To which sponsorship deals and agreements does the organisation have connections? Are these deals or agreements with ethically sound companies or movements? Do the organisation's activities cater for the cultural aspects of its user groups? Answering these questions honestly and rigorously will enable the organisation to assess whether its ethical practices need to change and if so, in what ways.

A final issue for sport development organisations to consider is how they distribute funding to sport and recreation projects, or who they support in the process of applying for funding. The obvious candidates applying for funding are voluntary sports clubs, school-based groups, and various leisure related community groups. The concern is to whom will the funding or support go? Will it be the organised, Clubmark-accredited sports club with all the trimmings, led by accountants and lawyers or the less organised, non-accredited community group, with a sound ethical agenda but lacking the structure and wherewithal to make major funding applications? It is likely that both would be given adequate support, but the funding distribution may be less equal (Hylton and Totten 2008).

For ethical factors, some questions that the sport development organisation might like to consider are: who do we support and why? Why do we support them and are there others that we need to focus on? Who are the less traditional groups that we should consider supporting? The issue is simple: is the sport development service as far-reaching and embracing of different group cultures and activities, and if not, how does the organisation take steps to begin that journey?

HOW TO STRUCTURE AN EXTERNAL ENVIRONMENT SCAN

There are many ways in which organisations can structure and record this process but we offer Table 3.1 on page 69 as an example of how it could be done, giving two examples from the social and technological factors of STEEPLE.

Avoid putting strategies and tactics down as opportunities, for example "we need a sports strategy" as an opportunity. The better analysis would be to have focused on government policy for sport as an opportunity. In the opportunities column is our ability to develop and influence local policy and key agencies. 'Production of a sports strategy' is the strategic option generated.

Clearly Table 3.1 would have many more entries for each factor, but the sample entries suggest one way in which the information can be presented. Many sport development professionals will be familiar with a tabular approach to setting out information, having done action plans, etc. and therefore adapting those that you have done before with the added context of an external environment scan will hopefully not be too troublesome.

E-V-R CONGRUENCE

As discussed in the last chapter it is important to match the values of the organisation with its environment (both internal and external) and the resources it has at its disposal, in order to ensure an effective strategy can be put in place to exploit strengths and opportunities and minimise threats as well as cover weaknesses. This is another reason why a detailed external scan can be so powerful, not only in terms of giving organisations the insight to take advantage of existing opportunities but also to create their own by identifying gaps in the external market. There will need to be a strategic fit between the organisation and the perceived gaps (linked to values) and the new opportunities must be relevant to the organisation's strengths and resources (identified via internal scanning) in order to become a key player in that area. Further acknowledgement of this process and how it is to be done will be covered in the next chapter.

Table 3.1 Example of STEEPLE using social and technological factors

STEEPLE factor	Level of importance (High (H), Medium (M) or Low (L))	Opportunities	Threats	Action and lead person/timescales
Social				
The Women's Sport and Fitness Foundation has recently conducted research that highlights how women and girls are still being given fewer opportunities in sport and physical activity than men and boys.	H	As a department we can strategically place ourselves as a beacon of good practice, with a specific strategic plan for developing awareness and participation in and for women and girl's sport.	There are fewer opportunities to gain specific funding for this work, and therefore the resourcing of any new strategic plans may hinder the desire to do this in an authentic and meaningful way.	A comprehensive review of our current provision as well as a scan of potential funding streams should be undertaken to enable us to produce a coherent and realistic strategy for improving the experiences and opportunities for women and girls in sport. Person responsible: Jean Bloggs Timescale: 6 months
Technological				
The explosion of new types of communication (Facebook, Twitter, etc.) means that society is communicating in different ways.	M	There is an opportunity to radically change and improve the way that we keep in touch with all of our stakeholders, ensuring we get messages and information out efficiently.	It needs to be appreciated that as widespread as these communication tools are being used there are still a lot of people relying on more traditional forms of communication. They may miss out on important information if our communication strategy does not consider the lack of access or inability to use these modern tools.	A communication strategy should be researched and written to incorporate the ways and means in which we communicate with stakeholders. Person responsible: Jean Bloggs Timescale: 3 months

SUMMARY

As stated at the outset, STEEPLE is one model that can be used to facilitate a scan of the external environment, but there are of course others (e.g. PEST, DESTEP, PESTLE) to be considered. The key point of this chapter is to show that only by engaging with this process in an authentic way can a sport development organisation expect to be successful in meeting the challenges and demands of the various stakeholders and conditions that impact upon their strategic thinking and service delivery. Being aware of these factors ensures an insightful understanding of present and future opportunities and threats, and hopefully allows you to stay one step ahead. Many successful entrepreneurs rely on such foresight to ensure they remain competitive and maintain the interest of their prospective customers. Not all organisations will consider the ethical factors as important as others, but this book urges practitioners to be as ethical and inclusive in their practice as possible, hence giving this aspect of the STEEPLE analysis equal prominence. Hopefully, those in charge of resources will appreciate the importance of doing the tasks needed for an effective internal and external environment scan, as although the activity itself may not generate income, strategic use of the outcomes will reap its own rewards longer term.

LEARNING ACTIVITIES

Combining aspects of a SWOT with the STEEPLE external environment scan, do the following:

> 1. For each STEEPLE factor consider the various opportunities and threats that factor presents for you and your organisation. Use the above table to action the activities that are necessary to respond to the opportunities and threats identified. If you have the time it would be worth engaging a number of people in this task and comparing and contrasting the results for a more rigorous and representative outcome.

The idea behind this exercise is that the opportunities that emerge can be exploited, whereas identified threats can be overcome with effective action plans. The key consideration is that as an organisation you are

70

aware of the opportunities and threats. It is not unusual for certain factors to create a longer list of threats or opportunities than others. This is acceptable as long as all factors have been afforded the same attention to detail.

REFERENCES

Bramham, P. (1994) 'Community Arts'. In Haywood, L. (1994) *Community Leisure and Recreation: Theory and Practice.* Oxford, Butterworth-Heinemann, pp. 83–110.

Bramham, P. (2008) Sports Policy. In Hylton, K. and Bramham, P. *Sport Development: Policy, Process And Practice.* 2nd ed. London, Routledge, pp. 10–24.

Capon, C. (2008) *Understanding Strategic Management.* London, Prentice Hall.

Carter, N. (2006) *The Politics of the Environment: Ideas, Activism, Policy.* Cambridge, Cambridge University Press.

Cashmore, E. (2005) *Making Sense of Sport.* 4th ed. London, Routledge.

Channel 4 (2008) *Kevin McCloud and the Big Town Plan.* Castleford, 2nd November.

Coakley, J. (2010) *Sports in Society: Issues and Controversies.* 10th ed. London, McGraw-Hill Higher Education.

Coakley, J. and Donnelly, P. (1998) *Inside Sports.* London, Routledge.

Coalter, F. (2007) *A Wider Social Role For Sport: Who's Keeping the Score?* London, Routledge.

Community Amateur Sports Club (2010) 'Cascinfo.co.uk: the definitive guide for community amateur sports clubs'. Available at http://www.cascinfo.co.uk/.

Cross, R. and Parker, A. (2004) *The Hidden Power of Social Networks: Understanding How Work Really Gets Done in Organizations.* Boston, Harvard Business School Press.

Directgov (2012) 'Criminal Record Checks: An Introduction'. Available at http://www.direct.gov.uk/en/Employment/Startinganewjob/DG_195809.

Doane, D. (2004) 'Good Intentions – Bad Outcomes? The broken promise of CSR reporting'. In Henriques, A. and Richardson, J. *The Triple Bottom Line: Does it All Add Up? Assessing the Sustainability of Business and CSR.* London, Earthscan, pp. 81–88.

Hartley, H. (2001) 'Legal Principles and Issues: managing disciplinaries in sport and recreation'. In Hylton, K., Bramham, P., Jackson, D. and Nesti, M. *Sport Development: Policy, Process and Practice.* London, Routledge, pp. 170–194.

Health and Safety Executive (2012) 'About HSE'. Available at http://www.hse.gov.uk/aboutus/index.htm.

Henry, I. (2001) *The Politics of Leisure Policy.* 2nd ed. Basingstoke, Palgrave Macmillan.

Heywood, L. (2007) *Political Ideologies: An Introduction.* 4th ed. Basingstoke, Palgrave Macmillan.

Home Office (2012) 'Equality Act 2010'. Available at http://www.homeoffice. gov.uk/equalities/equality-act/.

Houlihan, B. (2000) 'Sporting Excellence, Schools and Sports Development: the politics of crowded policy spaces'. *European Physical Education Review.* 6(2), pp. 171–192.

Houlihan, B. and White, A. (2002) *The Politics of Sports Development: Development of Sport or Development Through Sport?* London, Routledge.

House of Commons Library (2011) *Transport Policy in 2011: A New Direction?* London, House of Commons Library.

Hylton, K. and Totten, M. (2008) 'Community Sports Development'. In K. Hylton, and P. Bramham, (2008) *Sports Development: Policy, Process and Practice.* 2nd ed. London and New York, Routledge.

Independent Safeguarding Authority (2012) 'Welcome to the Independent Safeguarding Authority'. Available at http://www.isa.homeoffice.gov.uk/.

International Platform on Sport and Development (2012) 'What is Sport and Development?' Available at http://www.sportanddev.org/learnmore/what_ is_sport_and_development/.

Ledwith, M. (2005) *Community Development: A Critical Approach.* Bristol, The Polity Press.

Long, J. (2007) *Researching Leisure, Sport and Tourism: The Essential Guide.* London, Sage.

Mintzberg, H. (1979) 'The Structuring of Organizations: a synthesis of the research.' London, Prentice Hall. In Mintzberg, H., Ahlstrand, B. and Lamped, J. (1998) *Strategy Safari: A Guided Tour through the Wilds of Strategic Management.* London, Prentice Hall.

Mintzberg, H., Ahlstrand, B. and Lamped, J. (1998) *Strategy Safari: A Guided Tour through the Wilds of Strategic Management.* London, Prentice Hall.

Moisander and Pesonen (2002) Narratives of Sustainable Ways of Living: constructing the self and the other as a green customer. In *Management Decision.* 40(4), pp. 329–342.

Robson, S. (2008) Partnerships in Sport. In: Hylton, K. and Bramham, P. eds. *Sports Development: Policy, Process and Practice.* 2nd ed. Abingdon, Routledge, pp. 118–142.

Scott, J. (2000) *Social Network Analysis: A Handbook.* 2nd ed. London, SAGE Publications.

Smith, A. and Westerbeek, H. (2007). 'Sport as a Vehicle for Deploying Corporate Social Responsibility'. In: *The Journal of Corporate Citizenship.* 25, pp. 43–54.

Sport England (2011a) 'Active People Survey 5'. Available at http://www. sportengland.org/research/active_people_survey/active_people_survey_5/aps 5_quarter_two.aspx.

Sport England (2011b) 'Market Segmentation' Available at http://www.sport england.org/research/market_segmentation.aspx [Accessed 9th September].

Sport Leeds (2006) *Taking the Lead.* Leeds, Sport Leeds.

Torkildsen, G. (2005) *Leisure and Recreation Management.* London, Routledge.

Vidal, J., Stratton, A. and Goldenberg, S. (2009) 'Low Targets, Goals Dropped: Copenhagen ends in failure: deal thrashed out at talks condemned as climate change scepticism in action'. *The Guardian*. [Internet], 19th December. Available at http://www.guardian.co.uk/environment/2009/dec/18/copenhagen-deal.

CHAPTER 4

MAKING STRATEGIC CHOICES IN SPORT DEVELOPMENT

JAYNE WILSON

INTRODUCTION

Chapters 2 and 3 discussed the preceding stages of strategy development, firstly understanding the internal factors that influence how sport development organisations operate and secondly, appreciating the external context in which sports development activity takes place. In Chapter 3 we looked specifically at STEEPLE as a tool for analysing and interpreting the external environment in which we operate. Thompson's (2001) E-V-R congruence model was introduced and we have shown that the process of internal analysis helps strategic leaders in sport development to ensure alignment of V and R (values and resources) whilst the external scan (e.g. STEEPLE) self-evidently considers E (environment).

This chapter considers how the outcomes of internal and external analyses are used to inform strategic choices. In simple terms, choice is at the heart of strategy formulation, and the very nature of choice means that there must be a process which involves the development of potential options, evaluation and then selection and communication of the preferred one(s). In the real world the process of strategic choice is rarely so logical or straightforward and choice may be limited, particularly in public sector sport organisations where strategic decisions are politically determined or made at a more senior level in the organisation. It may be difficult to evaluate all potential options with the same degree of clarity at any one time; indeed choices that keep options open in a dynamic environment may be required! We should not lose sight of the fact that,

74

in order to ensure congruence with a turbulent *external* world, strategic choices may often need to be *internally* focused. For example, a chosen strategy may require new skills not currently available to the organisation (see Chapter 2) or a need to work with new or different partners. In this situation the best strategic options might involve a focus on internal improvement or resource development.

THE PURPOSE OF THIS CHAPTER

The purpose of this chapter is to give the reader an understanding of the key tools and processes that are used in the development of strategic options and to illustrate how they can be used in a sport development context. Meaningful engagement with this material increases the sport organisation's prospects of maintaining or achieving congruence. This chapter continues the trend established earlier in this book of applying carefully chosen business concepts to the world of sport development. For example, the thought process inherent to generic business strategies focused on growth, in terms of sales, income and profit can be adapted to develop strategies which focus on increasing participation in sport. The need for competitive advantage or for retrenchment or turnaround strategies, especially in a challenging economic climate, means that established tools of strategy development have a lot to offer the sport development profession.

This chapter takes the reader through a number of steps. Firstly, we consider effective use of tools to generate strategic options which build on internal and external environmental analysis. Secondly, we consider the generic strategic options proposed by Porter (1985) and demonstrate how the Ansoff (1957) product-market matrix can be applied to sport development in relation to growing sports participation. Next, we look at the evaluation of strategic choice: having developed a number of options how do we appraise them and select a course of action? Finally, we examine strategic vision and mission statements and their role and purpose in communicating strategic choice. Throughout we consider the contribution of these activities to E-V-R congruence.

DEVELOPING STRATEGIC OPTIONS AND CHOICE

In this section we consider some of the recognised strategy tools that help identify strategic options and shape strategic choice. We start by considering the outcomes of the different elements of SWOT analysis and use that as a basis for considering strategic options including Ansoff's product-market matrix and Porter's generic competitive strategies. We then consider resource-based options which focus on adding value from better, or different, uses of organisational resources. These will be considered from the perspective of developing and managing sport development strategy.

OUTCOMES OF SWOT ANALYSIS

Having considered internal strengths, weaknesses and other capabilities (Chapter 2) and assessed the opportunities and threats present in the external environment (Chapter 3) it is necessary to holistically analyse the elements of SWOT in order to generate strategic options. This activity can be used in a wide range of situations from the development of organisational strategy to personal development planning. It is a very useful exercise when considering organisational capability (the 'SW' – strengths and weaknesses – of SWOT) in terms of external drivers (the 'OT' – opportunities and threats – of SWOT, captured via STEEPLE or a similar environmental analysis). This further level of analysis produces strategic options for consideration:

- Strengths and opportunities (SO): can we capitalise upon our strengths to enable us to take advantage of the opportunities that exist in the external environment? Examples of this may include opportunities to address growing demand in activities the organisation has experience of providing. (Maintenance of E-V-R congruence.)
- Strengths and threats (ST): how can you take advantage of your strengths to avoid real and potential threats? For instance, a competent negotiator may be enlisted to stave off the threats of funding cuts by creating new partnerships. (Avoidance of strategic drift in the E-V-R congruence model.)
- Weaknesses and opportunities (WO): which internal weaknesses must you overcome or reduce to enable you to capitalise on

opportunities? Examples may include the training and development of staff to enable you to respond to new market opportunities. (Avoidance of conscious incompetence.)

■ Weaknesses and threats (WT): how can you minimise your weaknesses and avoid threats? This is often described as the development of defensive strategies. In the context of limited resources it may even be worth asking the question: should we even be involved in this area of work, particularly if there are other agencies or partners who could do it better? (Avoidance of a state of unconscious incompetence.)

Having considered the outcomes of SWOT and related analyses it is possible to generate and evaluate options for future strategic direction. It is important that a focus on both the internal and external environments is maintained throughout this process.

ENVIRONMENT-BASED APPROACHES TO DEVELOPING STRATEGIC OPTIONS

Porter's generic options

The generic strategies of Michael Porter (1985) were focused on competitive business environments and competitive advantage. As such, they were confined to business concerns rather than not-for-profit organisations and therefore their relevance for sport development organisations is open to exploration. They are called generic strategies because Porter claimed that there were only three basic strategies that a business could choose:

■ Cost leadership
■ Differentiation
■ Focus

In commercial terms, cost leadership is about managing your cost base effectively to enable you to charge an average price, whilst achieving above average profits: it is the 'no frills' approach. In sport development this can determine whether a service can even be offered, let alone at the requisite quality. Differentiation is focusing on specific segments of the market, those who are prepared to pay more for differentiated products and services. This may include considerations such as a better level of service. This is particularly apposite to sport development when we consider the many sedentary pursuits available to potential participants (Robson and McKenna 2013). Focus strategy (sometimes referred to as niche strategy) involves the identification of specific market segments and the development of strategies for each segment with which competitors will be unable to compete. Focus strategy can be achieved on the basis of cost focus and differentiation. National governing bodies of sport (NGBs) have a ready-made focus strategy as each is the key promoter of its sport, but for organisations with a more generic brief (e.g. local authority sport development teams, Youth Sport Trust) there is a need to identify specific market segments and the services to be offered to them. There are a number of limitations to these generic approaches, principally the risk attached to cost leadership and market positioning; the concept of differentiation given there is no insight into how to achieve it; and the difficulties of identifying niche markets and how to define them (Hendry 1990). The value of Porter's work, however, lies in the fact that it can be used for generating basic strategic options, particularly when it is important that public and voluntary sector sport organisations are not using valuable resources to compete with commercial sector provision. It can be a tool for sport development organisations to consider their 'market positioning' and to then consider resource-based options (discussed later in this chapter) to develop strategy. In E-V-R congruence terms it helps the sport development organisation to avoid in particular the state of conscious incompetence.

Ansoff's matrix

Ansoff's matrix is a tool to help develop product-market options to achieve business growth. Whilst the matrix has traditionally been used to grow income, sales, market share or profit it does have something to offer to sport as a strategic planning tool. Growing sports participation continues to be a focus of sports policy, regardless of whether you take the perspective of sport for sport's sake or sport as a tool for social good. Past investment in the Yorkshire region for instance, which was designed to grow participation has favoured projects concerned with mainly 'market penetration' and some 'product development', which result in a focus on existing markets. In other words, funding was being used to provide opportunities for those who were already participating, by

78

providing more of the same or opportunities to switch to new activities. Overall, despite significant investment, participation has not increased (Sport England 2011). The purpose of this tool is to encourage the development of a broader range of strategic options to grow participation. The concept of 'product' is intended to apply to all sport services, activities and programmes that are provided by the sports sector, and neither is it a prerequisite that they are purchased (see Kotler *et al.* 2010). Use of this tool can help a sport development organisation avoid strategic drift (the detachment of values and resources from the realities of the external environment).

The matrix (see Figure 4.1) combines existing and new markets with existing and new products to reveal four options for planning future strategy; it is purely a framework to shape future strategic choices. I will now explain each quadrant of the matrix.

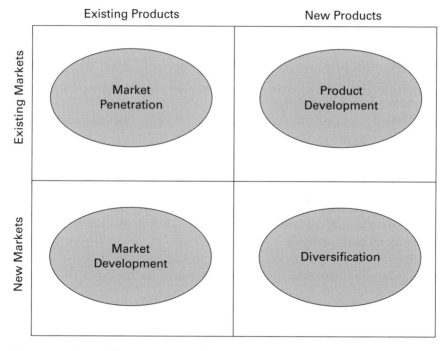

Figure 4.1 Ansoff's matrix. Ansoff (1957)

Market penetration

This strategy focuses on providing existing products into existing markets. The main objective is to increase the market share of current products, i.e. the number of people participating in sport and active recreation. This approach is very much 'business as usual' and 'more of the same'. Penetration is achieved by getting existing participants to do more e.g. by moving from nominally active to active, and by winning participants from 'competitors'. The issue of who our competitors are is debatable but for the purpose of this analysis it is useful to think of the competition as other discretionary leisure time activity. This is important as in planning for growth it is essential that we do not resource initiatives that merely create 'internal' competition in the sport and physical activity sector and do not therefore achieve an increase in terms of overall participation levels. This is the least risky method of achieving growth but is only likely to produce limited growth.

Examples:

- Promotional campaigns and incentives to increase participation, especially pricing offers such as 'buy one get one free'.
- Leisure card discount schemes.
- Inclusive gym membership that is better value than pay and play to encourage greater frequency of use.
- Development of sport coaching and development programmes aimed at providing opportunities to progress – e.g. Start, Stay and Succeed.
- Some initiatives aimed at target groups, for example 50+ sessions or women's only sessions that provide additional choice for those already participating.
- Facility development strategies, focusing on better distribution and appropriate numbers of facilities to meet demand.

Market development

Market development focuses on marketing of existing products to new market segments, often working with partners outside the sport and active recreation sector. The benefit of this approach is that it allows sport organisations to work within current areas of competence and to stay close to markets they are familiar with. In the context of our overall

80

aim of growing participation 'new segments' could be interpreted as those groups which are inactive or nominally active. The emphasis in this approach is on reaching new markets to achieve growth, rather than greater penetration of existing markets.

It is important that organisations know their *existing* markets. For example, in some sports clubs developing new markets may be as simple as creating a junior section or providing opportunities for beginners where there is evidence of demand. It is also appropriate to consider new markets as those in which we are currently operating but still learning. The use of sport and physical activity initiatives to contribute to other government agendas such as health, crime, educational attainment, economic vitality, children and young people exemplify this approach. In developing these new markets there will be a greater focus on 'marketing' the organisation to potential partners, as entry to these markets will be achieved through alliances with agencies already working in these policy areas.

Implicit in this approach is the need to understand and remove barriers to participation for certain market segments. The development of the Sport England Sport Market Segmentation Data (Sport England 2012c) provides sport development professionals with information that can inform market development strategies. Combining actual participation data from the Active People Survey (see Sport England 2011) with socio-economic data, it provides insights into attitudes, motivation and potential barriers to participation for adults. It also provides information about activities that each segment group would like to take part in. This means that it is now possible to take a more sophisticated approach to 'target groups'. For instance, we can move away from simplistic approaches such as targeting the 50+, given that the market segmentation data identifies eight different market segments over the age of 50, each with differing attitudes, needs and wants from sport and active recreation.

Examples:

- Active Women (Sport England): focusing on women from disadvantaged areas.
- Midnight Soccer Leagues: focusing on reducing antisocial behaviour.
- GP referral projects, involving sport development organisations working in partnership with the health sector.

- Cycling initiatives in partnership with Sustrans and highways and transport agencies.
- Playing for Success: literacy and numeracy projects with professional sports clubs.
- Fit for Football: health project using football as a vehicle for delivery.
- Armchair aerobics sessions in residential care homes.
- Sports participation events for charity, e.g. Race for Life, which has attracted high numbers of women who would not normally participate in jogging or running.

Product development

This involves the development of new products for existing markets for sport and physical activity. Specific options include the extension of existing product lines to provide greater choice, product replacement and innovation. For sport development this means being open to the adoption of new products rather than being involved in the research and development of new product lines. This approach can involve working with partners who can work with you to offer new products to existing markets.

Examples:

Product extension

- Expansion of exercise class programmes to include new ideas and to provide greater choice: e.g. boxercise, spin, fit ball, Zumba.
- Promotion of new activities such as street sports and lifestyle/ extreme sports such as free running.

Product replacement and innovation

- Facility development: new models of provision, upgrading and projects focusing on innovation and technological change (e.g. indoor ski slopes, synthetic surfaces, active playgrounds).

Projects focusing on capital developments, refurbishment and modernisation can have the characteristics of both market penetration and product development strategies. In some cases projects have been essential to *retaining* current participants in a climate of rising customer

82

expectations and increasing choice. The use of Sport England's Facilities Planning Model (Sport England 2012a), to identify shortfalls in provision and ensure that facilities are placed in appropriate geographical locations to maximise potential usage, is characteristic of market penetration approaches. However, in the development of new facilities there has been a clear objective to ensure that facilities meet modern day standards and rising customer expectations, a characteristic of product development strategies.

Diversification

This option involves the development of new products for new markets and is the most risky option as the strategy is likely to be outside the core competence of the organisation. Recent moves from 'traditional' sport projects to a broader physical activity agenda (Robson and McKenna 2013) exemplify this approach, but the area of work is still reasonably close to the core competences of the organisation and is in a related market. Partnerships and strategic alliances with other organisations in order to acquire the necessary skills and experience may be essential to ensure diversification strategies are successfully implemented.

It has become apparent that there has been an over reliance on investment on the supply side of participation, namely the provision of places and programmes designed to drive up participation. Clearly, the challenge now is to find new ways of creating demand for sport and physical activity, through supported behavioural change initiatives for those people who are currently inactive or on the 'subs' bench' and need a more diversified approach.

Examples:

- Health walks/Walking the Way to Health initiatives.
- Green gyms.
- Workplace health initiatives.
- Healthy sports stadia initiatives (e.g. York City FC/York City Knights).
- Active travel initiatives.
- Development of motivational interviewing skills of the sport and physical activity workforce and the development of new roles (e.g. health trainers, activators, peer group mentors).

It can be argued that there is one strategic option that the product-market matrix does not reveal, namely *withdrawal* from a particular market or markets (Lynch 2000). There may be circumstances when this option is appropriate, for instance:

- Products and services that are in the decline phase with little hope of recovery.
- Over-extension: offering too many services, including some which are under-performing and draining resources. It is important to remember that some services may exist because of policy priorities.
- It may be, however, that there are other providers better placed to deliver services, a voluntary sector sports club for example.

RESOURCE-BASED STRATEGIC OPTIONS

Resource-based approaches to developing strategic options are particularly important to public sector organisations in the current climate. Lynch (2000) argues that they are relevant when market opportunities are limited or the market is growing slowly, which is certainly true for sport participation. He also suggests that these approaches may be more appropriate when the organisation has limitations placed on resources by government, which applies to the vast majority of sport development organisations. Chapter 2 examined the analysis of internal resources, an important step in developing resource-based strategies which, in E-V-R congruence terms, helps to avoid conscious incompetence.

The value chain

Porter (1985) refers to the Value Chain and sources of added value that can exist either upstream or downstream. Upstream refers to the activities which add value early in the value chain, such as lower procurement or production costs. Downstream activities, such as research and development, distribution, customer service and investment in advertising and branding, add value later in the value chain. This concept is easily transferable to the world of sport development. For instance, sport development agencies play a significant role in adding value to the role of Community Sport Networks.

84

Cost reduction strategies

Strategic options for sport may also have to be concerned with cost reduction, particularly in response to reductions in public sector spending. For sport development organisations this may mean considering options to achieve economies of scale, outsourcing of specific tasks and focused use of resources on the activities likely to yield best results.

EVALUATING STRATEGIC CHOICES

So far we have examined some of the techniques that can be used to generate strategic options and the established strategic approaches available to sport development organisations. The next stage in the strategy development process is to evaluate these strategic options before making decisions on how it should respond to the external environment in which it operates. Thompson (2001:66) reminds us of the reality of making decisions in organisational contexts:

> We might like to think that strategic decisions would be taken objectively rather than subjectively. After all there is a host of useful techniques available to decision makers – if only they always had the time to use them!

> Then again it does not follow that using a selection of these techniques would provide consistent answers or priorities, leaving managers concerned to exercise judgement.

There is a vast array of tools in the strategic management literature to enable strategic options to be evaluated, many of which are financial in nature. However, it is possible to identify criteria that could be used as part of the evaluation process from the strategic management literature and adapt to our needs in sport development work. Lynch (2000:617) suggests six possible criteria: consistency, suitability, validity, feasibility, business risk and stakeholder attractiveness. Thompson (2001) points to appropriateness, feasibility, and desirability as the major issues. Bryson (1995) focused on strategy development in the public sector and identified sixteen criteria for evaluation clustered into administrative, results orientated and acceptability criteria. This literature can be summarised into the following questions for evaluating strategic choices.

Desirability, consistency and strategic fit:

■ Does the proposed strategic option fit with the current priorities of the organisation?
■ Will the approach be acceptable to our strategic leaders and other stakeholders?
■ Will the strategy fit with the current culture and values of the organisation? Will there be issues of cultural change?
■ Is it appropriate for the current economic and competitive environment in which we are operating?

From an E-V-R congruence viewpoint if all of these answers can be answered 'yes' we have evidence of a congruent sport development organisation.

Organisational competencies and resources:

■ Are the strategies proposed consistent with the existing skills and competencies, and have we factored in the need to develop or acquire new competencies?
■ Do we have the key resources (money, time, expertise) to deliver? For example, if developing new products or services do we have the resources to adequately develop and test our ideas?

Risks, returns and results:

■ What are the underlying financial assumptions and are they sound?
■ What will be the return on the financial investment, or cost benefit of the investment? In short, does it make financial sense?
■ What is the risk involved in pursuing this strategy, can we resource it, do we have the expertise to meet customer expectations, and will it have an adverse effect on customers, partners, stakeholders?
■ What are the future assumptions on which our strategy is based, and are there any external factors we cannot control (such as reduced external funding)?
■ Will the proposed strategy actually make a difference? Will it improve our performance and deliver the required results, and will it add value to what we do?

When evaluating strategic choices it is unlikely that any one option will be the most appropriate. Earlier, when we considered the role of Ansoff's matrix in developing strategies to increase participation it was clear that it was desirable to generate a range of options in our quest to increase participation in sport. Diversification strategies were identified as being potentially more risky and it was important therefore to use a range of strategies to increase participation. The above criteria should therefore be used "to search for an appropriate balance and trade off" (Thompson 2001:682).

It is unlikely that the full range of evaluation criteria will be applied to all potential strategic options so initial screening may be conducted – for example, to ascertain desirability. Only the most desirable options would subsequently be subjected to a full evaluation. Whilst this framework can be used to help evaluate strategic choices it must be remembered that it is not a replacement for sound judgement and experience. The questions are intended to enhance critical thinking and planning, but the intuitive question 'does it feel right?' still needs to be posed. Sound judgements come from a well-developed understanding of the external environment and the internal reality of the organisation.

Sport development work is largely delivered by public sector organisations, and as we have noted earlier strategic choices may be restricted because of political priorities. Additionally, in the face of funding difficulties, strategies may necessarily focus more on efficiency, effectiveness and value for money. Continuing this theme of evaluation and strategic choice it is important to understand that there are now tools emerging in the cultural sector which are appropriate to sport development professionals.

One of the key questions in the above evaluation criteria concerned the ability of the strategy to 'make a difference' and 'add value', or in current sport parlance to 'create a legacy'. For a number of years, publicly funded sport development work has had to demonstrate its ability to be 'outcome focused', contributing to broader government priorities for improved health, community safety, educational attainment and economic vitality. A significant evidence base known as the Value of Sport Monitor (Sport England 2012b) has been developed to guide sport development professionals in 'what works best' to deliver on government priorities, and is a useful tool in evaluating strategic choices.

There is now an increasing use of logic models (or logic chains) in sport development planning. A logic model illustrates the presumed relationship between resource inputs, activities, outputs and outcomes and the evidence to support them. They are used in the health sector to support the design of service interventions intended to create behaviour change, such as increased participation in physical activity. They provide a simple framework including much of the above, recommended criteria for evaluating strategic choices, particularly issues of resource and expertise. The value of logic models is that they test the assumptions and evidence base upon which strategies are predicated, and at the same time help plan for implementation and provide a structure for monitoring and evaluation. For a full discussion of the use and development of evaluation for sport development please see Chapter 6.

COMMUNICATING STRATEGIC CHOICE

In this concluding section we will consider how strategic choice and direction can be communicated to sport organisations' internal and external stakeholders. This introduces the concepts of vision and mission statements, values and strategic aims and objectives. It is important to understand the purpose of these and the relationship between them. Over the last couple of decades sport development professionals have been charged with producing a plethora of strategic plans. Experience suggests that this can be one of the most challenging parts of the strategy development process, particularly in terms of shelf life, so firstly we will explain the concepts before considering examples from actual strategies. From an E-V-R congruence perspective, an organisation without clearly articulated values risks becoming unconsciously competent and can slide towards becoming lost (wholly incongruent).

Vision and mission statements

Vision statements should define the future and describe what will be different as a result of the strategy. This typically captures how the organisation will be different, including its position in the market place, but also it can be about the impact the strategy has on the communities the organisation serves. This is particularly relevant to public and

88

voluntary sector sports organisations. Good vision statements will paint a clear and unambiguous picture of the future; they should be short, inspirational and memorable. Here are a few example vision statements taken from recent strategies developed by UK sport organisations:

> ... to unite a proud sporting nation, where every child is hooked on sport for life and Wales is a nation of champions (Sport Wales 2012).

> The creation of a world leading community sport system in England (Sport England 2008).

> Building active, healthy, successful and safe North Lincolnshire communities through increased participation in sport, physical activity and active recreation (North Lincolnshire Council 2007).

One of the challenges for sport development organisations when developing strategy, particularly local authorities, is the fact that they are often part of a larger organisation and the strategic vision has to reflect and support the overall vision of the council or local strategic partnership. The example from North Lincolnshire illustrates how the strategic vision for sport is meeting the council's priorities for health, educational attainment and safer communities, in addition to the national and regional priorities for sport. This is to ensure strategic fit with the work of other stakeholders, particularly those who are able to provide resources to support the implementation of the strategy.

It is useful when communicating a strategic vision to think about what success would look like, especially for external audiences. Below is an example of the critical success factors assigned to the North Lincolnshire vision. This is the first stage in setting out the performance criteria for the strategy:

> **Success** will mean that more people in North Lincolnshire are:
> - Aspiring to be physically active.
> - Taking part in sport, physical activity and active recreation.
> - Becoming involved as volunteers to help support opportunities for sport and active recreation.

- Walking and cycling more to get around (known as active transport).
- Satisfied with the opportunities for sport and active recreation that are available in their local communities (North Lincolnshire Council 2007).

Mission statements generally follow the vision and illustrate how the organisation will operate to deliver the vision. For example, a local authority leisure service which has a strategic vision to increase participation might develop a mission statement around the provision of a range of high quality, accessible services and sporting opportunities for the communities it serves.

> The mission reflects the essential purpose of the organisation, concerning particularly why it is in existence, the nature of the business it is in and the customers it seeks to serve and satisfy (Thompson 2001:89).

It is becoming increasingly common to see a statement of corporate or company values in addition to, or as an extension of a mission statement. These value statements focus on organisational behaviours, the principles which underpin how the organisation will work with its customers, partners and stakeholders and the expectations it has of its employees. This is well illustrated by the example below from England Athletics. Set against this mission statement:

> Working in partnership with the wider athletics family to create a vibrant, safe and progressive sport – embracing athletes of all abilities and from all communities – to grow the next generation of athletics champions (England Athletics 2008:1).

are the following corporate values:

- **Customer focus.** Athletes, coaches, officials, competition organisers, clubs, county associations, schools and all of the sports other volunteers are our customers. We are privileged to be the guardians of our sport in England and have been entrusted to manage its resources and finances on their behalf. We will strive at all times to exceed their expectations and ensure we deliver the best possible results.

90

- **Commitment to equality.** We are fully committed to the principles of equality and social justice for all of our customers. We will strive to ensure that everyone can participate in a safe and enjoyable environment free from the threat of intimidation, harassment, neglect and abuse.
- **Working together.** We can only achieve our goals through close and trusting partnerships with all members of the English athletics family. We will encourage and support the many expert groups and individuals that will help make the sport succeed.
- **Commitment to excellence.** We are focused on continuous improvement and we will work with our partners and customers to make English athletics a sport of which we can all be proud.
- **Pride in our heritage.** England has a proud legacy of success on the world athletics stage dating back over 100 years. Whilst acting as a force for modernisation and change, it is also our responsibility continue this legacy and ensure that our rich history will always be celebrated (England Athletics 2008:1).

This list of values does not offer a prescription for precisely *how* the mission will be achieved. Instead it offers a kind of moral code and provides pointers towards the organisational culture, or at least that to which the organisation's strategic leaders would like to see its employees, members and other internal stakeholders adhere. Having set out the overarching and underpinning drivers behind daily operations, the last step in the process of communicating strategic choice is the setting of the strategic aims and objectives. Vision and mission statements should provide clarity in terms of the desired future state of the organisation and those it serves as well as broadly defining how the organisation will operate to achieve the vision. Aims and objectives become more focused on what the organisation will be doing both in the short and longer term, providing the building blocks for strategy implementation.

An example is provided below from the North Lincolnshire Active Choices, Active Futures strategy. These aims illustrate what the focus will be and in addition introduce the headline targets by which the strategy's success will be measured. This is typical of many strategies developed by Community Sport Networks or local authorities as it aligns local goals with the national and regional priorities of Sport England for increasing sport participation at that time:

1   To increase overall participation in sport and active recreation in North Lincolnshire by 1% each year between 2007–2012.
2   To close the gap in participation of under participating groups by 25%. [These are women, older people, people with disabilities, people living in deprived communities and black and minority ethnic groups.]
3   To build local capacity to support opportunities for sport and active recreation (North Lincolnshire Council 2007).

Strategic aims such as these should be subdivided into objectives to enable operationalisation of these headline targets. This leads us to our final consideration relating to communicating strategic intent, namely the issue of the 'strategy document'. This needs careful thought as it can become a diversionary activity. Many strategies have been developed in our sector to satisfy requirements of government funding or improvement agendas, and in some instances they have merely occupied shelf space. For some, the glossy brochure becomes an end in itself, which may look impressive but often the content is somewhat lacking. It is far preferable to invest in research and thinking time, to ensure the strategy is developed on solid foundations and has partner commitment. The next chapter deals in detail with the vexed issue of strategy implementation.

From experience there are a number of key things to consider:

■   Our environment is fast changing: strategies written with a five-year time horizon quickly look dated. Communicate your strategy in a form that can be easily refreshed and updated. Consider web-based formats, for example, which promote interaction and networking and can be used to also report on progress and celebrate success in real time. Detailed action plans for implementation of the strategy will need to be reviewed every year; do not try to produce detailed five year plans.
■   Consider the audience for the strategy. Usually there are two completely different audiences, the professional network and the public. Local residents will not be interested in the detail; they just want to know what is going to be done and how things will be better. For partner organisations it is important that they have a strategy document that sets out the shared vision, mission, aims, objectives and the agreed action plans. Often the work that goes into evaluating the context, such as research, policy priorities and resource mapping

is valuable to all partners and should be harnessed for mutual benefit, but should not take over any published document.

- Often the most beneficial thing about developing strategies for sport and active recreation is the process involved. Few strategies in our sector are developed for one organisation; they are almost invariably partnership driven. Bringing partners together to shape shared vision and develop strategic objectives often brings more benefit than the final, printed plan! The important thing is to continue this way of working to help monitor progress, ensure timely review and to avoid strategic drift.

SUMMARY

This chapter has considered some of the tools that enable sport development organisations to benefit from a structured and detailed approach to developing strategic options. We have examined some of the established approaches to generating options from the broader strategic management field and tested their usefulness in the sport development environment. Ansoff's product-market matrix is a very useful tool in practice, helping to ensure that as a sector we are using all possible approaches to increasing participation and that we truly understand our markets for sport and physical activity. Generating the options is the relatively easy part; deciding on which options will be followed also needs a structured approach, so we have established a framework of common sense questions to underpin our choice of strategic direction. Finally, we have untangled the difference between strategic vision and mission and have considered the issues relating to the effective communication of strategic intent to partners and stakeholders. In E-V-R congruence terms we have seen how strategic choice based on thoughtful and regular analysis plays a major role in determining the sport development organisation's state of congruence (or otherwise). The next chapter examines the challenges of turning intentions into actions and ensuring that resources are expended on relevant activities.

LEARNING ACTIVITIES

Developing skills

National Occupational Standard A12 Contribute to Strategic Development in Sport and Active Leisure

Select ONE sport organisation that you know well from either:

the voluntary sector OR;

the public/not-for-profit sector OR;

the commercial sector.

1   Conduct an analysis of the external environment in which the organisation operates.
2   Conduct an internal analysis for your organisation which identifies key strengths and weaknesses, resources, capabilities and competencies.
3   Using the analysis developed above, generate a range of strategic options for the organisation to consider for the next five years.

Developing knowledge

National Occupational Standard A12 Contribute to Strategic Development in Sport and Active Leisure

Identify the vision and/or mission statements of three sports organisations.

1   Using your knowledge of what makes a good vision and mission statement, critically evaluate each one and where appropriate make recommendations for improvement.
2   You are helping to develop a strategy for a disability sport organisation whose purpose is to support sports clubs and organisations provide better opportunities for disabled people to participate in sport. Develop a vision and mission to share with the organisation and its partners.

94

REFERENCES

Ansoff, I. (1957) 'Strategies for Diversification'. *Harvard Business Review.* Sept–Oct, pp. 113–124.

Bryson, J. (1995) *Strategic Planning for Public and Non Profit Organisations: a Guide to Strengthening and Sustaining Organizational Achievement.* San Francisco, Jossey-Bass.

England Athletics (2008) *England Athletics: Growing Our Next Generation of Champions.* Birmingham, England Athletics.

Hendry, J. (1990) 'The Problem with Porter's Generic Strategies'. *European Management Journal*, 8, pp. 443–50.

Kotler, P., Armstrong, G., Wong, V. and Saunders, J. (2010) *Principles of Marketing.* 13th ed. Harlow, Pearson.

Lynch, R. (2000) *Corporate Strategy.* 2nd Ed. Harlow, Pearson Education.

North Lincolnshire Council (2007) 'Active Choices, Active Futures: vision and rationale'. Available at http://www.northlincs.gov.uk/leisure/sports/active-choices-active-futures/vision-and-rationale/.

Porter, M. (1985) *Competitive Advantage.* New York, The Free Press.

Robson, S. and McKenna, J. (2013) Sport and Health. In Hylton, K. ed. *Sport Development: Policy, Process and Practice.* Abingdon, Routledge.

Sport England (2008) *Sport England Strategy 2008–2011.* London, Sport England.

Sport England (2011) 'Active People Survey 5'. Available at http://www.sportengland.org/research/active_people_survey/active_people_survey_51.aspx.

Sport England (2012a) 'Facilities Planning Model'. Available at http://www.sportengland.org/research/market_segmentation.aspx.

Sport England (2012b) 'The Value of Sport Monitor'. Available at http://www.sportengland.org/research/value_of_sport_monitor.aspx.

Sport England (2012c) 'Market Segmentation'. Available at http://www.sportengland.org/research/marketsegmentation.aspx.

Sport Wales (2012) 'Our Vision'. Available at http://www.sportwales.org.uk/about-us/about-sport-wales/our-vision.aspx.

Thompson, J. (2001) *Understanding Corporate Strategy.* London, Thomson Learning.

CHAPTER 5

STRATEGIC PERFORMANCE MANAGEMENT 1: STRATEGIC IMPLEMENTATION

STEPHEN ROBSON

INTRODUCTION

It is by no means peculiar to sport development that huge amounts of time and effort are invested in the analysis and choice phases of the strategy process, only for the resulting document to gather dust on a shelf. However it has been a significant issue for the profession over the three decades of what might be termed its 'strategic awakening'. It may seem self-evident that "a good strategy is one that can be successfully implemented" (MacMillan and Tampoe 2000:188). So, in the light of so many strategic intentions failing to see the light of day (a classic example of which was the majority of the ten-year targets set out in England, the Sporting Nation (English Sports Council 1996)) this most optimistic of chapters, with its focus on getting things done, needs to be grounded in the reality of experience.

In Chapter 4, Jayne Wilson discusses good practice in articulating strategic choices through clearly written and appropriately disseminated strategic documents. As we were shown, a key focus of any strategic plan is to ensure buy-in from diverse stakeholders by outlining the rationale for decisions, but it and any associated materials must also provide a clear prescription for strategic implementation. In addition, the organisational capability must be in place to ensure successful delivery. There have been too many instances throughout the evolution of sport development whereby the sport development unit has been adept at desktop work and strategy production but not geared towards delivery. This may be thought of as an 'implementation gap'. The narrowing of this gap is a primary focus for this chapter.

96

It is useful at this early stage of the chapter to clarify the terminology which will be employed throughout. Wheelen and Hunger (2002:192) describe strategy implementation as "the sum total of activities and choices required for the execution of a strategic plan". Note their emphasis that the act of making choices does not end with the identification of strategic priorities. Action-focused words such as implementation, execution and delivery may (with care) be used interchangeably in the context of sport development. All stages of the strategic management process are (or should be) active and dynamic, but it is at the implementation stage that the 'physical' evidence of strategic thinking, in the form of improved outcomes for sports' many stakeholders, is brought to the fore. The other key concept to address at this point is the notion of strategy implementation as an internal change process. New strategic direction (ideally in recognition of the external influences discussed in Chapter 3) is frequently a driver for structural and budgetary change within the sport development organisation, and in politically-charged environments such as local authorities the reverse is often true. Implementation can therefore be thought of as much more than detectable changes to the organisation's outward-facing work with its customers and partners.

Numerous authors (e.g. Wheelen and Hunger 2002) accentuate this inextricable relationship between the formulation and implementation of strategy. Mintzberg and Waters (1998) were amongst the first to advance the notion that, particularly in the context of 'pure deliberate' strategies, significant aspects of the organisation's intentions remain unrealised at the end of the strategy cycle. At the same time, *emergent strategy* is the product of unforeseen events to which the organisation has had to respond. The resulting, realised strategy may therefore bear little resemblance to the vision of the future set out in the original document. As a consequence, on an ongoing basis, sport development professionals must ask whether the actions they are undertaking have relevance to either the initial vision or the current operating conditions. As with the rest of this book, flexibility is therefore an important concept to be explored in this chapter.

Given the above it is perhaps no surprise that many noble strategic intentions in sport development have lain unrealised. It is in many ways laudable that well-meaning professionals, all too familiar with the short-term thinking and political interference which can blight effective planning and implementation, have sought to gain the strategic commitment of stakeholders over three-, five- and sometimes ten-year periods, but they have frequently seen their good intentions founder. This tension between the short- and long-term planning domains is something of a standing joke in sport development, and offers a partial explanation for the failure of policymakers and practitioners to increase sport participation over the past thirty years (Sport England 2012). If implementation followed intent in a linear fashion, the long-term goal of steady, incremental increase in participation would be assured, with members of the sport development workforce acting in a uniform fashion, their efforts underwritten by consistent political and financial support. That this is manifestly not the case may be attributable to strategic implementation regrettably not having attained the status of a *core competency* in organisations (Pryor *et al.* 2007).

This chapter carries a positive message allied to practical solutions, to enable current and future sport development professionals to view strategic implementation through new lenses, using *Strategic Sport Development's* 4Ps theme as a guide. First, the aforementioned role of implementation as a *process* of change will be considered in depth. Is implementation merely the enactment of change, is it a consequence of organisational change or perhaps a cause of change? As we will see, it is most helpful to conceive of implementation as fulfilling all three roles to some extent. It is of equal importance to consider the *people* aspect: who implements sport development strategy? Unlike many commercial applications, it is often the case in sport development that the strategic leader co-ordinates and oversees a strategy formulation process on behalf of multiple stakeholders, the commitment of whom to implementing the strategy will determine its level of success. The seminal role of organisational culture, within and beyond the parent sport development unit, receives prominent coverage. Resistance to change is not the only cause of strategies gathering dust: linking the *product* and *practice* themes, this chapter acknowledges the historical vagueness of many sport development strategies. As we have already seen it is not enough to produce a 'textbook' strategy document and sit back whilst the world is changed for the better. SMART goals, targets and actions need to be monitored and refined on an ongoing basis to ensure their relevance and this chapter will propose workable approaches to this, using illustrative examples from contemporary sport development.

98

IMPLEMENTATION AND CHANGE

Let us begin by exploring the relationship between strategic intent and implementation in more depth. Thompson and Martin (2005) outline how conventional, hierarchical, militaristic approaches to strategy have diminishing relevance in the modern world. In sport development settings it is an incontrovertible truth that change must be owned not only by actors at all levels within the organisation, but also by those external customers and partners who will experience its impact. For MacMillan and Tampoe (2000), change needs to be considered in the context of culture, structure and processes. The start point for strategic leaders in sport development is to establish the extent of the change which will be required in these areas. For the majority who plan cyclically, the lessons of the preceding cycle having been absorbed, the decision needs to be taken whether the existing culture, structure and processes can largely support the achievement of new priorities, or whether transformative change is needed. In either case it is unlikely that existing working practices will survive unaltered. For example, when core funding for the network of County Sport Partnerships (CSPs) across England was all but removed, in the interests of survival many adopted a commissioning approach to their work, bidding for contracts to provide services to external clients. This major shift in priorities represented a challenge to core values and organisational culture – away from stimulating long-term change and achieving softer, developmental goals – in order to be able to deliver outputs for 'customers'.

Balogun and Hope Hailey (2004) propose a *context-sensitive* approach to change design. All sport development organisations are subject to constraints which need to be accounted for in change decisions. Options which were possible in the preceding strategy cycle may now be unavailable to the sport development organisation. Even if the sport development unit's or partnership's overarching vision and aims remain constant over a lengthy period, the way in which they are to be achieved may need to change dramatically. For example, in line with the above changes to CSPs' funding, Community Sport Networks (CSNs) were similarly affected by financial cuts. Originally established as part of Sport England's 'Delivery System' to provide strategic co-ordination for the delivery of sporting opportunities in defined localities, they too saw their funding radically diminished. The more robust CSNs, most able to continue their work following funding changes were those that had already existed, albeit in a different guise before the instigation of the Delivery System. Having had to jump through funding hoops the CSNs were subsequently all but abandoned, but many were able to coalesce around the values which had brought partners together in the first place. This somewhat dramatic example emphasises the value to practitioners and students alike of Balogun and Hope Hailey's (2004) *change kaleidoscope*, which accommodates the themes of culture, structure and process. This useful tool enables change options to be identified and evaluated within the envelope of existing constraints and enablers. There is not enough space here to apply it in full to sport development applications (hence you are encouraged to follow up on this), but its key features are highlighted below.

Design choices

At the centre of the model are the change path, change start point, change style, change target, change levers and change roles. We will assume, following the train of thought of this book, that strategic intent (the change start-point in this model) has already been ascertained via a bottom-up process (Huff *et al.* 2009), then the design choices relate to the implementation phase which, as we have already established, is in and of itself a change process. The change path is defined once the desired *type* of change has been identified in Table 5.1.

Inclusive sport development, by its very nature, should be a transformative activity in terms of its effect in communities, but strategic leaders must decide whether this necessitates such dramatic measures to be taken to change the organisation from within. Perhaps the ideal change path for many strategic leaders in sport development is evolution, an ongoing process which harmonises with the external demands placed upon the functional unit. This hopefully avoids the turbulence of a revolutionary approach but ensures that sport development resources are utilised in step with the needs of customers and partners. The change path having been chosen, Balogun and Hope Hailey (2004) assert that the *style* of change sits on a continuum between coercion at one end and education/delegation at the other. Strategic leaders would do well to recognise that sport development practitioners are characteristically independent thinkers with a passion for their vocation, thus a delegative approach is far more likely to glean the best results in the long term. We will return to this theme shortly.

100

Table 5.1 Types of change (adapted from Balogun and Hope Hailey 2004:20)

		End result	
		Transformation	*Realignment*
Nature	Incremental	**Evolution**	**Adaptation**
	Big bang	**Revolution**	**Reconstruction**

The change *target* relates to the level of the organisation at which to intervene: the design choice here is whether to focus solely on outputs or to seek to influence attitudes and behaviours. Much of the change literature (e.g. Wilson 1999) discusses managerial approaches which, in order to achieve the desired changes to organisational performance, attempt to enforce changes to attitudes and behaviours in an essentially top-down, directive fashion. Attitudinal and behavioural change can therefore be a means to an end (as is usually the case in conventional, sport development strategy contexts) or an end in itself. Strategic leaders in a local authority sport development unit, for instance, will commonly be able to depend upon colleagues' attitudinal commitment to working towards inclusive outcomes, often arrived at consensually. Desirable behavioural change should follow as a consequence of individuals' personal development in support of the new strategic direction.

The next two sections deal in more detail with the change *levers* and change *roles* elements of Balogun and Hope Hailey's model, examining the importance of organisational culture and considering the diverse implementation 'workforce' in strategic sport development. Intertwined with these themes is a discussion of the "organisational change context" (Balogun and Hope Hailey 2004:18), namely those factors which promote or constrain the organisation's ability to achieve its goals. The organisational change context consists of too many (namely eight) elements to cover in detail here; once again you are urged to investigate this further as an independent learning activity. Certain elements are more germane than others to this discussion of the implementation of sport development strategy, which is frequently undertaken at functional or departmental, as opposed to corporate level.

ORGANISATIONAL CULTURE AND CAPABILITY

Change *levers* are those interventions to be deployed across what Balogun and Hope Hailey (2004) characterise as technical, political, cultural and interpersonal subsystems. They are encapsulated within Johnson's (1988) famous *cultural web* model, which provides academics and strategic leaders alike with a means to map and account for the tangle of beliefs and assumptions which underpin organisational decisions and actions. The elements of the web are stories, symbols, rituals, power, organisation and controls. At the heart of the web is the *paradigm*: the underlying worldview of the strategic leader and her/his subordinates, which is both represented in, and shaped by the technical subsystem of organisational structures and control systems; the political subsystem of the distribution of power (formally and informally); and the cultural subsystem embodied in symbols, stories and rituals. The paradigm frequently acts as a filter (Johnson 1988) which influences interpretation of the complexity encountered in both the external and internal environments. For example, Robson (2001) found in an unnamed sport development unit in the north of England that the paradigm incorporated staff commitment to the 'cause' set against resentment towards stifling managerial practices. This tension impacted upon all aspects of the team's strategy implementation.

For successful implementation of sport development strategy, attention must be paid to each of the technical, political and cultural subsystems represented in the web: the day-to-day requirements for implementing strategy. Mapping the cultural web can provide new insights by questioning that which is taken for granted or has never been questioned (Johnson 2001). The technical subsystem is discussed in the next section; here, the political and cultural subsystems are considered. It is difficult to overstate the importance of the human factors embodied in the cultural artefacts known as symbols, stories and rituals. In many senses they are less tangible than formal structures, but they are the outward signs of the 'way of life' in the organisation and provide clues as to the values of the workforce at all levels. Identifying and interpreting symbols, stories and rituals is a crucial role of the strategic leader who wishes to achieve successful implementation. This is a complex task bearing in mind that these are manifested in different forms within and between individual teams and departments. Leeds City Council's sport development unit, for example, is one of the largest in the country and

102

strategic leaders oversee the development and implementation of numerous strategic plans (Leeds City Council 2012) across a range of sports and social objectives. The slick, professional symbolism of the unit's headquarters at the John Charles Centre for Sport may be intimidating if replicated at its community outposts around the city, where successful implementation depends upon the engagement of volunteers from diverse backgrounds.

Organisational stories or myths can be unheard outside the functional unit or may be shared in partnership settings. This activity is almost impossible for strategic leaders to control regardless of any interventions designed to address behaviours, but it must be acknowledged as it impacts upon the perception of the sport development unit in the external environment. The oral history of the service area, reputations of individuals and spoken perceptions of the current 'state of things' all offer useful predictors of the likely success of sport development strategy. In Robson's (2001) investigation, the nature and distribution of the stories surrounding the sport development unit evidenced a potential threat to successful implementation, as a clear sense of isolationism was communicated to the listener. Rituals or routines, meanwhile, are the 'way we do things around here', relating to official working practices as well as less formal activities which shape relationships between colleagues and teams. The execution of a new sport development strategy may present a challenge to established practices and staff may feel that their sovereignty is being threatened.

Closely linked to cultural factors is the political subsystem, namely the power structures within the team, unit, department and organisation. This is interwoven with, but should be considered separately from the formal organisational structures which are examined below, because power relationships can arise informally, with individuals possessing disproportionately high or low levels of actual power, regardless of published structures. Formal authority (the ability to wield power) is vested in individuals through the bureaucratic processes of the organisation. Strategic leaders in sport development have to appreciate and be able to negotiate their way through political processes within and beyond their organisational boundaries. This involves dealing with a range of power brokers from elected members to influential community figures. As this chapter deals with the transition from decisions into action, it can be assumed that necessary political mandates have been obtained for the new strategic direction, so we need to concentrate upon the influence of power upon implementation. In larger sport development units such as Leeds, strategic leaders must be conscious of unduly powerful individuals who can derail strategy implementation if preventative measures are not taken. The next section develops this theme further by taking into account the range of stakeholders from beyond the sport development unit whose power and influence are critical in enabling successful implementation.

Finally for this section, returning to Balogun and Hope Hailey's (2004) change kaleidoscope, two particularly relevant components of the organisational change context are *capacity* and *capability*. Whilst cultural analysis exposes the innate motivations of the workforce, assessing capacity and capability ascertains the readiness of the sport development unit to proceed with implementation. As with many concepts, they are defined in numerous ways across the body of literature. For the purposes of this discussion, capacity can be thought of in terms of the resources required to implement strategic intent. As was shown in Chapter 2, resource analysis is an essential activity to be undertaken when considering strategic options. Lack of sufficient resources such as staffing, finance, equipment, facilities, transport and time is one of the principal reasons for failure at the implementation stage. Strategic leaders should not commit to new programmes of work without having established whether the unit can 'afford' them in terms of all necessary resources. Capability can in some senses be thought of as a subset of capacity, with a particular focus upon the *skills* of the implementing workforce. Whether the change target is simply focused on outcomes, or whether behavioural change is desired, it is distinctly possible that change levers such as training, professional development and even modifications to terms and conditions of employment will be required. In the spirit of evolutionary change discussed earlier, the preferred position is one of ongoing, continuing professional development (CPD) so that the demands of executing strategic change are anticipated. A pioneering partnership between West Yorkshire Sport and Leeds Metropolitan University confirmed the role of CPD in ensuring successful implementation. Undergraduate students were recruited as Club Support Assistants (CSAs) to act as agents of change through the delivery of support to selected West Yorkshire sport clubs. Recruits received CPD on market segmentation, relevant legislation and so on, boosting their wider employment prospects in the process. Their intervention led the recruitment of almost 1000 new adult sport club members in the first year and contributed to West Yorkshire Sport's broader strategic goals for sport. In general the precise nature of the change levers to be deployed will be driven by the change target (Balogun and Hope Hailey 2004).

WHO DOES THE IMPLEMENTING?

The technical subsystem includes organisational structure, the formal system of task and reporting relationships which prescribes official lines of communication and confers responsibility at different levels. Since this discussion assumes that strategic decisions have already been arrived at, we need to consider the role of structure at *functional unit* level in facilitating co-operation between individuals and teams to deliver strategic sport development outcomes. Structural arrangements are often inherited, and strategic leaders' ability to manipulate them is mitigated by other aspects of the web. In the context of implementation, the notion of *responsibility* is paramount: abstract intentions are operationalised and tasks assigned to individuals and teams. Leaders must ensure that strategically vital activities do not fall into a vacuum such that no stakeholder can be held to account for their completion. A trawl of strategy documents produced by local authorities, NGBs and other sport development organisations reveals that the detail of precisely who is responsible for what is often absent.

As if it were needed, a further layer of complexity is added when considering the implementing workforce of sport development strategy. So far, in the interests of clarity the discussion has been focused predominantly at unit level. However, in sport development settings the implementation of strategy is rarely conducted purely by the sport development unit, particularly as the 'unit' often consists of one person! Whilst the ideal strategy development process should be inclusive and consensual, particularly in local authority settings, it is commonly the sport development unit which will 'carry the can' in terms of generating the product, namely the finished strategy document. However, it is highly likely that a multifarious and diverse network of stakeholders from beyond the organisational boundaries will be called upon to execute the strategy. This is what Alford (2001:7–8) refers to as "co-production beyond the producing unit", and accompanying its manifold benefits are a series of complex challenges to the strategy's curators.

Whilst this book urges strategic leaders to promote bottom-up decision-making and develop relationships of trust with paid subordinates, we acknowledge that more directive approaches are required at times, particularly when there are issues within the cultural subsystem. However, when the implementing workforce for sport development strategy includes volunteers, colleagues in partner organisations (some of whom may be in more senior positions) and elected members, a delicate balance must be struck which will test the strategic leader's negotiation skills. Alford (2001) refers to the leader's role as one of facilitating debate amongst stakeholders and orchestrating implementation: relatively soft language which emphases the required balancing act. A typical example of a sport development strategy with a strong partnership focus is Norwich City Council's Sport and Leisure Development Plan 2011–12 (Norwich City Council 2011). Here, external stakeholders as diverse as voluntary sport clubs, education providers, healthcare providers, police and wider sporting bodies are expected to contribute to the implementation of an ambitious strategy for sport and physical activity. Strategic leaders in Norwich have **no** formal authority to enforce strategic decisions or influence work programmes for personnel in these organisations.

Before proposing solutions let us develop this scenario further and take stock of the full magnitude of the challenge. Instead of applying Balogun and Hope Hailey's change kaleidoscope and Johnson's cultural web purely to the sport development unit, which may only consist of a small number of individuals, consider this amorphous mass of stakeholders as the 'organisation' and therefore how change decisions and cultural analyses may apply at this level. Whilst cultural artefacts will not have matured to the extent of those within a single organisation, elements such as routines, stories and power relations will certainly exist in a developed partnership, and a well-designed alliance will have an agreed 'organisational' structure. The benefits and challenges of the resulting mix of backgrounds, experiences, skills and knowledge can be at once exciting and daunting for strategic leaders in the host sport development unit. Ultimately the focus of implementation is upon getting the job done, so an approach has to be taken which accommodates the full range of motivations and working practices of the stakeholders, enabling them to play their part in delivering strategic outcomes. Extending the reach of implementation activity beyond the formulators of the strategy can help to achieve this, as well as representing a powerful inclusion tool.

106

The key to successful execution in settings as complex as this has been identified by Alford (2001) and others: strategic leadership. The term 'strategic leader', as opposed to 'manager', has been used deliberately throughout this chapter as it implies a more inclusive approach, less limited in terms of what can be achieved. Ideally the implementing workforce will constitute a 'leaderful' team (The Boston Consortium 2005), with many individuals able to share and appreciate the strategic vision, taking ownership of those aspects of implementation to which they have been assigned. Experience shows that this is not always the case, particularly where a sport development strategy is seen as a distraction (albeit an important one) from a professional's core business (e.g. a community development worker with a wider remit beyond sport) or where an individual's time may be severely pressured (e.g. a volunteer sports club chairperson). Here, the strategic leader(s) representing the host organisation must show empathy with the pressures faced by stakeholders, explain in meaningful terms the benefits of continued engagement, show flexibility and formally express appreciation for the contributions made. (Chapter 9 offers a full treatment of leadership in strategic sport development.) The unifying ingredient through which implementation can be achieved in such a messy environment is clearly constructed and skilfully communicated goals and action plans, the written articulation of the transition from ideas to delivery. These should be agreed by all stakeholders but their composition and publication should be handled by the host sport development organisation to ensure consistency and accountability. This chapter's focus now turns to good practice in this area.

FRAMEWORKS FOR SUCCESSFUL IMPLEMENTATION

Before examining in detail the ways in which workloads can be agreed and expressed, it is appropriate to challenge convention in terms of the way in which this process is managed. Getz, Jones and Loewe (2009) join many others in bemoaning the fact that the majority of business strategies fail to deliver the predicted results, citing familiar causes such as a lack of a meaningful connection between the "long-term time horizon of strategic thinking" (2009:18) and the more immediate, short-term requirements of action planning. They suggest a novel (and crucially, workable) approach to implementation: **migration management**. This embraces many of the principles already discussed in this chapter and elsewhere in this book, primarily that the reason for most strategies' failure is a lack of balance between maintaining a constant organisational purpose (see Chapter 2) and the realities of the external world. Migration management differs from traditional approaches to strategy implementation, which in sport development often involves attempts at the outset to define a work programme that covers the entire lifecycle of the published strategy. Bitter experience suggests that this is likely to result in poor use of scant resources, a need to backtrack or even the abandonment of strategic intentions, particularly in the later stages of the strategy's life. Instead migration management adopts a 'future-back' approach in which the desired future state is clearly identified and a migration path developed, showing the gaps which must be closed in order to reach it. The actions necessary to plug the gaps are made easier to ascertain. In applying the principles of migration management to strategic sport development we must of course be conscious of the numerous senses in which sport development differs from commercial settings, chief amongst which is the diversity of the implementing workforce, discussed earlier in this chapter. However, these principles can readily be applied and enable organisations to cope better with the chaotic and politicised environment in which they operate.

The headline aspects of migration management have been selected for the purposes of this chapter and you are strongly encouraged to read into it more deeply and apply it to the setting of interest to you. Getz, Jones and Loewe (2009) outline a seven-stage process for the development of the migration path. The first step, of **identifying the desired future state**, involves the activities discussed thus far in this book, including the identification of what is distinctive about the organisation and the services it provides. In sport development there is limited duplication as organisations can be distinguished from each other by geographical boundaries, specific sports, social objectives and so on. The desired future state includes not only a vision of what success means in the future, but also captures any transformations in terms of the skills, competencies and resources the organisation will possess at that time (see Chapters 2 and 4). Bearing in mind the nature of the environment for sport development it is suggested that the time horizon even for a 'crystal-ball gazing' exercise such as this should be kept relatively modest e.g. four–six years at most. The second step is the drawing up of a **first draft of a 'migration path'**, which is low on specific detail but which specifies implementation gaps and proposes a menu of gap-closing actions. Members of the implementation team (which, as we know in sport development may include wider stakeholders) ask whether the desired future state could be achieved in a matter of days or weeks. In the likely event that this is not the case they identify what is missing: the implementation gaps. In sport development settings this can include ingredients as diverse as the skill base (e.g. nobody trained in British Sign Language), reputation or credibility in target communities, lack of appropriate partners etc. Once identified, the **selection of gap-closing actions** can take place. This is, of course, the essence of strategy implementation, and the team may have to prioritise and select from a potentially bewildering array of options, the relevance of each of which can only be assured at that point in time. Getz, Jones and Loewe advise that a good mix of learning and execution actions should be sought: in other words, those activities necessary to enhance organisational capability, such as training and other forms of personal development, should be balanced against service delivery tasks (e.g. specific sport programmes in communities or participation in national initiatives).

Step four involves the **grouping of actions into four to six themes or clusters**. This is instrumental in determining the division of labour between individuals within a sport development unit (e.g. local authority) or functions within a department (e.g. in a larger national governing body of sport). This may be counter-intuitive to experienced practitioners who are accustomed to setting out areas of work in a linear fashion, using the broader purpose or vision and strategic aims as a guide. However, in this more traditional approach the existing structure of the organisation or department is prone to act as a principal driver for implementation decisions rather than the desired future state. The 'future-back' approach of migration management is more likely to generate perhaps unexpected but more valid solutions. In typical sport development settings clusters that might arise include organisational capability (staff development etc.), volunteer development, partnership development, access to external resources and so on, but in truth the possibilities are virtually limitless. Within each cluster it is then necessary to **sequence the action steps**. At this stage we are mapping the higher-level projects, initiatives etc. that are necessary to lead each cluster and therefore the organisation towards its desired future. Here it is important to **check overall consistency and interdependencies**, in other words you must take great care over sequencing to ensure that relationships between activities are accounted for. Using project management tools such as Gantt charts (see for instance Kerzner 2009) it is possible to paint a detailed picture of the roll-out of the activities needed to close all gaps, from first steps to the removal of the final gap. A project management approach also enables the identification and fine-tuning of time factors such as lead times, duration of activities and so on. Each of these high-level activities requires breaking down into its component tasks, the stage at which skilled *action planning* should be practised. This is discussed in detail shortly.

First we return to Balogun and Hope Hailey's model. The technical subsystem, besides organisational structure, incorporates something called *controls*. This is a somewhat misleading term as it principally seems to imply methods that may be used to restrict unauthorised activity such as surveillance and autocratic leadership. There is, however, more to this final component of the cultural web. Controls can be thought of more broadly as the means by which the organisation ensures and measures individuals' performance. This definition includes operational targets and can be an enabling device as much as it may be seen in some settings as a 'big stick'. With the emphasis on achievement rather than failure, however, and the opportunity for personnel at all levels to develop their own control mechanisms, the possibility of strategic intent being realised is greatly enhanced. A brief examination of a sample of sport strategy documents reveals a glaring inconsistency of approach, from the detailed action planning evident in Redditch Borough Council's Sport Development Plan 2010–13 (Redditch Borough Council 2010) to the much less prescriptive approach of the City of Plymouth (2010). As outlined throughout this chapter, the means through which sport development strategy implementation should take place must be context-specific and there is no fixed line of attack, but there are certain principles of good practice which should be universal and would lead to improved outcomes if applied across the board.

ACTION PLANNING FOR SUCCESSFUL IMPLEMENTATION

Following the identification and mapping of the high-level migration pathway, the next step in Getz, Jones and Loewe's (2009) process is to **develop the future state and migration path for *divisions and functions*.** Implicit here is that the future state for each of the key areas of work is

110

a necessary component of the overall future state the organisation is seeking to achieve. As discussed above it is prudent to adapt the Getz, Jones and Loewe approach to identify a shorter time horizon for the overall desired future state, but it is still useful to identify at least one intermediate future state (say two years into a four-year migration path) in order for progress to be checked. The intermediate future state should bear much closer resemblance to the overall future state than the organisation's start point. Migration path programmes can then be translated into specific projects and initiatives. In sport development settings this will often entail broader initiatives being disaggregated into actionable chunks. This is not an unfamiliar activity for sport development professionals, but the challenge of migration management is take a far more rigorous approach to assessing 'Why are we doing this?' Activities that do not contribute to the migration path have questionable value to the organisation and their continued resourcing must be in doubt. All other relevant activities must be subjected to meticulous action planning. Evidence from sport development strategy documents suggests that their writers are often skilled in the art of operationalising broader intentions, so with a migration management focus this should become a much more purposeful pursuit and a greater proportion of planned activities ought to be realised.

Chapters 4 and 6 discuss the hierarchical nature of strategic thinking and show how a progression should be constructed from the broad, philosophical underpinnings of the organisation and its work, through incrementally more concrete levels until actions can be generated (a simple example of which would be vision → mission → aims → objectives → actions). The various levels at which intentions are expressed can be thought of as philosophy, strategic intent, targets and operations. In support of this we need a consistent approach to nomenclature or terminology. The above inspection of published strategy unveils wildly variable practice. What are goals, targets, action plans, work programmes? Does it matter if the terms are used interchangeably? At the every least it would be of great benefit for strategic leaders to adopt a position on the meanings of these expressions in order to construct a framework for implementation that could be populated and actioned by all stakeholders. We also need to consider the distinctions and overlaps between the identification of *tasks* to be carried out (action planning) and the *targets* against which their success will be assessed (performance measurement), the latter of which is tackled in full in the next chapter. The two are inextricably bound, but this blurring of the boundaries often leads to fuzziness in the way they are enshrined in official sport development documents, resulting in neither being satisfactorily accomplished.

This extract (see Table 5.2) from a sample action plan contains the essential ingredients required to ensure that tasks are performed for the right reason and that the precise requirements of each action are set out. In essence the format will be broadly familiar to practitioners. There is no great mystery to action planning, a reasonably straightforward activity which is often undermined by the flawed strategic thought processes which precede it!

As shown in the detailed example below, tasks such as this one are embedded in wider strategic thought processes. In operational terms the essential information is present, identifying contributory activities, resource implications in terms of people, money and equipment etc. This approach conforms fully to the SMART model (Project SMART 2012), and crucially, *accountability* for tasks is an inbuilt feature. The next section provides a detailed, hypothetical example and shows how the value of an action planning approach such as this is enhanced when a greater common understanding of 'Why are we doing this?' is fostered through attention to the thinking which underpins both the change kaleidoscope and migration management.

MIGRATION MANAGEMENT FOR SUCCESSFUL IMPLEMENTATION: SPORT DEVELOPMENT EXAMPLE

This hypothetical example concerns a migration path towards increased sporting autonomy for communities. It is annotated throughout to demonstrate the connections to the change kaleidoscope and migration management. Let us begin by identifying a desired future state. For simplicity's sake we will assign the high-level migration path to a medium-sized, local authority sport development team in the fictional town of Beckett Park-on-Sea. A key part of the team's purpose and philosophy is:

To seek to achieve equity and inclusion in all sports opportunities.

Table 5.2 Extract from sport development operational plan

Ref. Planned action	How will this be achieved?	Target (what does success look like?)	Lead person	By when	Resources Unit cost	Total cost
1.1 Six-week coaching programme to be established for new boccia club	▪ Two hours of delivery ▪ Facility secured ▪ Head coach (Level 2) secured ▪ Voluntary Assistant Coach (Level 1) secured	Everything organised and booked to accommodate the new club	Disability Sport Dev Officer to lead with help from Jan Bloggs (club secretary)	10th December 2013	Facility hire 2 hrs @ £25/hr = £50 Head coach @ 2hrs @ £10/hr = £20+18% on costs = £23.60 x 6 weeks = £141.60 Assistant coach's travel expenses x 6 = £30 Equipment 2 x boccia sets inc ramps = £500	£721.60

Through consultation with external stakeholders (many of whom constitute the wider workforce which will implement the strategy) it has been determined that the desired future state is thus:

> **Vision** (*i.e. the desired state of community sport development team in five years' time*): To stimulate greater self-determination amongst community sports organisations in Beckett Park-on-Sea.

> **Aim 1** (*this particular aim deals with an intermediate future state half way along the migration path for the Club Development aspect of the sport development organisation's work*): To support six new sports clubs to achieve Clubmark status.

> **Objective 1.3** (*one of several objectives which contribute to the achievement of Aim 1*): To achieve a minimum of twenty newly qualified, female, Level 2 football coaches by September 2014.

The first of these actions relates to the internal capabilities of the organisation (linked to resources in the E-V-R congruence model) and shows that CPD is often a critical part of the migration path. It also connects to the change target aspect of Balogun and Hope Hailey's model: by affecting this internal change (to the competency of the member of the team responsible for the coaching programme), the likelihood of the desired external change being achieved is greatly heightened. The second action is more visible as it is externally directed but is underpinned by the internal change. Taken together these sample actions show that the migration path is a combination of tangible and more subtle steps towards the desired future state. Such an approach also places the resources in the hands of those responsible for the delivery of that part of the migration path and makes a significant contribution to the development of a productive organisational culture. Clearly the full version of this action plan would need to be revisited on a regular basis to ensure the relevance and currency of planned activities.

SUMMARY

In no small way a key purpose of this chapter was to demonstrate that it is with good reason that fixed, long-term approaches to strategy implementation in sport development have been largely discredited. In

114

Table 5.3 Adapted sport development operational plan

Ref.	Planned action	How will this be achieved?	Target (what does success look like?)	Lead person	By When	Resources Unit cost	Total cost
1.3.1	Provide project management training for Coaching Development Officer	▪ Identification of development needs ▪ Attendance at CIMSPA training course ▪ Shadowing of senior project manager ▪ Feedback and review	Development needs identified and met	Coaching DO and line manager	End March 2013	One place at CIMSPA project management training course = £395	£395
1.3.2	Coaching panel to identify existing, female Level 1 coaches to enter development programme	▪ Invite community football clubs to nominate Level 1 coaches for development programme ▪ Coaching panel to discuss programme and approve nominations	At least 30 coaches to commence programme	Coaching DO and coaching panel	End September 2013	No additional expenditure	N/A

researching the chapter I found numerous examples of obsolete sport development action plans hiding in the Internet's nooks and crannies, monuments to good intentions that were overtaken by events beyond their authors' control. An action plan template has been offered, but in truth the tool is only of use to the practitioner who takes time to appreciate the context within which implementation occurs. Balogun and Hope Hailey's work provides a means for achieving this, whilst Getz, Jones and Loewe offer a mechanism by which strategic leaders can navigate the tortuous path towards the attainment of the wider sport development vision.

The other principal reason for the chapter was an attempt to elevate the status of strategic implementation in sport development. A keener appreciation of 'Why are we doing this?' might just help to unlock better outcomes for communities through more effective and focused implementation. The next chapter should therefore be treated as a partner to this one, since implementation will succeed in the short term only if performance management is not dynamic and responsive. What we do today, whether it succeeds and whether we are able to detect that success should influence what we decide to do tomorrow. In the ever-changing sport development environment this seems particularly apt.

LEARNING ACTIVITIES

Developing skills and knowledge

In keeping with aspects of National Occupational Standard A44 Manage a Project (Management Standards Centre 2008), clear communication with stakeholders is necessary for effective strategic implementation. So, for a sport development organisation with which you are familiar:

1   Identify a desired future state (e.g. five years from now) for an important aspect of the organisation's work and determine which departments, functional units and/or areas of work require migration paths towards that future state.
2   Choose one of these migration paths and construct one aim plus a series of objectives (aim = *what* needs to be achieved in order for that migration path to contribute to the vision; objectives = *how* the aim will be achieved).

116

3   Choose one of the objectives and create a detailed action plan to enable it to be achieved. Referring to Balogun and Hope Hailey's (2004) change kaleidoscope, ensure that necessary internal changes are mapped as well as outward-facing activities.

REFERENCES

Alford, J. (2001) 'The Implications of "Publicness" for Strategic Management Theory'. In Johnson, G. and Scholes, K. eds. (2001) *Exploring Public Sector Strategy*. Harlow, Pearson Education.

Balogun, J. and Hope Hailey, V. (2004) *Exploring Strategic Change*. 2nd ed. Financial Times, Prentice Hall.

The Boston Consortium (2005) 'The Leaderful Concept'. Available at http://www.leaderful.org/leaderful.html.

City of Plymouth (2010) *Sports Development Plan 2010–13*. Plymouth, City of Plymouth.

English Sports Council (1996) *England, the Sporting Nation*. London, English Sports Council.

Getz, G., Jones, C. and Loewe, P. (2009) 'Migration Management: an approach for improving strategy implementation'. In *Strategy and Leadership*. 37(6), pp. 8–24.

Huff, A., Floyd, S., Sherman, H. and Terjesen, S. (2009) *Strategic Management*. London, Wiley.

Johnson, G. (1988) 'Rethinking Incrementalism'. In *Strategic Management Journal*. 9, pp. 75–91.

Johnson, G. (2001) 'Mapping and Re-Mapping Organisational Culture: a local government example'. In Johnson, G. and Scholes, K. eds. (2001) *Exploring Public Sector Strategy*. Harlow, Pearson Education.

Kerzner, H. (2009) *Project Management: A Systems Approach to Planning, Scheduling, and Controlling*. Hoboken, NJ, John Wiley & Sons.

Leeds City Council (2012) 'Sport Development'. Available from http://www.leeds.gov.uk/Leisure_and_culture/Sports_clubs_and_centres/Sports_coaching.aspx

MacMillan, H. and Tampoe, M. (2000) *Strategic Management: Process, Content, and Implementation*. Oxford: Oxford University Press.

Management Standards Centre (2008) *A44 Manage a Project*. London, Management Standards Centre.

Mintzberg, H. and Waters, J. (1998) 'Of Strategies, Deliberate and Emergent'. In Segal-Horn, S. ed. *The Strategy Reader*. Oxford, Blackwell, pp. 20–34.

Norwich City Council (2011) *Sport and Leisure Development Plan 2011–12*. Norwich, Norwich City Council.

Project SMART (2012) SMART Goals: a clear route to success. Available at http://www.projectsmart.co.uk/smart-goals-objectives.html

Pryor, M., Anderson, D., Toombs, L. and Humphreys, J. (2007) 'Strategic Implementation as a Core Competency: the 5P's model'. *Journal of Management Research.* 7(1), pp. 3–17.

Redditch Borough Council (2010) 'Sports Development Plan 2010–2013'. Redditch, Redditch Borough Council.

Robson, S. (2001) 'The Public Sector, Best Value and Local Authority Sports Development'. In Wolsey, C. and Abrams, J. (2001) *Understanding the Leisure and Sport Industry.* Harlow, Pearson Education, pp. 3–17.

Sport England (2012) Active People Survey 6. Available at http://www.sportengland.org/research/active_people_survey/active_people_survey_6.aspx

Thompson, J. and Martin, F. (2005) *Strategic Management: Awareness and Change.* London, Thomson Learning.

Wheelen, T. and Hunger, D. (2002) *Strategic Management and Business Policy.* 8th ed. Upper Saddle River, NJ, Pearson Prentice Hall.

Wilson, D. (1999) *A Strategy of Change: Concepts and Controversies in the Management of Change.* London, Thomson Learning.

Stephen Robson

CHAPTER 6

STRATEGIC PERFORMANCE MANAGEMENT 2: EVALUATING STRATEGIC SPORT DEVELOPMENT

KIRSTIE SIMPSON

INTRODUCTION

With a recent history of policy focus on evidence-based service improvement (i.e. Comprehensive Area Assessment), and a future that looks set to concern strategic commissioning of services, the role of performance management in driving improvement becomes increasingly relevant. However, if there is to be a greater focus on user experience and neighbourhoods as is intimated by the philosophy of a 'Big Society', then the method and implementation of managing and measuring performance is directly affected. As Coalter (2006) argues, a process-led approach to what can be described as monitoring and evaluation can contribute to staff development and capacity building, as well as greater organisational integration and more coherently designed and consistently delivered programmes. This links to aspects within Chapter 7 on strategic partnerships where a typology of partnerships is offered; performance management is relevant here as practitioners often indicate that monitoring, but more specifically evaluation, is far too difficult to do when working within the myriad of organisations that utilise sport in a variety of ways in the community.

As expressed in Chapter 7, if partnerships are developed with high levels of critical consciousness on the part of the sport development practitioner (SDP) then these relationships allow, and fundamentally demand, the growth of trust, respect and cohesion within communities (Gilchrist 2003). This 'bottom-up' thinking is fundamental to 'bottom-up' strategic planning and therefore to the implementation and subsequent evaluation of successful strategy. With this community-led approach in mind, readers of this chapter will critically engage with theory-driven evaluation looking specifically at the logic model of evaluation proposed by Coalter (2002), as well as examining performance management from more generic perspectives. Further links to the concept of critical consciousness (Freire 1996) are proposed, and a model of strategy-as-theory and strategy-as-action is presented.

By way of introduction, this chapter features a clear link between the processes of performance measurement and performance management. Performance measurement is concerned with gathering data to evidence the extent to which targets (however expressed) are being fulfilled. Performance measurement forms part of the more comprehensive performance management process, whereby these data are considered and utilised to evaluate the project in some way. It is helpful at this point to identify the terms *inputs*, *outputs* and *outcomes* as these are often defined (within strategic documents) in different ways. For the purpose of this chapter, these are taken to mean the following:

> **Inputs** – those resources (i.e. human, physical and financial) that are used within the identified strategy/project.
>
> **Outputs** – the intended short term result of the strategy or project, usually linked to the strategy's stated objectives. For example, this might be expressed as the number of participants attending a specific training opportunity.
>
> **Outcome** – the intended long term change (generally in behaviour) that is anticipated through the strategy or project. To follow on from the example given above, this may relate to the consequences (i.e. what happened next) of attendance at said training opportunity.

In this chapter, the *people* aspect of the 4Ps model concerns the SDP and the extent to which this individual embeds the philosophy and *processes* of monitoring and evaluation in their *practice*. The absence of *product*, i.e. appropriately evaluated *practice,* which is utilised in the development of strategy, is of key concern. The chapter will take the reader on a journey which begins and ends with the SDP and will emphasise how important it is for colleagues to understand how evaluation can evidence change. This is, of course, prefaced by the assumption that the SDP is undertaking appropriate action, at an appropriate time, working in an appropriate way with the relevant community.

LACK OF CLEAR DIRECTION

The job title Sports Development Officer (SDO), commonly used throughout the 1980s and 1990s was a misnomer. The community sport development process was, and is, the preserve of many, not of the few. Paid roles such as facility manager, physical education teacher, coach, youth worker and unpaid ones such as supportive parent are an integral part of the process and essential to its success (however that is defined and managed), even for those individuals who might not recognise the development of sport as an end objective for either themselves or for their organisation.

Historically, the aim for most public sector SDOs (now referred to as SDPs by the industry and within this book) was to increase the levels of participation in sport within the geographical boundary of the local authority for which they work, regardless of whether or not this made any sense in sporting terms. The development of sporting excellence was rarely on their agenda and work with the mainly voluntary NGBs was rare. Support in terms of understanding this work was often limited as no one above or around these officers had any similar experience. Sport development became another chiefly local authority function. The SDP alternated between doing and providing (coaching and leading) and organising (administration). Most were not employed at a level where an overview of sport-related work was evident or where influence of others was possible. It is argued therefore that this lack of strategic leadership, in addition to a lack of SDPs actually understanding the change (in participation) they might be creating, has led to a whole generation of SDPs not knowing whether they have made any difference within the community they have worked. This difference would generally constitute an increase in participation, not always documented, measured or understood in any meaningful way.

This gap, both in terms of knowledge and competence, continued to expand in width and depth when sport development practice broadened to include using sport to tackle other agendas such as social exclusion. In essence, there were lots of keen, enthusiastic professionals undertaking sport development work, mostly funded by the tax payer, who felt what they were doing was right but had no way of understanding whether it was making any sort of difference at all. Hughes and Traynor (2000) suggest that it is commonplace for practitioners working in communities to argue that their work cannot be evaluated fully. Interestingly, Hughes and Traynor support this assertion from a community development perspective, stating that the myth that community initiatives cannot be evaluated needs to be challenged, that community development practitioners have as much obligation as anyone else to measure the effectiveness of social interventions.

LACK OF EVIDENCE

The benefits of being physically active in terms of health promotion and disease prevention are well documented (Department of Health, 2004) yet despite this, actual activity levels remain low (Department of Health 2003; Department of Health 2005; Sport England 2011a). In addition, the benefits of being physically active in terms of *sport* have not been articulated in the same way; it is hardly surprising therefore that one of the challenges for sport development resides in the paucity of longitudinal data on the long-term outcome or impact of interventions. There appears to be a strong belief on the part of SDPs in what sport can do (as suggested by comments in the previous section) but unfortunately not enough empirical data to support these beliefs (Collins *et al.* 1999; Robins 1990; Coalter 2001; Coalter 2002; Coalter 2007).

There have been a number of academic reviews undertaken on participation which discuss similar concerns. For example, Foster *et al.* (2005:2 in Coalter, 2007:20), in a systematic review of research on psychological and ecological factors relating to sports participation, conclude that there is "insufficient high quality research evidence about the reasons why adults and young people do and do not participate". Ironically, traditional sport development has been concerned mainly with sporting outcomes related to increasing participation and development of skill yet there is still no agreement about how best to gather data in this regard. Optimistically, Sport England (2011b) states:

> There is a growing body of evidence that sport can deliver benefits across a wide range of public policy agendas. What is

122

missing is easy access to the most up to date research combined with 'state of the evidence reviews' of its strengths and weaknesses

Both the Active People Survey (Sport England 2011a) and the Taking Part Survey (Sport England 2008) are helpful to a degree when discussing participation in sport though there is debate amongst academics on the validity of data collection methods in each case (Lynn 2011). Any increase in participation has been the only measure of 'effectiveness' of any given strategy and even this basic information is not collected consistently at project level (Collins *et al.* 1999; Coalter *et al.* 2000).

A number of what might be termed 'community outcomes' have often been presumed in the development of both policy and action in sport development; for example, increased social capital, community cohesion and regeneration. These outcomes however, are rarely systematically articulated and even more rarely monitored or evaluated. For example, Collins *et al.* (1999:3), in an analysis of literature on sport and social exclusion, found only 11 studies from 180 that had "...anything approaching rigorous evaluations and some of these did not give specific data for excluded groups or communities". This is a worrying picture and superficially appears to highlight concerns that SDPs are not interested in what development or change happens as a result of their work. This is an issue to which we will return later in the chapter.

THE PLANNING PROCESS

The lack of rigorous evaluation-in-practice evident in sport development is aggravated by an absence of systematically derived knowledge about evaluation practice itself and the resulting scarcity of investigations that attempt to ascertain whether "theoretical prescriptions and real-world practices do or do not align" (Miller and Campbell 2006:297). The absence of consideration of real world practice in this regard is fundamentally important to busy SDPs who require easy, straightforward ways of attempting to understand what has happened as a result of their work; the importance of praxis needs to be highlighted here.

As has already been outlined in the book thus far, the process of planning would appear to be relatively straightforward in functional, linear terms: analysis, choice, action and evaluation. Johnson, Scholes and

Whittington (2009:270) state that planning processes are the "archetypal administrative control" and really concern the control of resources, although they go on to say that bottom-up planning is often more helpful. Dugdill, Graham and McNair (2005) suggest that monitoring and measuring must be given as much thought as the intervention itself in the planning stages, and they usefully indicate that a way to understand this is that each action (within an intervention) requires a collection of evidence. It is argued that initially this evidence would relate to outputs which logically, over time, would be useful in ascertaining the outcome of the project. With the inclusion of evaluation in the planning process in mind, once organisations have undertaken environmental analysis, both internal and external, and have identified a number of strategic choices, these choices can be evaluated initially in relation to three key success criteria: suitability, acceptability and feasibility (Johnson, Scholes and Whittington 2009). To summarise these:

- Suitability refers to whether a strategy relates to the organisation's strategic position (as identified by purpose and rationale of the strategy, internal and external analysis and stakeholder expectations and cultural influences). This is critical to the SDP, although it is difficult to apply as often SDPs are attempting to fulfil a number of strategies (of which they may or may not be aware) through partnership working. This may mean that the SDP is not considering the suitability of this (partnership) approach i.e. the chosen 'strategy' in a systematic way.
- Acceptability concerns the performance outcomes and the extent to which these meet stakeholder expectations. As already stated, real evidence of coherently developed outcomes has seemingly eluded sport development: focus, possibly through necessity has tended to be on output not outcome.
- Feasibility orients around whether the strategy could work in practice. There is generally little evidence in sport-related strategies that any sort of feasibility process has been undertaken. In fact, it is rare to find a sport-related strategy with evidence of analysis of any kind.

Johnson, Scholes and Whittington (2009) consider that the success or failure of strategies will fundamentally be related to these three success criteria. It makes sense to analyse the intended strategic approach to ascertain whether this is the most appropriate strategy to follow.

124

However, for the majority of SDPs, this is simply not an option; timescales, and the rate at which success (in whatever form) is expected to be delivered do not allow time for this critical reflection. Are we to conclude then, on the basis of the comments above that the majority of sport-related strategies are not successful? At the very least, it is possible to intimate that sport-related strategies do not stand up well to scrutiny from a theoretical strategic management perspective.

To support this assertion, there would appear to be little evidence that any form of planning process is implemented consistently within what might be described as the sport development industry. This may be due to a lack of awareness of the processes of monitoring and evaluation or a reluctance to be accountable for interventions that may be identified as failing (Bloyce and Smith 2010). Establishing clear aims and objectives for any strategy document, and therefore intervention, is critical; without these how can SDPs claim to have been successful? Aims and objectives allow for targets to be established, against which progress can be monitored and measured and ultimately evaluated. Sport development as a term implies change (through the use of the word development); if this change cannot be measured how do we know that it has occurred? As the Audit Commission (2000:6) helpfully states:

> What gets measured gets done. If you don't measure success, you can't tell success from failure. If you can't see success, you can't reward it. If you can't reward success, you are probably rewarding failure. If you can't see success, you can't learn from it. If you can't recognise failure, you can't correct it. If you can demonstrate results, you can win public support.

'M-AND-E'

It could be argued that monitoring and evaluation activity in sport development has for a considerable time been collapsed into one term – m-and-e – with practitioners seemingly struggling to identify what is supposed to be done in the name of monitoring and evaluation. M-and-e is often referred to as a process in the singular, not as two complementary, though distinct processes. In addition, it is well documented (e.g. Bloyce and Smith 2010) that sport development practice has *not* been based on evidence generated through rigorous evaluation but has been, it can be argued, based on a need for sport development professionals to 'do the right thing' (to serve their own interests) rather than to do it right. This view would appear to be supported by earlier comments from Collins *et al.* (1999) and the limitations of this insular way of working can be better understood through consideration of the concept of critical consciousness.

DEVELOPING A CRITICAL CONSCIOUSNESS

The concept of critical consciousness was first developed by Freire (1996) in his work 'Pedagogy of the Oppressed'. Freire worked with people in the third world, teaching them to read and noted how oppressed these people were in a number of ways: for example, in his view, teachers do not communicate but provide information which students digest; knowledge is a gift bestowed by those who consider themselves knowledgeable to those they consider are not. For the benefit of this chapter, critical consciousness has been interpreted to relate to how SDPs are able to perceive inequalities and take action against them, working in partnership with the local community. The partnership working aspect of this is considered in more detail in the next chapter.

To expand, it is the view of the author that SDPs may implement interventions with which they feel comfortable (with regard to their personal sphere of experience in sport and their core values) which ultimately leads to initiatives based on low levels of critical consciousness. This would be consistent with the concept of thoughtless action as opposed to thoughtful action proposed by Ledwith (2005); this is discussed in more detail in Chapter 7. It can be argued that SDPs, are in the main, extroverts, leaders and certainly tend to have a passion for sport (Nesti 2001). It is therefore unsurprising that SDPs often struggle to engage individuals who have had negative experiences in sport or who are inherently disempowered in sports settings; this 'lack of passion' would not be something with which some SDPs were familiar. This almost evangelical position, believing wholeheartedly in sport and all it claims to achieve, raises a number of questions: How does this passion translate to understanding and empathising with communities or individuals who have no interest in sport and from this, generating 'thoughtful action' (Ledwith 2005)? And furthermore, how does this relate to SDPs being able to objectively evaluate the effectiveness of these initiatives? Do SDPs have the requisite levels of knowledge/skill to undertake evaluation or is the process of evaluation the issue? More worryingly for the future of sport development, does the way sport is managed, structured and delivered mean that evaluation is not the priority it should be? This chapter will continue with a definition of the processes of monitoring and evaluation and will then debate how effectively these processes are utilised in sport development.

MONITORING

Monitoring is the straightforward process of checking progress against specific, measurable objectives. It is impossible to monitor progress if the basis of the strategy (i.e. purpose and subsequent aims and objectives) is not in place. What is being monitored and why may well be the basis of useful discussion prior to any monitoring being undertaken, however this cannot happen if there are no clearly articulated aims/objectives in the first place! Performance indicators are often used as a method to understand the extent to which objectives, and therefore aims, have been achieved. This is much more likely to be a process that SDPs choose to use (or are required to undertake by funders such as Sport England) as it can more easily be put into practice. Taking registers of attendance at the beginning of sessions is the norm as well as the collection of relevant details – address, postcode, emergency number etc. – but can this information be used in any meaningful way to understand the effectiveness of the intervention? Could SDPs utilise data to understand where the 'market' for their intervention may be? A register can monitor attendance as an output but as a document for understanding participants it is limited. The SDP does not know why participants choose to attend, simply that they do. Further investigation is required if SDPs are interested in anything more than numbers; this is highlighted in more detail within the performance management case study in Chapter 11.

There are benefits to looking at monitoring data, some of which have already been alluded to. Looking at addresses, the SDP is able to ascertain the postcode from which participants have travelled and subsequently, by deduction, can isolate neighbourhoods with zero attendees. Performance indicators are intended to indicate the level of performance (in theory, against identified aims and objectives) at that point in time when data are collected and allows the SDP to monitor whether performance is on track, below expected levels or higher than anticipated. This has tended to be where the process of 'evaluation' stops or stalls for the majority of sport development interventions, since if the target numbers (e.g. of attendees) are not met funding can be withdrawn, thereby halting any potential to understand what happened. Potentially, a lack of attendees could signal an inappropriate target to start with and not necessarily a lack of interest on the part of the relevant community.

Historically, the focus of monitoring in a sport development sense has been about increasing participation by engaging specific 'target' groups (particularly when funding has been secured via regeneration sources), and until relatively recently with the introduction of the Active People Survey and the Taking Part Survey, SDPs have been forced to focus only on their contribution to a range of vague, poorly articulated 'bigger pictures'. This situation has been less than satisfactory in terms of building a comprehensive evidence base for sport development, not least because the actual practice of monitoring is so varied, disparate and poorly executed.

EVALUATION

The process of evaluation is directly linked to understanding the data collected through the monitoring process and using this knowledge to understand any change (e.g. in behaviour) that has occurred. Evaluation is complex in that the process (of developing the intervention) and the output/outcome should be evaluated, i.e. what did we do (and was that useful in and of itself) and what changes (e.g. in behaviour) were observed in the short term (output) and long term (outcome)? The former is more easily evaluated than the latter as this may take months or even years of gathering longitudinal data. This is where the importance of clear aims and objectives becomes obvious, as does an understanding of basic data collection techniques.

Over recent years there has been pressure on SDPs to evidence increases in participation, lessened slightly by the advent of the Active People Survey which is designed to provide this evidence in a relatively easy-to-access way. Disappointingly, the reasons for this increase (or otherwise) do not seem as important to policymakers and therefore emerging SDPs have not been able to benefit in real terms from good practice that must exist. Consequently, this has meant that SDPs have not been required to collect data that informs them about why individuals choose to participate (or not) and this has resulted in poorly informed strategies and interventions. It is argued that there has been an over-emphasis on quantity and getting people through the door and less of an emphasis on quality and ensuring individuals actually continue to participate in the long term. This is exemplified in the case study presented in Chapter 11 on the Cheshire and Warrington County Sport Partnership.

That said, it is not easy or straightforward to measure outcomes. In an international example, Coalter (2002; 2004; 2005) has used projects concerning HIV/Aids to understand how sport can contribute to this significant agenda through the notion of sport-in-development. These projects focus on ensuring processes rather than outcomes are measured, and by doing so a hypothetical chain to the intended outcome is created. The link between these processes and the initial development of aims is crucial. This book's chapters on internal and external analysis raise the importance of the articulation of clear, relevant aims that ultimately provide the framework against which strategy can be monitored and evaluated. In addition, it is difficult to ascertain the level of consultation undertaken for the majority of publicly funded sports-related strategies in the UK as this does not feature consistently within the published documents. This might give an indication as to the level of critical consciousness observed by these organisations in relation to the communities they strive to serve and therefore the validity of the stated aims of the strategy.

Aims can be defined as aspirational statements relating to where the organisation would like to 'get to', i.e. aims should clearly express what the organisation hopes to achieve in the longer term. These may be broad and should be organisation-wide (in strategic terms). Aims should relate to the overall purpose of the organisation and link directly to stated outcomes of the work of the organisation. In other words, aims should relate upwards (in a linear strategy) to the organisation's mission, purpose and vision and downwards to relevant objectives, outputs and outcomes (i.e. statements of intended action that will enable the organisation to fulfil its aims and thus the mission, purpose and ultimately vision). With this in mind, the arrows in Figure 6.1 could point up or down.

This logical, linear link should be self-evident in the deliberate way the strategy has been written and produced, although this does require time

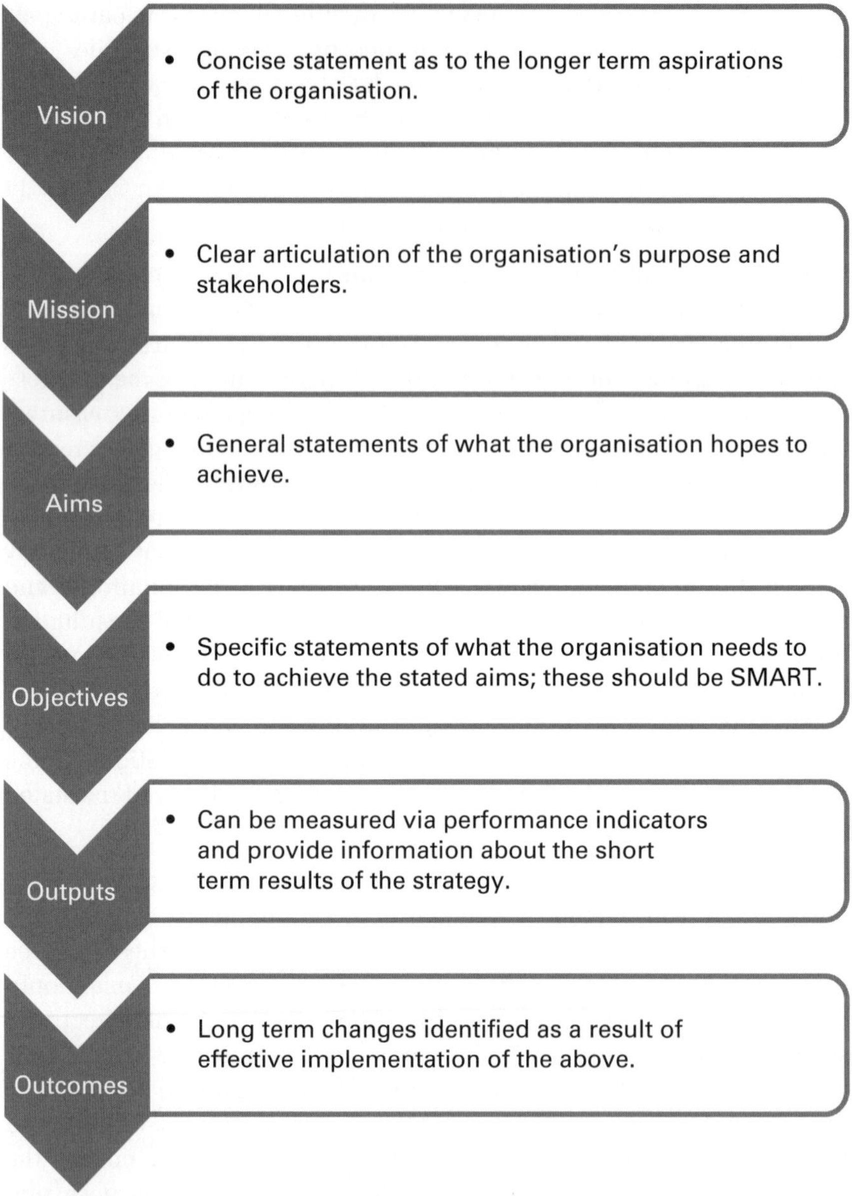

Vision • Concise statement as to the longer term aspirations of the organisation.

Mission • Clear articulation of the organisation's purpose and stakeholders.

Aims • General statements of what the organisation hopes to achieve.

Objectives • Specific statements of what the organisation needs to do to achieve the stated aims; these should be SMART.

Outputs • Can be measured via performance indicators and provide information about the short term results of the strategy.

Outcomes • Long term changes identified as a result of effective implementation of the above.

Figure 6.1 The linear relationship between different elements of deliberate strategy: towards consistent definitions

130

and energy to be spent on fulsome analysis and careful planning, as outlined in previous chapters. That said, this does not mean to imply that strategy development is cumbersome and long-winded; it is about SDPS being flexible, knowledgeable and consistent in their approach to strategy, even thinking strategically when planning on a day-to-day basis.

Understanding the purpose of the organisation is crucial in identifying relevant aims and objectives and without these there is no way of ascertaining success from failure. Having a solid foundation in the form of appropriate aims and objectives, developed by the community in which the strategy will be implemented is fundamental to the process of evaluation, as without this building block the strategy is effectively flawed. You cannot evaluate a project if you do not know what 'change' you are attempting to create. As Bloyce and Smith (2010) contend, objectives evident in the development of the 'sport for good' and 'development of sport' agendas have been based on a lack of consistency and clarity in policy. In their view, objectives have been overly ambitious, often uncritical and, in essence, they have been a statement of faith and therefore difficult to measure.

LANGUAGE BARRIERS

Coalter (2002) argues that monitoring and evaluation should be considered at the planning stage, i.e. when setting organisational aims and objectives. This connects to Dugdill, Graham and McNair's (2005) contention that each action (within an intervention) requires a collection of evidence. Problematically, the language used in strategic sport-related documents is not consistent; terms such as *aims* and *objectives* are used interchangeably, also including *targets*, *goals*, *outputs* and *outcomes* to name but a few. This lack of apparent consistency in nomenclature makes it difficult to analyse what sport organisations want to achieve; the language used almost appears to be what 'should be said' or 'what is expected' rather than useful, meaningful statements of what the organisation hopes to achieve and by when from a strategic perspective. The Introduction chapter identified the use of consultants in the development of strategy, so the language used within a strategy might not even be familiar to members of the organisation due to it being written by an external contractor. This is only one view amongst many but the point is well worth considering, particularly when ascertaining the strength (or otherwise) of the evidence base for sport development. It has already been noted that lack of ownership or 'attitudinal commitment' (Chapter 5) is a live issue in the implementation of strategy and this apathy, or possible detachment, tracks through into monitoring and evaluation activities.

Attempting an inclusive planning process is made more complex when working with others who possibly have very little or no experience of strategic thinking or planning, for example, when SDPs work with specific residents from a disadvantaged area. Working with communities in this way may well challenge SDPs' interpersonal skills, as well as their knowledge and understanding of developing strategy. This is where the concept of critical consciousness becomes extremely important, in order to ensure that the SDP does not become the 'oppressor', forcing residents to do 'what's best for them' just to make sure 'outputs' are achieved. As Turner (2009) discusses at length, in this type of situation language or jargon may be used to unintentionally baffle or overpower, not empower, with professionals bombarding the local residents with projects that 'would be good for them'. Sadan and Churchman (1997) also suggest planning with a community should be empowering and conducted in a way that is non-directive, resident-focused, de-centralised, open-ended, and reflective. This approach is fundamentally different to that taken in the past by many sport-related workers. The focus has been (and arguably remains) about increasing participation in the short term and with this in mind, SDPs have tended to approach interventions with a 'quick-win' attitude which dis-empowers the community, is not resident-focused and ultimately has not actually increased participation.

If you accept the logical, linear relationship between the elements of strategy (which enables us to understand how to evaluate the process more readily) then planning should be as important as the product or outcome of the strategy, with the two concepts of process and outcome not becoming polarised. This point is also relevant to those SDPs who have not been involved in the conception of a strategy they are tasked to implement; as a result SDPs often do not see how their role fits with the organisational strategy and the document itself remains unread and unused.

132

THEORY-DRIVEN EVALUATION

Coryn *et al.* (2011:1) describe evaluation theories as prescriptions that state "what evaluators do or should do when conducting evaluations". Theories of this type make comment on evaluation purposes, users and uses, who participates in the evaluation process and to what extent, general activities or strategies, method choices, and roles and responsibilities of the evaluator. Most academic evaluation theories have been derived from practice (Chelimsky 1998) and really only came to prominence after 1990 when Chen's seminal book titled *Theory-Driven Evaluations* was published.

Theory-driven evaluation has gathered momentum conceptually, methodologically and theoretically through works such as Chen and Rossi (1992), Rogers (2000, 2008), and Weiss (1995, 1997a, 1997b, 1998, 2004a, 2004b) yet there remains a lack of consistency in nomenclature, an issue already identified in the terminology of strategy. With this in mind, theory-driven evaluation is sometimes referred to as programme-theory evaluation, theory-based evaluation, theory guided evaluation, theory-of-action, theory-of-change, programme logic, logical frameworks, outcome hierarchies, realist or realistic evaluation and more recently, programme theory-driven evaluation science (Coryn *et al.* 2011). Despite an apparent lack of common vocabulary, the theory-driven general approach to evaluation has been utilised for and by organisations such as the W.K. Kellogg Foundation (2004a, 2004b) to evaluate a community change programme, but the utilisation of this type of approach in sport (development) has not been taken seriously.

Rogers (2000) constructively identifies theory-driven evaluation: conceptually this type of evaluation should explicate a programme theory or model and empirically this type of evaluation should seek to investigate how programmes cause intended or observed outcomes. The former is useful both from an academic and vocational perspective but the latter requires further thought and discussion as it is not common practice in sport development. Rogers (2000:5) goes on to define programme theory-driven evaluation as being based on "...an explicit theory or model of how the program causes the intended or observed outcomes and an evaluation that is partly guided by this model" and programme theory really forms the basis of this. Programme theories are typically represented diagrammatically or graphically, specifying relationships between actions, outcomes and other relevant factors and may be relatively simplistic linear models or much more complex contextual models. For example, a simple linear model would tend (amongst other things) to identify inputs, action and outputs (together forming a programme process theory) and then initial outcomes, intermediate outcomes and then long-term outcomes (representing programme outcome theory).

Coalter (2002) proposes a logic model that considers the programme planning process. This model illustrates the linear progression from consultation through to strategic outcomes, identifying what Coalter terms as outputs, sporting outcomes, intermediate outcomes and strategic outcomes. It is useful for practitioners at this stage to identify how this process may be evidenced, given previously mooted concerns (Dugdill, Graham, and McNair 2005). Utilising evidence gained at each stage of this process, as suggested by Dugdill, Graham, and McNair (2005) would enable SDPs to convince colleagues as to the consequences of the action undertaken at all stages. Over time, these data can be used to support claims in a more comprehensive way than would currently appear to be the case. Please see Table 6.1 on page 135.

A linear approach was taken by the London Borough of Newham in its evaluation of Newham's cultural and sporting programme (London Borough of Newham 2007). In July 2004, Newham Borough Council commissioned ECOTEC Research and Consulting to assist with the evaluation of their cultural and sporting offer. ECOTEC was charged with identifying impacts whilst acknowledging that a number of interventions and external factors would be impacting on data at any one time. Newham took the view that it is "more productive to explore how and why a programme is contributing to overall change in an area" (p.17) and utilised a "logic chain" (p.20) to illustrate how a programme will achieve its objectives. During 2004, Newham and ECOTEC developed the Newham-ECOTEC Assessment Technique (NEAT), a detailed evaluation model that enables the council to measure programme outcomes through the selection of nationally recognised indicators that are applied systematically and consistently across projects.

Early iterations of programme theory have tended to favour the linear approach such as that taken by Coalter (2002) and the London Borough of Newham (2007), though writers on theory-driven evaluation such as Chen (2005) and Rogers (2008) have advocated the use of more complex, non-linear models. A sport-related example of a more ecological

134

Table 6.1 The programming planning process and sources of evidence

Action	Potential evidence	Link to other chapters
Consultation with stakeholders	Completed questionnaires, video diaries, voting slips	Chapter 1 Introduction Chapter 7 Strategic Partnerships
Organisational/process outcomes	Development of new partnership (paper evidence could be the partnership terms of reference, minutes of meetings etc.)	Chapter 2 Internal Analysis Chapter 7 Strategic Partnerships
Programme aims and objectives	Clearly written, jointly agreed aims and objectives, a shared strategy document	Chapter 4 Strategic Choices Chapter 5 Implementation
Baseline data for indicators	Jointly agreed use of data from sources such as Active People Survey or Taking Part Survey	Chapters 2 and 3 Internal and External Analysis Chapter 7 Strategic Partnerships
Inputs	Jointly agreed, clearly stated recources including human, financial and physical	Chapter 4 Strategic Choices
Outputs: measurable indicators	Jointly agreed, clearly stated expected results	
Sporting outcomes: Targets Sporting inclusion	Actual increase in participation (repeated use of Active People Survey), completed questionnaires from the beginning and end of the intervention	
Intermediate outcomes: Targets Individual/group impacts Aspects of social inclusion	Questionnaires from specific points in time after interventions, indicating changes in attitude or behaviour from participants	
Strategic outcomes Social/community development	Changes evident over time with regards to the collation of all evidence identified above	

Source: Adapted from Coalter (2002); Dugdill, Graham, and McNair (2005).

approach is proposed by Brackenridge *et al.* (2011) whereby a logic model for the Football Association's (FA) Respect pilot is presented. This study considers both the process and outcomes of the FA's Respect project, acknowledging guidance from the Institute of Public Policy Research on key factors that influence the success of behaviour change programmes.

It is important to recognise the relationship between concepts identified within the programme planning model using economy, efficiency and effectiveness (Coalter 2002) as many methods of evaluation relating to the strategic management body of knowledge refer directly to the general idea of accountability. For example, Coulter (2008:221) identifies four methods of evaluation: corporate goals; efficiency, effectiveness and productivity measures; benchmarking; and portfolio analysis. Economy, effectiveness and efficiency are central to understanding accountability in relation to value for money. Economy is concerned with the lowest cost option, with the highest possible quality of service. Expectations of quality and cost need to be agreed with all concerned in the development of the strategy. Efficiency relates to the ratio of outputs to the inputs, and effectiveness relates outputs to outcomes (Coalter 2002).

Put simply, outputs relate to measurable aspects of the process of implementing the strategy. For example, in the sport development context this would include the number of training courses organised, the number of participants, and the number of opportunities provided; attendance registers or basic surveys following attendance would collect these data. Outputs tend to be short-term and although usually easy to measure, tend to only partly contribute to the overall aim(s) and therefore ultimately outcome(s) of the strategy.

Outcomes are defined by Coalter (2002) in two ways, as intermediate outcomes and social/community outcomes. Intermediate outcomes relate to the way in which participants are affected by participation in programmes within the strategy; specifically changes to their attitude or behaviour. This may include a non-participant becoming a participant, increased levels of health and fitness and increased self-esteem and self-confidence. These intermediate outcomes are crucial and build on outputs, thus (optimistically) feeding forward into social/community outcomes. This type of outcome can be measured by some form of 'before and after' data gathering exercise.

Where community-wide claims are made by the strategy, the organisation has to collect baseline data on the aspects in which an improvement is

136

expected. The key concern when evaluating these social/community outcomes (such as reduction in overall levels of crime, improved quality of life etc.) is that it is very difficult to prove cause and effect. In 'Shaping Places through Sport', Sport England (2008) describes how sport can enable the delivery of local priority outcomes namely:

- Developing strong, sustainable and cohesive communities;
- Improving health and reducing health inequalities;
- Improving life chances and focusing the energy of children and young people;
- Reducing anti-social behaviour and fear of crime;
- Increasing skills, employment and economic prosperity.

It is difficult to ascertain, though this rhetoric from Sport England is unequivocal, exactly *how* SDPs on the ground could (categorically) state that sport has contributed to the outcomes Sport England outline *without* undertaking local level monitoring and evaluation. As outlined previously in Table 6.1, this local level data information is made more accessible by the collection of data throughout the process of strategy implementation. However, making the cause and effect link between short-term output and longer-term outcome is difficult. SDPs have to begin to understand their role in the destiny of the wider industry. If colleagues continue not to understand the changes that have (potentially) occurred within the implementation of strategy then the future of community sport development in particular looks bleak.

TOWARDS AN UNDERSTANDING OF STRATEGY-AS-PRACTICE

It is important to understand strategy as both theory and practice; ensuring that tools for collecting and understanding data are readily available and easy to use, whilst at the same time being clear about what data are necessary to effectively identify aims, objectives, outputs and possibly even outcomes. Using the elements of strategic management as described by Johnson, Scholes and Whittington (2009:13—14), Table 6.2 attempts to enable practitioners and students alike to develop knowledge and skills in performance management and thus be in a more informed position when practising strategic thinking. The column on the left of the table identifies the different stages of the strategy process, but more importantly the box on the right of the table is concerned with action

Table 6.2 Understanding strategy-as-practice

Strategy-as-process	Strategy-as-practice
Strategic approach	Ensuring consultation with stakeholders uses the six dimensions of the planning process (Hughes and Traynor 2000) in order to empower the community to which the strategy applies:
	▪ non-directive intervention; ▪ resident-focused; ▪ de-centralised decision-making; ▪ open-ended task definition; ▪ community as subject; ▪ reflective practitioner.
	Record these processes in a straightforward way.
Strategic analysis	Where are we now? What are we doing and why? Where do we want to be? Doing it right first time – doing it thoroughly and sensitively.
	Using critical consciousness.
	Understand issue – participant/non-participant perspectives. Use of consulting techniques/community audit, for example Participatory Learning and Action (Pretty *et al.* 1995).
	Analysis (internal/external environment). Use of SWOT and STEEPLE.
	Use of all available data; for example Active People, Market Segmentation (Sport England 2012a), stakeholder mapping and cultural web.
	Resources – application for funding needed?
	Partnership working preferred/required?
	Monitoring processes – what data can be collected and for what purpose?
	Evaluation processes – consider linear or non-linear planning model and outcome model.

Table 6.2 Understanding strategy-as-practice (continued)

Strategy-as-process	Strategy-as-practice
Strategic choices	How might we get there? What direction should we travel in, taking all of our analysis into account?
Developing a programme process theory	Using critical consciousness.
	Choice of intervention – what options are there? Community involvement?
	How will we know we have achieved our aims?
	Programme process theory – what change (in behaviour/in attitude etc.) are we expecting/anticipating?
	Monitoring processes – what data can be collected and for what purpose?
	Evaluation processes – consider of linear or non-linear planning model and outcome model.
Strategic implementation	What do we need to do? Who will be responsible for creating action? How will we know when we're there? 'Just getting on with it' and 'doing it right'.
	Using critical consciousness.
	Develop overall aims that are clear and related to organisational purpose.
	Develop SMART objectives that enable the achievement of the overall aims.
	Further develop methods of monitoring.
	Further develop methods of evaluation.
	Implement objectives.
	Use of project management tools e.g. Gantt charts.

Table 6.2 Understanding strategy-as-practice (continued)

Strategy-as-process	Strategy-as-practice
Monitoring progress of implementation	Are we there yet? Are we there yet? Are we there yet?
	Using critical consciousness.
Developing a planning process theory	Monitor progress against objectives (and therefore overall aims) – may include use of performance indicators or targets.
	Measurement of outputs.
	Formative evaluation (i.e. evaluation during the intervention). Asking how is everything going? As expected or otherwise?
Evaluation	Is there a better way to get there? Could we go even further? What might we do differently next time?
Developing an outcome process theory	Using critical consciousness.
	Summative evaluation of objectives against overall aims.
	Assessment of initial outcomes.
	Understanding what went well and what did not, including the processes used to develop the strategy in the first place.
	Quantitative (i.e. numbers-based, e.g. %) and qualitative (i.e. text-based, e.g. attitudes and opinions) methods may be used to ascertain progress.
	Use of formative (i.e. during) and summative (i.e. at the end of the intervention) evaluation to enable change.
	Understand the issue better – participant/non-participant perspectives.
	Feedback understanding to next iteration of intervention if relevant/necessary.
	Assessment of intermediate outcomes.

and thought; i.e. what strategic practitioners need to begin to consider and then put into practice when developing strategy.

It is useful at this juncture to remind readers that although the strategy process can be viewed in a linear way the process should be viewed as flexible and dynamic. SDPs should open their minds to thinking about strategy in different ways, utilising the process and associated questions in Table 6.2 as a guide. This table is merely illustrative of the different elements of strategic thinking as this might relate to the practice of strategic sport development.

THE SYSTEM OR THE PROCESS?

Monitoring and evaluation is difficult. The two processes require resources; particularly time. The processes require SDPs to plan effectively with the relevant stakeholders and then consider, objectively, what has happened during the course of the intervention. Finally SDPs need to ascertain, utilising any monitoring data gathered, the extent to which aims and objectives have been achieved. This process needs to become second nature within the industry for the evidence-base of sport development to increase.

It could be assumed that the majority of SDPs, within a graduate industry, would have completed a dissertation or sustained research project and therefore could reasonably be expected to understand basic data collection and interpretation. Admittedly, the process undertaken as part of university study will be different to that required in the 'real world' but why does it appear that SDPs are not using this knowledge base and skill set to effect change in the workplace? It could be argued that, if levels of participation are to be increased, SDPs require further skills that enable the effective planning and setting of realistic objectives that can then be measured simply and at minimal cost.

The policy focus on increasing numbers of participants merely encourages SDPs to target 'easy hits'; working with segments/ communities that already participate to some degree. In order to achieve the outcomes identified by Sport England, SDPs need to understand why a large percentage of the population aged 16+ currently does not participate, subsequently setting realistic objectives that can be measured and evaluated in terms of making a contribution towards longer term outcomes. Are we, therefore, expressing concern regarding 'the system' as opposed to 'the process' of monitoring and evaluation? To effect real change, SDPs have to take responsibility for their part in that change which means understanding why their intervention has been successful or otherwise and on what basis. It is crucial that SDPs understand the need to gather data that evidence success, a process which can be used to maintain and develop priority work areas. That said, data gathering should not be onerous and should clearly link to the project's aims and objectives.

STRATEGIC COMMISSIONING OF SERVICES

Strategic commissioning of public services seems to be gaining momentum within government, with Local Government Improvement and Development (LGID) developing this as a policy theme. Users and communities should be placed at the centre of all decision-making about their community in order to produce more relevant outcomes via strategic needs assessment, options appraisal, monitoring and managing performance (Allen 2010). This focus on localism, central to which is evidence from sources such as the Active People Survey, Active Places Power, market segmentation and the Facilities Planning Model, should enable communities to set clear outcomes that are relevant to them, and thus should ensure more ownership of the process by the community. This rhetoric places great emphasis on the role of the SDP appropriately engaging 'the community' in an inclusive manner; much more difficult and time-consuming than it sounds. Communities are not homogenous masses but are made up of individuals with different opinions and motives, and any work in this regard should consider the principles identified by Hughes and Traynor (2000).

To support this move towards a 'Big Society', Sport England identifies a Strategic Planning Framework for Sport and the creation of five groups of approved suppliers in (i) strategic planning, (ii) needs assessment, (iii) playing pitch strategy, (iv) town planning and (v) sport specific (Sport England 2012b). A number of consultants have been pre-procured in order to try to save time and the cost of procurement. Sport England considers the organisation of the five panels in this period of austerity to be about best value for money (i.e. minimising costs of procurement) although it does seriously limit the choice local authorities (and therefore local communities) have in terms of developing and writing strategy. Consultants are often used by local authorities to write strategic documents, given the time constraints on local authority officers but the irony of this, in relation to 'Big Society', is that the use of consultants potentially takes decisions further away from the community, not bring them closer. SDPs have to work hard in this era of austerity to ensure that the community voice is heard, which ultimately should lead to more effective strategy implementation and thus more successful interventions. This success needs to be recorded in some way and to do this SDPs are encouraged to use processes such as those identified in Table 6.2.

SUMMARY

More SDPs at every level in the industry need to begin to think strategically about their work. This means moving beyond their love or passion for sport and working effectively with communities to empower individuals and create change. As Coalter (2007:7) states,

> ...there is a need to think more clearly, analytically and less emotionally about 'sport' and its potential. This might be difficult for sport evangelists, for those who have invested much in their professional repertoires, for those wanting cheap and simple answers (if not solutions), for generalist civil servants with limited understanding of 'sport' (but a desire to do something) and those operating in a still marginal policy area with demanding, if often ill-informed masters.

Hughes and Traynor (2000) suggest community practitioners frequently state that their work cannot be evaluated but there is a clear need for this type of intervention to be evaluated as rigorously as any other type of project. Tables 6.1 and 6.2 are designed to bring concepts of strategic management to life in order to support SDPs in the production of an evidence chain. In a time when organisations are under increasing pressure to evidence how well they are doing in order to survive, monitoring and evaluation needs to be built into all strategic processes to ensure successful interventions, high quality work and clear, evidenced change.

LEARNING ACTIVITIES

Developing skills

Review a recent intervention with which you have been associated: were you able to clearly identify the main aims and objectives?

Describe the techniques you used/could use to monitor the intervention effectively. How would you use this information to usefully evaluate the extent to which the intended aim of the project has been achieved?

Developing knowledge

In your view, explain why sport development professionals may benefit from a culture of evidence-based practice.

What would be the advantages and disadvantages of this type of approach to the sector as a whole?

What implications do you think this approach would have on how sport development professionals are developed e.g. sport development/sport-related degree material?

REFERENCES

Allen, N. (2010) 'Strategic planning for sport'. In *Sports Management*. 4, pp. 32–34.

Audit Commission (2000) *Aiming to Improve the Principles of Performance Measurement*. London, Audit Commission.

Bloyce, D. and Smith, A. (2010) *Sport Policy and Development: An Introduction*. London, Routledge.

Brackenridge, C., Pitchford, A. and Wilson, M. (2011) 'Respect: results of a pilot project designed to improve behaviour in English football'. In *Managing Leisure*. 16 (3), pp. 175–191.

Chelimsky, E. (1998). 'The role of experience in formulating theories of evaluation practice'. *American Journal of Evaluation*. 19(1), pp. 35–55.

Chen, H. (1990) *Theory-driven Evaluations*. London, SAGE.

Chen, H. (2005) *Practical Program Evaluation: Assessing and Improving Planning, Implementation and Effectiveness*. London, SAGE.

Chen, H. and Rossi, P. (1992) *Using Theory to Improve Program and Policy Evaluations*. Westport, Greenwood Press.

Kirstie Simpson

Coalter, F. (2001) 'Realising the Potential of Cultural Services: the case for sport'. London, Local Government Association.

Coalter, F. (2002) 'Sport and Community Development: A Manual Research Report'. No 86. Edinburgh, sportscotland.

Coalter, F. (2004) 'Future sports or future challenges to sport?' In Sport England Driving up participation: the Challenge for Sport. London: Sport England.

Coalter, F. (2005) 'The Social Benefits of Sport: an overview to inform the community planning process'. Edinburgh, sportscotland.

Coalter, F. (2006) 'Sport-in-development: a monitoring and evaluation manual'. London, UK Sport.

Coalter, F. (2007) *A Wider Social Role for Sport: Who's Keeping the Score?* London, Routledge.

Coalter, F., Allison, M. and Taylor, J. (2000) 'The Role of Sport in Regenerating Deprived Urban Areas'. Edinburgh, Scottish Office Central Research Unit.

Collins, M., Henry, I., Houlihan, B. and Buller, J. (1999) 'Sport and Social Inclusion: a report to the Department Of Culture, Media and Sport, Institute of Sport and Leisure Policy'. Loughborough, Loughborough University.

Coryn, C., Noakes, L., Westine, C. and Schroter, D. (2011) 'A Systematic Review of Theory-driven Evaluation Practice from 1990 to 2009'. *American Journal of Evaluation.* 32(2), pp. 199–226.

Coulter, M. (2008) *Strategic Management in Action.* NJ, Pearson Education.

Department of Health (2003) 'Health Survey for England'. London, Department of Health publications.

Department of Health (2004) 'Choosing Health? Choosing Activity: a consultation on how to increase physical activity'. London, Department of Health publications.

Department of Health (2005) 'Choosing Activity: a physical activity action plan'. London, Department of Health publications.

Dugdill, L., Graham, R. and McNair, F. (2005) 'Exercise Referral: the public health panacea for physical activity promotion? A critical perspective of exercise referral schemes; their development and evaluation'. In *Ergonomics.* 48(11–14), pp. 1390–1410.

Foster, C., Hillsdon, M., Cavillo, N., Allender, S. and Cowburn, G. (2005) 'Understanding Participation in Sport: a systematic review'. London, Sport England. In Coalter, F. (2007) *A Wider Social Role for Sport: Who's Keeping the Score?* London, Routledge.

Freire, P. (1996) *Pedagogy of the Oppressed.* 2nd ed. London, Penguin Books Ltd.

Gilchrist, A. (2003) 'Linking Partnerships and Networks'. In Banks, S., Butcher, H., Henderson, P. and Robertson, J. eds. (2003) *Managing Community Practice: Principles, Policies and Programmes.* Bristol, The Policy Press, pp. 33–54.

Hughes, M. and Traynor, T. (2000) 'Reconciling Process and Outcome in Evaluating Community Initiatives'. In *Evaluation.* 6(1), pp. 37–49.

Johnson, G., Scholes, K. and Whittington R. (2009) *Fundamentals of Strategy.* London, Pearson Education.

Ledwith, M. (2005) *Community Development: A Critical Approach*. Bristol, The Polity Press.

London Borough of Newham (2007) 'Shaping Sustainable Communities Through Culture and Sport: an evaluation of the London Borough of Newham's cultural and sporting programmes 2006–2007'. Newham Borough Council.

Lynn, B. (2011) 'Conflicting Data on Sports Participation'. *The Guardian*. Available at http://www.guardian.co.uk/sport/2011/apr/06/conflicting-data-sport-participation-olympics. (Accessed Wednesday 6th April 2011).

Miller, R. and Campbell, R. (2006) 'Taking stock of empowerment evaluation: an empirical review'. *American Journal of Evaluation*. 27, pp. 296–319.

Nesti, M. (2001) 'Working in Sports Development'. In Hylton, K., Bramham, P., Jackson, D. and Nesti, M. eds. *Sports Development: Policy, Process and Practice*. London, Routledge, pp. 195–213.

Pretty, J., Guijt.I., Thompson, J. and Scoones, I. (1995) 'Participatory Learning and Action: A Trainer's Guide'. IIED, London.

Robins, D. (1990) 'Sport as Prevention: the Role of Sport in Crime Prevention Programmes Aimed at Young People'. University of Oxford, Centre for Criminological Research occasional paper no. 12, Oxford.

Rogers, P. (2000) 'Program Theory Evaluation: not whether programs work but how they work'. In Shufflebeam, D., Madaus, F. and Kellaghan, T. eds. *Evaluation Models: Viewpoints on Educational and Human Services Evaluation*. Boston, MA: Kluwer, pp. 209–232.

Rogers, P. (2008) 'Using Programme Theory to Evaluate Complicated and Complex Aspects of Interventions'. In *Evaluation*. 14, pp. 29–48.

Sadan, E. and Churchman, A. (1997) 'Process Focused and Product Focused Community Planning: Two variations of empowering professional practice'. *Community Development Journal*. 32(1), pp. 3–16.

Sport England (2008) 'Shaping Places Through Sport'. Available at http://www.sportengland.org/support_advice/local_government/shaping_places.aspx.

Sport England (2011a) 'Active People Survey 5'. Available at http://www.sportengland.org/research/active_people_survey/active_people_survey_5/aps5_quarter_two.aspx.

Sport England (2011b) 'The Value of Sport Monitor'. Available at http://www.sportengland.org/research/value_of_sport_monitor.aspx.

Sport England (2012a) 'Market segmentation'. Available at http://www.sportengland.org/research/market_segmentation.aspx.

Sport England (2012b) 'Strategic Planning Framework for Sport'. Available at http://www.sportengland.org/facilities_planning/planning_tools_and_guidance/strategic_planning_framework.aspx.

Turner, A. (2009) 'Bottom-up Community Development: Reality or rhetoric? the example of the Kingsmead Kabin in East London'. *Community Development Journal*. 44(2) April, pp. 230–247.

Weiss, C. (1995) 'Nothing as Practical as Good Theory: exploring theory-based evaluation for comprehensive community initiatives for children and families'. In J. Connell, J., Kubisch, A., Schorr, L. and Weiss, C. eds. *New approaches to Evaluating Community Initatives: Volume 1, Concepts, Methods, and Contexts*. New York: Aspen Institute, pp. 65–92.

146

Weiss, C. (1997a) How can theory-based evaluations make better headway? In *Evaluation Review*. 21, pp. 501–524.

Weiss, C. (1997b) 'Theory-based Evaluation: Past, Present and Future'. In Rog, D. and Fournier, D. eds. *Progress and Future Directions in Evaluation: Perspectives on Theory, Practice and Methods: New Directions for Evaluation.* 76, Winter. San Francisco, Jossey-Bass, pp. 34–41.

Weiss, C. (1998) *Evaluation: Methods for Studying Programs and Policies.* 2nd ed. Upper Saddle River, NJ, Prentice Hall.

Weiss, C. (2004a) 'On Theory-based Evaluation: winning friends and influencing people'. In *The Evaluation Exchange.* IX, pp. 1–5.

Weiss, C. (2004b) 'Rooting for Evaluation: a cliff notes version of my work'. In Alkin, M. ed. *Evaluation Roots: Tracing Theorists Views and Influences.* Thousand Oaks, CA: SAGE, pp. 153–168.

W. K. Kellogg Foundation (2004a) *Evaluation Handbook.* W.K. Kellogg Foundation.

W. K. Kellogg Foundation (2004b) *Using Logic Models to Bring Together Planning, Evaluation and Action: Logic Model Development Guide.* W.K. Kellogg Foundation.

CHAPTER 7

STRATEGIC PARTNERSHIPS

KIRSTIE SIMPSON AND JANINE PARTINGTON

INTRODUCTION

Although this is a chapter about partnerships, no one definition or model of this well-used term is supported over another. As Ballach and Taylor (2001:6) propose, this concept is "variously identified as interagency, inter-professional, collaborative or joined-up working, joined-up thinking or a whole systems or holistic approach". In the interest of clarity, this chapter will analyse strategic partnerships and alliances where two or more organisations collaborate: sharing resources and activities to pursue a strategy (Johnson, Scholes and Whittington, 2008:353). Organisations involved in sport development may also form strategic alliances internally, for example, cross-departmental working within a local authority, and informally, for example, communities of practice (Wenger and Snyder 2000). Ultimately, however, the view taken in this chapter is that partnerships are about people, regardless of how many individuals are involved and whom they represent. This is justified by Gilchrist (2003:35) who comments that policy needs partnerships and partnerships require people. Inevitably, relationships between those SDPs responsible for managing partnerships is crucial, and therefore the *people* aspect of the 4Ps model is particularly relevant to this chapter as we consider the importance and variety of stakeholders in the sport development *process*. We argue that the *practice* of partnership can be as important as the *product* that emanates from said partnership. The nature of partnership in sport development is complex and multi-faceted and can be linked to Checkland's (1999) notion of layered thinking, identified within the Introduction. Due to a paucity of

148

existing material, this chapter applies academic frameworks from the strategic management body of knowledge to relevant sport development examples. Amongst other theoretical frameworks, the Power/Interest matrix (Scholes 2001) will be used to help understand the complex relationships evident in sport development, and the PiiSA framework proposed by I&DeA (2009) will be considered in relation to a case study example. But first it is necessary to consider why and how partnership working has become so embedded in sport development practice.

WHY WORK IN PARTNERSHIP?

Numerous authors have written about the benefits of partnership working in relation to sport development (e.g. Frisby, Thibault and Kikulis 2004; Shaw and Allen 2006; Robson 2008; Parent and Harvey 2009). These benefits are neatly summarised by I&DeA (2009) as: a more connected and better connected service delivery; more effective service delivery to local communities; opportunity to participate in wider discussions about improving quality of life; enhanced profile and credibility; increased and effective use of resources; access to wider expertise; potential for learning and sharing knowledge and a greater opportunity to inform and influence decision-making. Partnership working has become increasingly common in sport development over the last twenty years as a result of social, economic and political pressures, along with increased competition for resources both internally and externally (Frisby, Thibault and Kikulis 2004). Partnerships within sport development have become a potential solution to a lack of resources, and a way of fulfilling organisational goals. They are also frequently underpinned by positive expectations, as Kanter (2003:227) states:

> Partnerships are initially romantic...their formation rests on hopes and dreams – what might be possible if certain opportunities are pursued.

With such emotional and financial investment, it is therefore crucial to understand how organisations can work together effectively through people in order to successfully achieve the intended outputs and outcomes identified in strategy documents. There may be a clear tension between the document's producers and the document's implementers, which can impact upon the type of partnerships formed and their subsequent success. Aspects of this tension have been discussed in previous chapters on implementation and performance measurement.

In addition to the benefits of partnership working, Frisby, Thibault and Kikulis (2004) highlight several negative consequences of poorly managed partnerships such as staff dissatisfaction, an inability to deliver quality services to the public, a loss of credibility and future difficulties in retaining and attracting partners. Partnerships also cost money to develop and maintain, therefore unsuccessful partnerships do not offer value for money, thus alliances should not be entered into without due diligence. In the same way that there has been widespread recognition of 'initiative overload' in sport development, it can be argued that SDPs have also been affected by 'partnership fatigue' (Houlihan and White, 2002), partnership working becoming the main focus of their role, thereby over-extending capacity and resource. It is crucial that SDPs are provided with the skills, knowledge and power to create effective and appropriate partnerships and are empowered to walk away from ineffective ones.

THE BUSINESS OF PARTNERSHIP

Coulter (2008) describes how organisations can establish strategic relationships with suppliers or distributors (vertical integration); with a competitor (horizontal integration); or with an organisation in a related industry (related diversification). Colleagues in sport development regularly establish these types of relationships. For example, SDPs often work with suppliers (such as adidas, one of the official sponsors for the London 2012 Olympic Games, who not only provided the kit for 2012 Olympic Games but also the kit for the Sports Makers volunteer initiative, a 2012 Legacy programme); with competitors via activities such as the StreetGames network where national governing bodies (NGBs) work together at regional festivals; and organisations in related industries such as the collaborations that exist between many local authority sport development teams and local health care professionals.

All three of these types of relationship could be deemed to be strategic partnerships, albeit with each one having a different structure and purpose. Furthermore, Coulter (2008) goes on to describe three types of strategic partnerships, these being joint ventures, long-term contracts and strategic alliances. In sport development all three of these types of partnership exist

150

though would not, possibly for political reasons, be described in this formal, private sector 'speak'. **Joint ventures** are formalised alliances where two or more individual organisations remain separate but set up a new organisation which is jointly owned or governed. An example that exists in sport development is County Sport Partnerships (CSPs). Over the past ten years, each county in England has developed these independent charitable organisations following funding and political support from Sport England and the co-operation and agreement of associated local authorities. Typically, CSPs are managed by boards, which have representation from each 'member' local authority and provide governance for the CSP.

Long-term contracts lock a supplier into a long-term relationship that hopefully benefits both organisations, for example, Rochdale Metropolitan Borough Council and their cultural trust Link4Life. A 15-year agreement exists between these two organisations in order for Link4Life to provide services in four main areas: arts and heritage; entertainment; fitness and health; and sport and leisure. An annual 'contract charge' is paid by Rochdale Metropolitan Borough Council to the trust for delivery of these services against an agreed standard of performance (Link4Life 2011).

Coulter (2008:212) considers **strategic alliances** as separate to joint ventures in that a new organisation is not formed: "instead the partnering organisations simply share whatever they need, in order to do whatever they want to do". For example, formal networks such as local or regional development forums attended by representatives of local authorities and NGBs as required. Community Badminton Networks are a prime example of this. They operate in local areas and involve the strategic co-ordination and development of badminton opportunities between partners such as the NGB, local authority, clubs, facility providers and any other interested parties (Badminton England n.d.). In addition, Johnson, Scholes and Whittington (2008:360) describe strategic alliances as a method by which strategies can be pursued; this can include formal, inter-organisational relationships (such as Coulter's joint ventures) but may also be very informal with "loose arrangements of co-operation." The complexity of partnership working is demonstrated here as sport development officer posts (often an example of a joint venture) can be developed through informal networks such as those that exist between local authorities and NGBs. This may involve pooling of resources or joint funding applications, but crucially the arrangement has occurred as a result of informal networking rather than through a formally structured, politically endorsed network.

A fourth type of partnership can be identified as **communities of practice**. Wenger and Snyder (2000:139) describe these as "groups of people who are informally bound together by shared expertise and passion." Typically, these congregations are self-organised and form their own leadership as opposed to being formed to fulfil a specific goal and operating within formal working procedures or hierarchies. They are flexible and formed to suit the specific purpose for which they were developed, rather than being structured around existing organisational alliances or synergies. Communities of practice can range from something as simple as a group of SDPs meeting regularly to discuss work activities, to more complex networks of organisations, for example, sports clubs from within the same geographic area meeting regularly to discuss club development. Communities of practice can lead to the development of more formalised partnership arrangements as described above, but fundamentally the emphasis is on individuals and organisations learning together and making their work more effective. As Wenger and Snyder (2000:143) argue,

> ...the strength of communities of practice is self-perpetuating. As they generate knowledge, they reinforce and renew themselves. They give you both the golden eggs and the goose that laid them.

Clearly, the range of partnerships in existence within sport development is broad. What is unclear however, is the degree to which partnerships are viewed by SDPs as either an effective mechanism for working or an inconvenience. Are, for example, SDPs drawn towards partnership working because of its benefits, because of political pressure, or through the motivation to be part of a team and share responsibility for the achievement of targets?

A POLITICAL TOOL OR AN INNATE SENSE OF TEAM?

Houlihan and Lindsey (2008:225) indicate that the emergence of

> ...more formal partnership working can be seen, to an extent at least, as a development of existing delivery practices which were given substantial additional momentum from the Labour government elected in 1997.

152

However, it could be argued that sport-related partnerships became politically important after the publication of Game Plan (DCMS/Strategy Unit 2002), written and developed by two government departments, the Strategy Unit and the Department for Culture, Media and Sport (DCMS), fulfilling New Labour's 'joined-up thinking' philosophy. As former Prime Minister Tony Blair suggests in the Foreword of the document (DCMS/Cabinet Office 2002:5):

> It [Game Plan] highlights the central importance of Government working closely in partnership with those that provide sport – national governing bodies, clubs, schools, local authorities, the voluntary and the private sectors – to help deliver key outcomes. We cannot drive that step change in participation alone.

Not only was this a political endorsement, but it set out a clear framework for delivery of national sports objectives, namely partnership working. As Friend (2006:261) suggests, there is an expectation that different government departments (and by extension those QUANGOs funded via exchequer resources) should collaborate rather than compete wherever their agendas converge or overlap, in order to act in the best interests of the public.

Over the course of the last two decades, it can be said that partnership working has become a tool that has been promoted through policy and duly used by sport development professionals to address participation nationally, regionally and locally. This way of working is so deeply ingrained that SDPs who do not engage in partnership working are often viewed as unorthodox or a 'loose cannon'. The public funding of the majority of initiatives was, and is, based on the premise of working with others so the focus on developing 'teams' of professionals within partnership frameworks has been to a degree inescapable. Crucially, the trend towards partnership working is not unique to sport development and has become a central tenet of local government activity too. Whilst joint working between departments is nothing new, the development of Local Strategic Partnerships (LSPs) under New Labour was a significant shift towards joint working at a strategic level locally, and further embedded partnership working as *the* way to do things. It is also possible to argue that broader local government structures such as LSPs were major influences on the subsequent Community Sports Networks (CSNs), a Sport England-led initiative to create structures, or what Lindsey (2006) describes as inter-organisational networks, that would advocate for, and on behalf of sport and physical activity at a local level. CSNs would also seek to encourage more collaborative working between agencies and departments through jointly delivered projects and initiatives. Not only did CSNs take on board the bureaucracy of LSPs and their structure (typically being organised around similar themes), more significantly perhaps they embraced all agencies operating at a local level that had an interest in sport and physical activity. For the first time this took the emphasis away from local authorities as the only local driver of sport development and CSNs sought to seek alliances with other major organisations such as Primary Care Trusts who often had compatible goals. The challenge for many CSNs was not only to ensure adequate representation from community organisations in order that community needs became as integrated into their strategic plans as those of the larger organisations, but also that the CSN itself was integrated in the strategic planning of LSPs, and was not left isolated with little influence or opportunity to bid for resources.

One of the issues manifested in CSNs was varied commitment levels between partners. Friend (2006:265) discusses the differences between 'symmetrical partnerships' (where all organisations are of a similar size and ilk, for example, a number of schools working together to deliver and co-ordinate the National School Games Programme at a local level) and 'asymmetrical partnerships' (where a diverse range of organisations of different size, structure and resource work together, such as a CSN). This difference highlights the difficulties experienced in the latter where differing organisations are expected to subscribe to a set of shared objectives, yet often have to manage "competing motivations from other sources, limiting the extent to which these declared partnership goals can be realistically pursued." Lindsey's (2006) research on local partnerships, focusing upon the New Opportunities for PE and Sport programme, argued that political pressure to form partnerships often resulted in short timescales for their establishment. This pressured those overseeing the development of the partnership to select convenient and reliable partners, rather than those who might offer greater reward but with whom a relationship did not exist. Whilst this arrangement might result in agreement, it will not result in effective implementation.

The driver for the establishment of CSNs was not necessarily the opportunity to bring key stakeholders together to rationalise and co-ordinate provision of sport and physical activity or to reduce risk, but to draw down resources in the form of funding from Sport England. This is yet another example of policy – rather than need – driving the formation

154

of partnerships. Whilst Frisby, Thibault and Kikulis (2004) argue that partnerships offer a reduced risk when resources are pooled, the relationships between members of the CSN (and similarly within other partnership types) could become soured when those resources are redistributed, creating potential competition amongst partners for a share of those resources. Ironically, political support for CSNs has subsequently waned, and they are no longer endorsed by Sport England. It is unclear how many CSNs are still active. Some local partnerships considered the often complex structures a useful way of strategically planning provision, but many CSNs have slid into oblivion and are now no more than a distant memory. This 'disposability' of partnerships once they are deemed to have served their purpose often comes at a cost, leaving community partners disillusioned and frustrated. Despite this, the political pressure for partnership working was continued under the Coalition government, although the financial climate created by public sector budget cuts has resulted in partnerships becoming resource-driven rather than outcome-driven. As Asthana, Richardson and Halliwell (2002) argue, resources are a necessary ingredient of partnership working but the provision of financial resources is an insufficient condition for establishing partnerships.

This focus on securing resources has served to further disempower SDPs from utilising partnerships to create and implement strategy, instead creating an environment where partnerships are crucial for survival. Clearly, policy is still driving partnerships, but not necessarily for the right reasons! There is also an increasing political pressure on ensuring community involvement in partnerships and service delivery. The 'Big Society' policy espoused by the Coalition government seeks to redistribute power from the state to local communities, encouraging the development of new partnerships between the state and those organisations funded by the state (such as NGBs) with communities (Conservative Party 2010). Whilst this offers the potential to consider and integrate local needs and issues into service delivery, it also creates potential for tokenistic gestures of co-operation and bottom-up working.

'COMMUNITY VOICES'

All of that said, the rhetoric of much policy since the 1960s claims the inclusion of community voices with local residents being involved in decision-making. The reality of this is that communities have often been marginalised or 'consulted' via third sector officers or other paid professionals (Hastings *et al.*, 1996; Taylor 1998; Anastacio *et al.* 2000 in Banks *et al.* 2003). Partington and Totten (2012) argue this tokenistic approach only serves to further disenfranchise local communities, as the information they provide is rarely considered when making strategic decisions, which subsequently become about the needs of the organisations (and the staff within them) rather than the needs of the community that the strategy or intervention is targeted at. Frisby and Millar (2002) caution against community partnerships where the pretence of devolved power becomes a way of 'off-loading' services to communities as a cost saving measure. This serves as a warning to the Coalition government and their focus on developing a 'Big Society' and verges very close to what Berner and Phillips (2005:20–1) describe as a "neo-liberal wolf dressed up as a populist sheep" boosting "the self esteem of the poor by letting them take care of themselves." This could be seen as a somewhat cynical use of partnerships to reduce the burden on the state.

Conversely, Vail (2007) describes a successful partnership in Canada that focused on developing grassroots tennis participation between Tennis Canada, local tennis clubs and local community champions that successfully utilised principles of community development to identify community needs and involve community members in decision-making, management and delivery of the intervention. Whilst not without its problems, the partnership resulted in significant increases in participation and much improved relationships between the clubs and their local community. Gilchrist (2003) describes this process of 'building bridges' across community boundaries as an important part of community practice. Informal networking is crucial to ensuring indigenous participants can articulate community needs within a partnership setting. These informal practices enable local people to develop confidence and status both within and outside of the community. However, as Skinner (1997) warns, in order for genuine community involvement to occur, communities may need help to become organised and establish democratic and inclusive structures to ensure that community representatives are actually accountable to their 'community' and possess the skills necessary to contribute fully to the partnership. This not only requires the SDP to recognise the importance of undertaking capacity building work and possess the requisite skills to do this, but it also requires the SDP to have the ability to establish appropriate and

Kirstie Simpson and Janine Partington

equal relationships with community representatives. An inappropriate approach coupled with the use of specialist language and jargon can build barriers between staff and community members, and can result in community members feeling excluded and disempowered (Turner 2009), a situation that is clearly not conducive to effective partnership working. As such, it is important at this stage to consider the skills necessary for partnership working within the sport development sector.

SKILLS FOR PARTNERSHIP WORKING

It could be argued that the political environment in which the sport development professional operates is considered secondary to the personal or cultural ideology that surrounds the industry. As Nesti (2008) indicates

> ...sports development is for lovers of sport. It is not a safe and sensible career option like accountancy or law. This is personal. Employers should not recruit or promote anyone looking for a career in sport, only those still in love with it.

Certainly, there is a presumption that SDPs inherently possess the necessary skills to effectively work in partnership. This is reflected in job descriptions available online and, for example, in the summary job description available via Graduate Prospects, a typical work activity for a Sport Development Officer is described as "developing a range of partnerships" (Graduate Prospects 2011). By taking the view that sport development practitioners have an innate sense of 'team', it would seem that taking a partnership approach would be second nature to those attempting to create real change within a community; however, personality aside, one way of managing change has been to utilise partnerships, real or otherwise, in order to secure scant resources in a (naturally) competitive field. An opposing view of this would be that SDPs are passionate about sport because they enjoy sport themselves and value the (competitive) nature of it, therefore the consideration of others before oneself would not be something that would be natural to this type of SDP. There is also a tendency, perhaps due to the 'team' element of working in partnership, to purposely develop partnerships with other agencies and staff with whom you have an established personal relationship or shared philosophy (in a similar vein to the development of communities of practice), whilst avoiding those with whom you have little personal connection, irrespective of the strategic value of that partnership.

Being objective in partnership working is clearly a desirable aspiration, but unrealistic as personal values inevitably impact upon, and possibly cloud judgement (Lindsey 2006). Indeed, criticisms of the ineffectiveness of past partnerships allied to the "fragmentation, fractiousness and perceived ineffectiveness of organisations within the sport policy area" (Houlihan and Green 2009:678) adds to the doubt about SDPs' 'natural' abilities to work collaboratively. It is argued throughout this book that core sport development skills orient around team work, leadership and communication. In order to be strategically effective, SDPs need to be able to talk to colleagues within and outside of their organisation in an appropriate way, i.e. an empathic understanding or appreciation of the colleague's environment is needed to ensure that the two individuals (let alone the two departments or organisations) are working together with the same purpose. The ability of SDPs to foster "win-win thinking", where alliances contribute to the strategic aims of each partner organisation, hinges on a SDP's ability to communicate, influence and negotiate sometimes complex alliances (I&DeA 2009:10).

There is a clear role here for the utilisation of National Occupational Standards (SkillsActive 2010), the most relevant in this case being A324, *Develop productive working relationships with colleagues.* This Standard concerns the development of working relationships with colleagues, both within the SDP's own organisation and with external colleagues, and the associated outcomes, behaviours and knowledge necessary to fulfil successful relationships. Higher education also has a key part to play; specifically the way that students engage with external organisations and the extent to which the degree or any work experience undertaken prepares them for communicating with individuals who may well have a very different set of core values. This leads us to consider the pedagogy of partnership working. Is this more about the art of leadership than partnership per se?

THE PEDAGOGY OF PARTNERSHIPS

When developing strategy it is crucial that a shared purpose is developed between partners as without this a shared vision and relevant aims and

Kirstie Simpson and Janine Partington

objectives cannot be devised. A lack of planning and strategic thought can lead to poor performance and misunderstanding between partners. Therefore, for the partnership to be effective, the shared agenda (of the two colleagues and therefore the two or more organisations) has to be more important than any individual agenda. This is different to thinking about the activities undertaken by the partnership, as the intrinsic value of good partnership working should be rated highly in and of itself. In practical terms, this means that the sharing of information and expertise, possibly leading to long-term communities of practice and co-operation, is often more valuable than short-term agreements to access funding or resources.

Robson (2008:136) identifies what he describes as "boundary spanning" which deals with the transfer of information between organisations. SDPs themselves are in fact boundary spanners and assume the role of key communicator and leader; this can only work well when this individual has the requisite skills in leadership, communication and negotiation. If an organisation is insular in its approach to strategy and no form of external analysis is undertaken, then it is likely that a 'silo' mentality will be reflected in their work. If this approach is taken, the SDP will work alone in the delivery of the proposed strategy, metaphorically placing themselves and their organisation in an 'implementation silo'. See Figure 7.1 below.

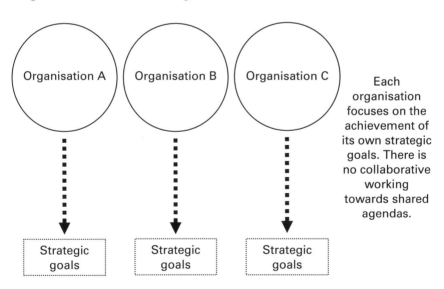

Figure 7.1 Silo mentality in practice

The ability to bring organisations together and promote partnership working is increasingly important in sport development as there is an implied requirement to create change through sport. This change can only occur if and when SDPs are able to cross organisational boundaries to create effective, strategic partnerships and act as boundary spanners, as shown in Figure 7.2 below. This approach lifts the SDP out of the metaphorical silo and enables their thinking and delivery to be collaborative.

Stage One: The SDP act as a boundary spanner; bringing multiple organisations together to identify common strategic goals

Stage Two: Collaborative working between organisations in pursuit of shared strategic goals

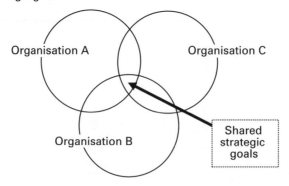

Figure 7.2 SDP as boundary spanner, working towards collaboration

160

Figure 7.3 demonstrates the principle of boundary spanning in relation to the development of badminton at a local level. In this example, the Regional Badminton Development Officer is acting as the boundary spanner to create a strategic alliance between Badminton England, a local authority (Bury Metropolitan Borough Council) and the local school sports partnerships. The outcome of this strategic alliance was the establishment of a new junior badminton club within Bury. This development contributed towards the achievement of strategic goals common to all three organisations, namely the creation of opportunities for increased participation, improvement and development of the local sporting infrastructure (specifically in relation to Badminton) and the development of school-club links. Without the input of the boundary spanner, acting as an initial bridge between the organisations, it is unlikely this outcome would have been achieved as each organisation would have been constrained by working within its self-imposed silo.

It is important to note that any organisation could follow any one method of strategy development, either taking a silo approach or working collaboratively, or a combination of these. The approach taken would firstly depend on organisational culture (see Chapters 2 and 5 for a more thorough analysis of this), and secondly, it would depend on the philosophy of the individual (the boundary spanner) charged with that area of work. The methods indicated in the figures above may not be mutually exclusive, i.e. SDPs may develop collaborative partnerships over a period of time, either having started from a silo mentality themselves or having worked with organisations with historically embedded silo mentalities.

Given that sport development has evolved into a graduate 'profession', a lot of SDPs are middle-class either by origin or by education (Pitchford and Collins 2010) and therefore will need to work very hard to ensure colleagues in local communities see them as equals and not as middle-class 'do-gooders'. Certainly, the skills required to work in collaboration with local communities using a community development approach requires SDPs to be embracing, empowering, involving and mobilising (Vangen and Huxham 2002 cited in Vail 2007:575). An 'I know better than you' attitude is certainly unlikely to generate trust between stakeholders or foster a mutually beneficial partnership. SDPs working in this way could be described as boundary builders rather than boundary spanners. Shaw and Allen (2006) stress that trust is vital to the success of partnerships, particularly in terms of having confidence

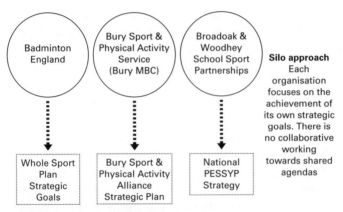

Silo approach
Each organisation focuses on the achievement of its own strategic goals. There is no collaborative working towards shared agendas

Stage One: The Regional Badminton Development Officer acting as a boundary spanner to identify common strategic goals between the NGB, local authority and SSP

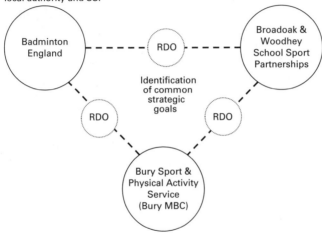

Stage Two: Collaborative working between organisations in pursuit of shared strategic goals resulted in the establishment of Bury Topflight Junior Badminton Club

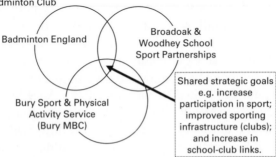

Figure 7.3   Boundary spanning in action

162

in a partner to undertake work or act on behalf of that partnership. A lack of trust often breeds a lack of action, rendering the partnership ineffective and no more than a talking shop.

TYPES OF STRATEGIC SPORT DEVELOPMENT PARTNERSHIPS

In order to act as a successful boundary spanner, SDPs require an understanding of the purpose and structure of partnerships so that they are able to support the development of effective alliances. This requires them to possess 'critical consciousness' which Shor (1993:32) describes as the "dynamic between critical thought and critical action." Placed along a continuum of critical consciousness, partnerships with a high level of this commodity may be expected to have a focus on outcomes (for example, a joint venture where partners are equally engaged with mutually agreed outcomes). Partnerships with a low level of critical consciousness, meanwhile, will be process oriented and may well, for example, be termed 'paper' partnerships (partnerships in name only, in which organisations have come together purely because they need to be seen to do so in order to complete a funding application or simply gain access to a community).

There has been an increase in academic theorising around partnerships in sport development, which has resulted in several attempts at the classification of different partnerships (such as Lindsey 2006 and Parent and Harvey 2009). A potential typology of strategic partnerships is provided for debate in Table 7.1.

The SDP may well be operating or involved with a number of different types of partnerships, as identified above, at any one time depending on the work they are undertaking. This exemplifies the complexity of the work of the SDP, the essential requirement being the ability to spin lots of plates at the same time!

MANAGING PARTNERSHIPS: A FRAMEWORK FOR DISCUSSION

The I&DeA (2009) specifies four factors for successful partnership working. These are P – purpose, ii – to influence and be influenced, S – structure and systems and A – action (PiiSA). This framework forms the basis of a balanced scorecard approach to evaluating the quality and

Table 7.1 Potential typology of strategic partnerships

	HIGH ← → LOW		
Critical consciousness			
Culture (based on Reid and Iqbal 1996)	Collaborative ←		→ Competitive
Focus	Outcome based on a jointly developed sense of purpose	Output with a specific sense of purpose for at least one 'partner'	Process focus with a superficial sense of purpose
Approach	'Bottom-up' and 'endogenous' (McQuaid 2000) with genuine dialogue between partners resulting in a sustainable partnership that leads to 'thoughtful action' (Ledwith 2005) being undertaken.	Some dialogue occurs between partners, but this is likely to be unequal and does not always result in successful collaboration or implementation	'Top-down' and 'exogenous' (McQuaid 2000). A paper trail is created as 'evidence' of the partnership, but collaborative working is tokenistic and often results in 'thoughtless action' (Ledwith 2005)
SDP leadership style (see Chapter 9 on Strategic Leadership)	Authentic-transformational leader	Transactional leader	Pseudo-transformational leader
Resulting partnership type	– Joint Venture – Community-led	– Presumed – Mutual appreciation – Delivery partnerships	– Paper – Enforced

likely effectiveness of partnerships. It also provides a useful tool for the management of partnerships which will enable SDPs to create and develop effective working relationships.

Creating partnerships

This concerns the P of the PiiSA framework and the extent to which the partnership has a clear sense of purpose. Effective partnerships will continuously work to clarify the nature of the relationship, ensuring a shared vision/purpose at all times. This is enhanced when colleagues are able to express specific constraints, what they and their organisation wish to achieve, as well as the level of commitment to shared objectives. In relation to Figure 7.1, it could be argued that partnerships with a highly developed sense of purpose are more likely to have a high level of critical consciousness, assuming that all partners are working collaboratively. Asthana, Richardson and Halliday (2002), writing about Health Action Zones, argue that partnerships are frequently established due to political pressure, rather than 'real need'. This can subsequently impact upon the commitment of partners towards that partnership, and can compromise the willingness of stakeholders to input resources to support the work of the partnership. Clearly, there must be a consideration of why the partnership is being formed and its purpose in order to avoid the establishment of 'thoughtless' partnerships. Parent and Harvey (2009) suggest a model of partnership working that encourages practitioners to consider three stages of partnerships: partnership antecedents, partnership management and partnership evaluation. Partnership antecedents are essential to partnership success and include, amongst other factors, the organisation's culture, motives for involvement, and the external environment.

Understanding and influencing partnerships

The ii of the PiiSA framework relates to how colleagues are influenced and can be influential. This has to be linked to the skills SDPs have in negotiation and basic communication, as well as the extent to which they are capable boundary spanners. It is important in effective partnerships that all parties are able to communicate in an environment of trust so that genuine dialogue can take place; as I&DeA (2009) states dialogue should be characterised by honesty and authenticity, with individuals seeking to understand each other's position and identifying courses of action that meet the needs of all those present. In practice, however, partnerships often become dominated by one or two partners who have control of resources, with strategic decisions about the use of those resources being undertaken outside of partnership meetings (Asthana, Richardson and Halliday 2002). Clearly, this does not make for an open and honest dialogue between all stakeholders, and would impact on levels of trust between partners. The use of informal networks to share information outside of the formal partnership once again results in the exclusion of stakeholders who sit outside of these networks. It also means that information used to make decisions is incomplete and potentially biased, resulting in poor decisions being made which ultimately impair the effectiveness of the partnership.

It is difficult to see how a partnership that is developed in a top-down fashion can be effective in this sense. Again, an individual's skills are at the heart of success. This relates neatly to the power/interest matrix (Mendelow 1991), a management tool that can be used by organisations to ascertain the relative power and interest of key stakeholders in a strategy or intervention.

Stakeholder mapping allows practitioners to understand the political interplay between stakeholders and be better prepared to manage the impact of changes in one stakeholder on the other stakeholders (Johnson, Scholes and Whittington 2009). The matrix should be used to first map out the current positions of stakeholders to show how they line up in terms of the extent of their power and interest, before a second map is produced showing the desired positions of stakeholders in order for the strategy or intervention to be successful. Sources of power include the control of resources, charismatic leadership and possession of knowledge, status and hierarchy (Scholes 2001). Indicators of interest are harder to define but within a sport development environment may include verbal expressions of interest, shared organisational goals and objectives, common geographical focus, and political pressure or status. Interest should be represented by (+) for, against (−) and neutral (0) in terms of how the stakeholder may feel about the strategy or intervention. For example, whilst a community group may have interest in local authority plans to develop a community sports project in their area, they may have low power in relation to the strategy or intervention, so their interest would be negative (due to feeling initially excluded from the

Kirstie Simpson and Janine Partington

development of the project). However, the local authority, if following community development principles, would have a desired position where the community group has high power (and is actively involved in establishing community need and in decision-making regarding the project) and subsequently positive, rather than negative interest (due to increased ownership and involvement of the project).

Figures 7.4 and 7.5 show both the initial and desired power/interest matrix applied to the previously discussed badminton development group in Bury, Greater Manchester. Figure 7.4 below shows the power/interest matrix applied to this situation, specifically at the point before the establishment of the Bury badminton development group. An explanation of each organisation's interest levels is also provided:

■ Badminton England and Bury Sport & Physical Activity Service have both high interest and power. The establishment of a development group fits with both organisations' priorities and they currently hold the resources (in terms of staff time and local knowledge) to drive the establishment of the development group.

		Interest	
		Low	**High**
Power	**Low**	A (monitor with minimum effort) Participants (0) Primary Care Trust (0) Bury MBC sport and leisure facilities (0)	B (keep informed) Adult and social badminton clubs (+) Individual coaches (+)
	High	C (keep satisfied) Broadoak and Woodhey School Sport Partnerships (0) Greater Sport (+)	D (key players) Bury Sport & Physical Activity Service (+) Badminton England (+)

Figure 7.4   Initial power/interest matrix pre-establishment of the Bury badminton development group

- The two School Sport Partnerships at this stage of development have low interest but high power. They are not formally involved with the establishment of the development group but retain high power due to their role in providing competitive sports opportunities, school-club links and identifying talented young people. They are neutral about the development group at this stage as their priorities remain focused on the achievement of the (now defunct) PE and School Sport for Young People (PESSYP) strategy rather than broader sport development objectives.
- Greater Sport (County Sports Partnership) also has low interest and high power, but is 'for' the establishment of a development group as it helps address their strategic objective of driving up opportunities for participation in sport across the sub-region. It has high power due to its role in channelling potential resources to local authorities and its role as the organiser of the regional Youth Games event which forms part of the badminton talent pathway.
- The adult and social badminton clubs and individual coaches have high interest due to their commitment to, and participation in the sport, but they also have low power, as they do not possess the resources or power to influence how the development group is established. The individual coaches are 'for' the development group as it may create opportunities for work, whereas the interest level of the club is unclear as there may be suspicion attached to the formation of a formal network, with it being viewed as a potential threat.
- At this stage, participants, Bury's sport and leisure facilities and the Primary Care Trust have low interest and low power. They have not yet been formally involved in the establishment of the development group and are concentrating on their own strategic objectives.

Scholes's (2001) analysis of stakeholder maps identifies nine 'typical' power/interest matrices. These identify where the weight of the dominant stakeholder influence lies and Scholes acknowledges that in many cases in the real world there will be a combination of some of these nine typical maps. Scholes argues that the maps are useful ways to identify political priorities and potential support for an initiative, activity or strategy. The map shown in Figure 7.4 provides an example of a 'lone champion' or in the case of Bury Sport & Physical Activity and Badminton England two 'lone champions'. As Scholes (2001) states there are many strategies which succeed through the support of one or two powerful champions who drive through the implementation phase.

168

In this situation, it is important that the interest of these champions is maintained. Potential threats to the success of this approach include a loss of power (for example, significant funding cuts) or loss of interest (for example, a change in national sports policy and related objectives) within a 'champion'. In order to minimise this risk, efforts need to be made to broaden the base of support for the strategy by increasing the interest of other stakeholders (from box C) or building the power base of supporters (from box B) (Scholes 2001). Figure 7.5 illustrates the desired power/interest matrix for the badminton development group.

■ On the desired power/interest matrix those organisations shown in italics have moved boxes as a result of the work of the two champions towards the establishment of the badminton development group. This work has not only led to an increase in support for the group amongst other organisations (broadening the base of support) but the formation of a new organisation, namely Bury Topflight Badminton Club which not only provided new opportunities for junior badminton but also acted to strengthen the power base of supporters.

| | | Interest | |
		Low	High
Power	**Low**	A *(monitor with minimum effort)* Participants (0)	B *(keep informed)* Other adult and social badminton clubs (0) Individual coaches (+) *Primary Care Trust (0)*
	High	C *(keep satisfied)* Greater Sport (+) *Bury MBC sport and leisure facilities (+)*	D *(key players)* Bury Sport & Physical Activity Service (+) Badminton England (+) *Broadoak and Woodhey School Sport Partnerships (+)* *Bury Topflight Badminton Club (+)*

Figure 7.5   Desired power/interest matrix for the Bury badminton development group

- As a result of the clear links to the national PESSYP strategy and provision of school-club links, the two School Sport Partnership programmes have moved from box C to box D and are now key players in the development of badminton within Bury.
- The Primary Care Trust has moved from box A to box B due to its interest in the outcomes of the work of the development group in response to their objective increasing adult participation in physical activity, specifically the increase in numbers of adult and social clubs providing badminton opportunities and the development of 'No Strings Badminton' sessions.
- Bury sport and leisure facilities have also moved from box A but unlike the Primary Care Trust they are now positioned in box C. As a result of the work of the two champions of the strategy, they have bought into the 'No Strings Badminton' initiative and now run two of these sessions within their facilities. As a result of this funding arrangement with Badminton England, they need to be kept satisfied in terms of getting value for money from the 'No Strings' sessions and being regularly informed of any future opportunities or threats resulting from the work of the development group.
- The status of the adult and social badminton clubs has changed from being unknown to neutral. At this stage the focus of the development group has primarily been on developing junior provision and 'No Strings' sessions. These have led to the establishment of new adult and social clubs, but there has not been a direct impact on these clubs in terms of how they operate, so at this stage they remain neutral rather than for or against the strategy.

The map in Figure 7.5 resembles a 'dream ticket' according to Scholes (2001) where there are several champions of the strategy and no powerful opponents. Potential threats to the continuing success of the development group include complacency amongst key players (Scholes 2001). It is also crucial that they keep the other organisations and players informed and satisfied; for example, if the 'No Strings Badminton' sessions were to be unsuccessful it is likely that Bury sport and leisure facilities would lose interest in the strategy and possibly be unsupportive of future ventures. There is also the potential for conflict between partners should the strategic objectives of key players change, for example if Badminton England changed its priorities from increasing participation to focusing solely on talent identification and development. This could potentially

170

lead to conflicting agendas with other key players, and also impact on the relationships with the other organisations shown on the matrix.

Supporting partnerships

The S within the PiiSA framework focuses on structure and whether the systems that the partnership is developing are fit for purpose, i.e. whether the structure/system being developed is dynamic and flexible enough to meet changing demands of the partners and/or the intervention. Successful partnerships will have structures that enable and empower rather than disable and disempower those involved. This also relates to the power/interest matrix on the previous page where the badminton development group needs to be flexible to meet the demands of a wide range of partners. Without an ability to do this, it is unlikely that the development group would benefit from the support base it currently possesses or be able to implement its strategy as successfully.

This aspect of partnership work has to be supported by education and training, so the extent to which those immediately involved in the partnership have the requisite skills to support others to support themselves more effectively is important. This means that SDPs (and others) have to micro-manage the system to ensure that it remains fit for purpose and at the same time recognise their individual weaknesses, in order that the partnership is able to continue to be effective; a positive cycle of development if you will. As Frisby, Thibault and Kikulis (2004) warn, many partnerships fail to meet expectations because little attention is paid to managing the web of partner relationships that emerge. Their research on organisational dynamics in partnerships within leisure service departments discovered that the three structural dynamics that created issues within partnership were: a lack of planning and policy guidelines, unclear roles and reporting channels and insufficient resources. Frequently, partnerships are neglected once established and almost expected to function effectively with no maintenance or attention. It is also common to find that there are no leadership structures in place, with no single partner taking responsibility for driving the partnership forward and 'gentlemen's agreements' taking the place of formalised actions/decisions. Shaw and Allen (2006) describe this as a 'lack of management intensity' where partners are unwilling to intervene in the management of the partnership. Conversely, they also counsel against over-management, in particular a hierarchical arrangement, which may also blunt the partnership's effectiveness. Therefore, it is essential to establish a common framework for working that achieves both a balance between over- and under-management, but that also establishes clear partnership goals and communication channels and provides internal accountability.

Taking action

Action is the final factor of the PiiSA framework and reflects the organisation's capacity to take action in terms of resource and capability. This element requires organisations to be clear about outputs (and therefore overall outcomes) and the objectives required to achieve these outputs in the short term. Taking action is the hardest element of partnership working. Frequently partnerships are very successful at producing strategic documents, but poor at making decisions and implementing them (Asthana, Richardson and Halliday 2002). Clearly, without the partnership generating outputs and outcomes it will be less able to develop a broad support base for its work or attract potential partners to invest in that partnership. Producing results was, and is crucial to the success of the badminton development group shown in Figure 7.5 and has allowed it to gain political support for its work, namely from other departments within Bury MBC and also the Primary Care Trust. This not only raised the group's profile but has also created the possibility of additional resources for its work. In addition, I&DeA (2009) warns against the development of 'talking shops' which can ultimately lead to a lack of action and frustration amongst partners, and crucially a complete failure to implement strategy.

Partnership appraisal

The PiiSA framework allows those working within partnerships to assess and appraise the effectiveness of their relationships. One of the common weaknesses within sport development is a lack of willingness to terminate partnerships when they have served their purpose or are not fulfilling expectations. Instead, SDPs contribute to pre-existing feelings of partnership fatigue by continuing to undertake partnership business, even in the form of meetings that have become talking shops

Kirstie Simpson and Janine Partington

and therefore achieve very little, because of an inability to 'pull the plug'. Whether this is due to pressure to work in partnership wherever possible or due to the members of the partnership each being unwilling to suggest termination is unclear. What is evident is that partnerships without purpose continue to be a drain on already stretched resources. Parent and Harvey (2009) argue that evaluation of partnerships is frequently forgotten despite the fact that an honest appraisal of successes and failures can have the potential to result in future improvements. Unfortunately, resources spent on evaluation are often seen as taking resources away from delivery, and thus, not prioritised. Utilising an action learning approach to evaluation, for example, creates a cyclical process of evaluation and promotes continuous improvement.

SUMMARY

If developed in the right way, with high levels of critical consciousness, partnerships allow, and fundamentally demand the growth of trust, respect and cohesion within communities (Gilchrist 2003). Within community settings, strategic sport development should be concerned with long-term, sustainable change and 'thoughtful action' (Ledwith 2005) and in order for this to be achieved, the SDP needs to have appropriate skills (i.e. be an authentic transformative leader) and utilise partnerships effectively in order to enable communities to fulfil their own potential. The value of real collaboration over and above working in silos (or, in fact, in paper partnerships) should not be underestimated in the war against physical inactivity.

LEARNING ACTIVITIES

Developing skills

For a partnership you have knowledge of, attempt to locate organisations within a power/interest matrix. You should initially attempt the current version of the matrix and then move onto articulating the desired future state. You should focus specifically on identifying how this future state will be achieved.

Developing knowledge

Using the proposed typology of partnerships as well as the PiiSA framework, analyse the strengths and weaknesses of a partnership with which you are familiar. You should identify improvements to practice wherever possible.

REFERENCES

Anastacio, J., Gidley, B., Hart, L., Keith, M., Mayo, M. and Kowarzik, U. (2000) 'Reflecting Realities: participants' perspectives on integrated communities and sustainable development'. Bristol, Policy Press/Joseph Rowntree Foundation. In Banks, S., Butcher, H., Henderson, P. and Robertson, J. eds. (2003) *Managing Community Practice: Principles, Policies and Programmes.* Bristol, The Policy Press.

Asthana, S., Richardson, S. and Halliday, J. (2002). 'Partnership Working in Public Policy Provision: a framework for evaluation'. In *Social Policy and Administration.* 36(7), pp. 780–795.

Badminton England (n.d.) 'Community Badminton Networks'. Available at http://www.sysport.co.uk/downloads/CBN%20Leaflet.pdf.

Ballach, S. and Taylor, M. (2001) *Partnership Working: Policy And Practice.* Bristol, The Policy Press.

Banks, S., Butcher, H., Henderson, P. and Robertson, J. eds. (2003) *Managing Community Practice: Principles, Policies And Programmes.* Bristol, The Policy Press.

Berner, E. and Phillips, B. (2005) 'Left to their own devices? Community self help between alternative development and neo-liberalism'. *Community Development Journal.* 40 (1), pp. 17–29.

Checkland, P. (1999) *Soft Systems Methodology: A 30-Year Retrospective.* Chichester, John Wiley & Sons.

Conservative Party (2010) 'Big Society, Not Big Government'. London, Conservatives.

Coulter, M. (2008) *Strategic Management in Action.* 4th ed. NJ, Pearson Education.

DCMS/Cabinet Offfice (2002) 'Game Plan: a strategy for delivering Government's sport and physical activity objectives'. London, The Strategy Unit.

Friend, J. (2006) 'Partnership Meets Politics: managing within the maze'. *International Journal of Public Sector Management.* 19(3), pp. 261–277.

Frisby, W. and Millar, S. (2002) 'The Actualities of Doing Community Development to Promote the Inclusion of Low Income Populations in Local Sport and Recreation'. *European Sport Management Quarterly.* 2(3), pp. 209–233.

Kirstie Simpson and Janine Partington

Frisby, W., Thibault, L. and Kikulis, L. (2004) 'The Organizational Dynamics of Under-managed Partnerships in Leisure Service Departments'. *Leisure Studies.* 23(3) April, pp. 109–126.

Gilchrist, A. (2003) 'Linking Partnerships and Networks'. In Banks, S., Butcher, H., Henderson, P. and Robertson, J. eds. (2003) *Managing Community Practice: Principles, Policies and Programmes.* Bristol, The Policy Press, pp. 33–54.

Graduate Prospects (2011) 'Sports Development Officer'. Manchester, Graduate Prospects. Available from: http://www.prospects.ac.uk/sports_development_officer_job_description.htm.

Hastings, A., McArthur, A. and McGregor, A. (1996) *Less than Equal? Community Organisations and Estate Regeneration Partnerships.* Bristol, The Policy Press.

Houlihan, B. and Green, M. (2009) 'Modernization and Sport: the reform of Sport England and UK Sport'. *Public Administration.* 87(3), pp. 678–698.

Houlihan, B. and Lindsey, I. (2008) 'Networks and Partnerships in Sports Development'. In Girginov, V. ed. *Managing Sports Development.* Oxford, Butterworth-Heinemann, pp. 225–242.

Houlihan, B. and White, A. (2002) *The Politics of Sports Development: Development of Sport or Development Through Sport?* London, Routledge.

I&DeA (2009) 'Making Partnership Work Better in the Culture & Sport Sector'. London, I&DeA.

Johnson, G., Scholes, K. and Whittington, R. (2008) *Exploring Corporate Strategy: Texts and Cases.* 8th ed. London, Prentice Hall.

Johnson, G., Scholes, K. and Whittington, R. (2009) *Fundamentals of Strategy.* London, Prentice Hall.

Kanter, R.M.(2003) *The Frontiers of Management.* Boston, Harvard Business School Press.

Ledwith, M. (2005) *Community Development: A Critical Approach.* Bristol, The Policy Press.

Lindsey, I. (2006) 'Local Partnerships in the United Kingdom for the New Opportunities for PE and Sport Programme: a policy network analysis'. *European Sport Management Quarterly.* 6(2) June, pp. 167–184.

Link4Life (2011) 'About Link4Life'. Available at http://www.link4life.org/index.cfm?fuseaction=c.showPage&pageID=34.

McQuaid, R. (2000). 'The Theory of Partnerships. Why Have Partnerships?' In Osbourne S. ed. (2000) *Public-Private Partnerships: Theory and Practice in International Perspective.* London, Routledge. pp. 9–35.

Mendelow, A. (1991) 'Environmental Scanning: the impact of the stakeholder concept'. In *Proceedings from the second international conference on information systems.* pp. 407–418.

Nesti, M. (2008) 'Challenging Yourself to Challenge Others'. *The Leisure Review.* Available from http://www.theleisurereview.co.uk/articles08/nesti.html (accessed May 2008).

Parent, M. and Harvey, J. (2009) 'Towards a Management Model for Sport and Physical Activity Community-based Partnerships'. *European Sport Management Quarterly.* 9(1), March 2009, pp. 23–45.

Partington, J. and Totten, M. (2012) 'Community Sports Projects and Effective Community Empowerment: a case study in Rochdale'. *Managing Leisure*. 17, January 2012, pp. 29–46.

Pitchford, A. and Collins, M. (2010) 'Sport Development as a Job, a Career and Training'. In Collins, M. ed. (2010) *Examining Sports Development*. Abingdon, Routledge, pp. 259–288.

Reid, B. and Iqbal, B. (1996) 'Interorganisational Relationships and Social Housing Services'. In Malpass, P. ed. (1996) *Ownership, Control and Accountability: the new governance of housing*. Harlow, Longman.

Robson, S. (2008) 'Partnerships in Sport'. In Hylton, K. and Bramham, P. eds. *Sports Development: Policy, Process and Practice*. 2nd ed. Abingdon, Routledge, pp. 118–142.

Scholes, K. (2001) 'Stakeholder Mapping: a practical tool for public sector managers'. In Johnson, G. and Scholes, K. eds. (2001) *Exploring Public Sector Strategy*. Harlow, Pearson Education Ltd, pp. 165–184.

Shaw, S. and Allen, J. (2006) "It basically is a fairly loose arrangement...and that works out fine, really." Analysing the Dynamics of an Interorganisational Partnership'. *Sport Management Review*. 9, pp. 203–228.

Shor, I. (1993) 'Education is Politics: Paulo Freire's critical pedagogy'. In McLaren, P. and Leonard, P. eds. *Paulo Friere: A Critical Encounter*. London, Routledge, pp. 24–35.

SkillsActive (2010) 'National Occupational Standards for Sports Development'. Available at http://www.skillsactive.com/training/standards/level_3/sports_development.

Skinner, S. (1997) *Building Community Strengths*. London, Community Development Foundation.

Taylor, M. (1998) 'Combating the Social Exclusion of Housing Estates'. In *Housing Studies*. 13(6), pp. 819–832.

Turner, A. (2009) 'Bottom-up Community Development: reality or rhetoric? The example of the Kingsmead Kabin in East London'. *Community Development Journal*. 44(2) April, pp. 230–247.

Vail, E. (2007) 'Community Development and Sport Participation'. *Journal of Sport Management*. 21, pp. 571–596.

Vangen, S. and Huxham, C. (2002) 'Enacting leadership for collaborative advantage'. Glasgow, University of Strathclyde Graduate School of Business.

Wenger, E. and Snyder, W. (2000) 'Communities of Practice: the organizational frontier'. *Harvard Business Review*. January–February, pp. 139–145.

Kirstie Simpson and Janine Partington

CHAPTER 8

POLITICS, POLICY AND SPORT DEVELOPMENT

LEE TUCKER

INTRODUCTION

It is important to acknowledge at the outset of this chapter that there is a deliberate intention to be provocative and maybe even controversial at times in order to challenge conventional thinking within sport development. This is necessary if we are to initiate a process of change that gets sport development professionals (SDPs) to think and act in alternative ways to impact upon historical problems within society, through sport.

Sport development professionals are familiar with the notion that sport and politics are inseparable, contrary to many lay persons' view that they should not mix. Sport development operates within a highly politicised climate. Whether this is via the partisan politics of central and local government, or the inter- and intra-organisational wrangling experienced in national governing bodies of sport (NGBs), sport development professionals have to lead the strategic management process as a response to policy decisions with which they may not agree but to which they are beholden. The actions of the coalition government in 2010–11 illustrate emphatically how decisions made in Westminster impact upon all aspects and levels of sport. The ideologically driven concept of the 'Big Society' meant that responsibility for many activities including sports provision is handed to local communities and partners, although many feel without the necessary resources to do so (Richards 2011 and Goulding 2011). Sport England and the Youth Sport Trust were two of the major organisations to be hit hard by government cutbacks, the ramifications of which reverberated around every nook and cranny of the UK's sporting infrastructure. So, for those naïve enough to still claim that politics and sport do not mix: think again!

This chapter provides the reader with a critical examination of the current political climate for sport development in all its guises. A brief history of government policy in this area will be offered, but the main thrust of the chapter will be the questioning of existing policy and practice and how this may be challenged through sport development strategy into the delivery of meaningful opportunities. Mainstream political ideology (Leach 2002) will be presented and critiqued in terms of its relevance to sport development. The critique and challenge of established policy-practice relationships will incorporate an argument for the implementation of more bottom-up approaches to sports policy. This will complement the critical aspects of consultation and empowerment covered in Chapters 10 and 11.

It is important to define some key concepts that will permeate the chapter. 'Political' and 'politics' will be used in two ways: first, they will be used to consider politics at a macro level and how political parties influence policy and strategy primarily via their adopted ideology (what some people would call 'politics with a big P'). Alternatively, these terms will be also used to discuss micro or issue politics of individuals and groups and the way political viewpoints influence decisions and ways of life (what some call 'politics with a little p'). An important distinction should also be made between policy and strategy. Davies (2000:26) does this by stating that:

> Whereas, policy defines the company's goals and objectives and its operational domain, strategy decides how the company's goals and objectives will be achieved, what operational units will be used to achieve the company's goals and objectives, and how those operational units will be structured. Strategy also determines what resources will be needed to achieve the company's goals and objectives and how these resources will be acquired and used. Strategy is a design or plan that defines how policy is to be achieved.

Hegemony is another concept that is central to any discussion of political action and ideology. Adamson (1980:170) states that one aspect of hegemony is "the consensual basis of an existing political system within

Lee Tucker

civil society". Williams (1977:108) discusses the way in which hegemony relates "the whole social process to specific distributions of power and influence" and how this therefore impacts upon people's everyday lives in very practical ways. An analysis of contemporary society highlights how hegemonic processes are at work in the way in which major challenges such as the global economic crisis are handled. Despite the widespread belief that bankers and the financial sector were to blame for the economic recession in the late 2000s (Prynn 2008), 'ordinary' tax payers bore a heavy burden and saw their public services cut. This is rationalised by those in power (the dominant hegemony) as necessary for all to share the burden, yet many of the same bankers were still accruing millions of pounds in salaries and bonuses (Treanor and Wearden 2011).

Members of the hegemonic elite who lead society attempt to influence others to accept and strive to be like them, i.e. to be successful within a meritocratic (work hard enough and you can reach the top in your chosen profession), capitalist system. This subscription to the market economy, the basis of the dominant hegemonic ideology of neo-liberalism in the western world (Schwarzmantel 2008), means that any alternative view is seen as deviant and often stigmatised. This is just one (simplified) example of how hegemony works, but it is endemic within all aspects of society and contributes to the 'acceptable' intolerance of others. The consensual adherence to certain political parameters as well as the indoctrination into a popular culture that encourages consumerism, fragmentation and individuality are key factors in how a dominant hegemonic system manifests itself in the outlook and attitudes of society. The attention given to socialism in this chapter will consequently be seen as controversial because of the press it has received from the dominant hegemony in the West, deriding it as "yesterday's political philosophy" (Whannel 2008:223). However, Stalinist Russia, Maoist China and related systems were based on many *antisocialist* principles such as the suppression of a free press, the militarised labour and the banning of political dissent and oppositional parties (Eagleton 2011) and should not deter us from analysing the many positive contributions that socialism can bring to an improved sporting system and more equal society (Whannel 2008).

The final key concept to be defined, already used within this introduction, is ideology. Schwarzmantel (2008:25) offers this definition of the term:

An ideology is thus totalistic: it presents, at least in its fullest form, a broad range of views which cover the central aspects of how society should be organised, answering such questions as what the role of the state should be, what forms of difference and differentiation between people should be accepted, and which rejected. In the widest possible sense an ideology thus offers answers to the question of what kind of world is desirable.

For Bramham (2001:9) "political ideologies are best described as reflections of the world and reflections on the world". An ideology can belong to an individual or be shared within a political party, etc. This is significant when discussing political influence on sport development as it dictates how sport is perceived, managed, funded and supported from central to local government and beyond.

HISTORY

Evidence of the symbiotic relationship between politics and sport can be tracked through key events and policies throughout the last fifty years. The Wolfenden report of 1960 made links between sport and the tackling of youth crime; the International Olympic Committee (IOC) and others excluded South Africa from competing in international sport due to apartheid; back in the UK a new initiative called Action Sport was introduced in the early 1980s in response to inner city riots; and the social inclusion agenda created the foundations of policy generated by the Policy Action Team 10 in the late 1990s (Houlihan and White 2002). Alongside these examples is the intervention of politicians and other influential people on behalf of the nation, as witnessed in the attempts of the British Prime Minister and Prince William to woo FIFA delegates into awarding the 2018 men's FIFA World Cup to England. The list goes on but these are a few of many examples of political activity and policy impacting upon sport or the use of sport as a means to political ends.

Paradoxically, despite such widespread recognition by politicians and others of the value of sport, the resources needed to exploit the full potential of sport rarely follow. This will resonate with the majority of sport development professionals throughout the UK who are continuously faced with the challenge of being tasked to positively impact on their communities/sports on a shoestring budget that is

180

normally one of the first to be hit in times of austerity. National examples have been highlighted above (Sport England and the Youth Sport Trust) but at a more local level the impact of the coalition government's 2010 cuts of School Sport Partnerships and local authority sport development units are additional examples of services being hit despite the excellent work being done by many of these professionals. The wider economic conditions inevitably permeate decision-making throughout all aspects of social policy, however, the political ideology of the governing party has a profound affect on shaping the landscape that determines the decisions which impact on sport development. Therefore, it is to political ideologies that we now turn in more depth.

POLITICAL IDEOLOGIES – MAINSTREAM PARTY POLITICS

There seems little point in modern day politics to attempt to detect the subtle differences between the leading political parties in the UK. This is due to a merging of many ideological positions of the Conservative, Liberal Democrat and Labour parties. Western capitalism is a major determinant of many of the policies of the three major parties, and their reliance on big business or other significant investors means that in order to attain a position of power, concessions must be made to appeal to those in dominant hegemonic positions within society. All political parties seek to rub shoulders with the successful sport stars of the day and demonstrate to the populace that they are associated with that success. All parties claim to value sporting institutions and traditions and how sport itself contributes to communities and the nation as a whole. Yet despite this political convergence there are still differences between the policies of the parties and how they envision the provision and purpose of sport.

To highlight the policy differences that remain it is straightforward to demarcate the shift in policy of the 2010 coalition government from that of New Labour. The coalition's preoccupation with competitive sport contrasts with that of New Labour who channelled funding into grass roots participation via the aforementioned School Sport Partnerships, Specialist Sport Colleges and other local delivery agents, although one of the aims was still to see talented athletes emerge from the system (a more comprehensive insight into the various policies and themes under New Labour is given by Houlihan and White (2002)). The significant ideological difference, particularly between the Conservative party and New Labour is the Conservatives' focus on competitive sport with the introduction of 'The School Games' (DCMS 2011). The original policy of the coalition government was the withdrawal of funding specifically for school sport. Although, this was later partially reversed to the approval of organisations, such as the Youth Sport Trust (2011), this decision gave an insight into the ideological drive of the government (and in particular of the Conservative party). What was presented as conferring independence and the withdrawal of state control quite effectively represents Conservatism and its encouragement of individualism. This may have suited some but judgements on whether or not to support sport in any serious way were to become dependent on the background and character of those in decision-making positions within schools.

This lack of intervention by the Conservative-Liberal Democrat coalition is encapsulated in the ethos of the aforementioned 'Big Society'. Putting more responsibility and accountability upon individuals within communities offsets the government's reduction in capital and revenue support for many initiatives: this is ideological and not, as was claimed, essential. Values of sport relate closely to capitalism through the pursuit of success via competition against others. The strong and capable succeed whilst the weak (incidentally the overwhelming majority) fail. So, in any period of austerity there will be success stories. There will be media coverage and support of such enterprise; popular TV programmes such as Dragon's Den and The Apprentice will popularise the myth that anyone can achieve anything, but these will be the exceptions to the rule and not the norm. A contrasting ideology which, as stated above, many believe belongs in the political archives, is that of socialism, an argument for which was made convincingly by Gary Whannel firstly in *Blowing the Whistle: the Politics of Sport* (1983) and in his more recent text *Culture, Politics and Sport: Blowing the Whistle Revisited* (2008).

SOCIALISM

Firstly, it is important to recognise that there are many different forms of socialism: many on the left perceive this as a problem in itself. Anarcho-socialism, market socialism, green socialism, socialist feminism are a few of the variants (the list goes on but a useful outline of the different doctrines can be found in Wright (1986)). However, many of the sources mentioned in this chapter also give a good insight into the philosophical and practical arguments for socialism. A common endeavour of all socialists is to bring about change in the world that attempts to eradicate much of the inequality that exists under capitalism. Eagleton (2011) claims that:

> Capitalism has created more prosperity than history has ever witnessed, but the cost – not least in the near-destitution of billions – has been astronomical. According to the World Bank, 2.74 billion people in 2001 lived on less than two dollars a day. We face a probable future of nuclear-armed states warring over a scarcity of resources; and that scarcity is largely the consequence of capitalism itself...Capitalism will behave antisocially if it is profitable for it to do so, and that can now mean human devastation on an unimaginable scale. (2011:8)

As with the mainstream political parties it is too complex to deal with the minutiae of each strand of socialism here, so instead a generic analysis of socialism and how this differs from the mainstream will be offered. To help achieve this, a generic socialist perspective will be adopted to give a brief critique of how the political and sporting systems work in tandem to perpetuate the cyclical nature of inequality and oppression. This will incorporate many aspects of issue politics as well as a contestation of the macro politics that reign in modern western society. Although not always explicitly about sport it is crucial to acknowledge the wider socio-economic and socio-political issues that impact upon sport development and the need for such issues to be considered if a society that offers real hope to people through sport is to be created.

For most people the need to work to survive is a daily challenge and for many this results in a life of poverty: figures show that almost a third of children in the UK live beneath the poverty line (Ledwith and Springett 2010). For most rational people it would seem ridiculous that such poverty can exist at one end of the spectrum whist others have such wealth at the other end: a report by Credit Suisse in 2010 stated that 0.5% of the world's population owned well over a third of the world's wealth (Credit Suisse Research Institute 2010). There are numerous other facts and figures which reveal the astonishing ability that those powerful individuals and organisations have to actually abolish world poverty. An example of this is the incredible amount of money avoided and evaded in tax havens as reported by Shaxson (2011) which, if brought back into the mainstream economy, could make a huge difference to many lives. Critics often state that the world's poorest people live better now than ever due to capitalism. However, it is accepted that the same case was made for slavery (Chomsky 2011) and during Stalinism but it did not make it right. So why is there not more of a challenge to such a system? Critics have asserted that those in power (the dominant hegemony) are devious in the way that they engage the media, convey political messages of hope and create an image of the undeserving poor that renders the majority to blame themselves for their own destitution (Hall 2011). David Cameron's problematisation of multiculturalism in 2011 is one example of how the working class are encouraged to turn on each other and blame issues like immigration for example, for many of society's problems, rather than addressing the absurd disparity of income between the richest and poorest in society (Socialist Worker 2011).

How does this process manifest itself in sport? Once again, analysis of the media is helpful here. Through the use of the media, sport is sexualised, racialised etc. and therefore used to reinforce the representation of the 'other' whilst simultaneously fragmenting the potential of a united working class. Sport itself is used as an opiate (Hargreaves 1986) to distract the working class from their often mundane lives. So, the build up to big sporting events and the dramatic representation of national victories or losses are distracters which help to quell the focus of attention on the dominant hegemony. Yet, without a coherent and collective movement to meaningfully challenge this system we often let our anger dissipate and let the Wimbledon tennis tournament, the Ashes cricket or FIFA World Cup become the main focus of our lives away from work and other commitments. This is not to say that these sporting events are not impressive spectacles but they are also part of the armoury that helps to blunt the effectiveness of a counter hegemonic resistance (focus, organisation and motivation) to a system that perpetuates the existing hegemonic order.

Veal (2010) discusses the various models that are used to inform decisions on sport policy (power-based models, corporatism, rationality models and so on) but a key feature here is that choices are always constrained due to the need to protect vested interests. The elitist and corporatist models that he covers seem to have been a particular feature of the 2010 coalition government, evidenced by the educational academies set up by business entrepreneurs and the return to a focus on elite sport.

The impact of all of the above on sport development professionals is that we are in a constant state of flux, working under the conditions of life-limited governments and the changing social conditions that emerge (sometimes in response to government policy). Of key interest here is that as sport development professionals we all carry our own political persuasions. As professionals we are often instructed to avoid bringing our personal politics to work but this can be seen as just another way of protecting those in power from an inquisitive majority. Instead, it could be argued that practitioners have a duty to their profession to politicise the young people (and others) that they encounter through sport in order to defend and resist, but also to demand and fight for an improved democratic structure of sport that authentically pursues an equal playing field for all. Whether this is in the classroom, on the sports field or through youth forums, getting people to actively engage in the political system has significant potential and can ultimately have a significant impact on the future of sport and society.

PRACTICAL POLITICS

It is understood that some of the ideas and arguments above seem idealistic and that this is not overly helpful in addressing the actual, day-to-day issues and power dynamics faced by most sport development professionals. Yet, it seems incontrovertible that the majority of people working in the industry are aware of their responsibility to create a better future for the communities that they serve. Therefore, gaining access to those communities is essential for any sport development professional. Once this is achieved there is an opportunity to engage people in the more radical areas of community development and bottom-up provision. Getting people to question their living conditions, including the root causes is something that the radical educationalist Paulo Freire (1972) introduced to many areas of South America in the 1970s and has since become a popular blueprint for the engagement of people in a more bottom-up approach to education. The same principles are available to sport development professionals. Getting people to discuss their own subjective positions within society, and working alongside others to generate improvements is critical if people are to make genuine differences to their lives.

A football coach going into a community for eight weeks and teaching a few skills is not going to have any long-term impact on any individual or community. However, somebody with the necessary skills, working in a community whose inhabitants have expressed a desire for change and equipping them with the knowledge and skills to cater for themselves (and therefore not being dependent on the 'professional' in future) is an example of a bottom-up provision that benefits those involved. This is similar to the experiences of many when seeking to obtain funding. Sometimes the arduous nature of funding application forms can deter all but the most knowledgeable or determined person from completing the process. There is a skill to this process, but one which is required by members of the community. Reliance upon others must be avoided if long-term sustainability is to be achieved. Using sport as a mechanism to draw people together and discuss their personal/community issues is another way in which a Freirean approach can be facilitated.

This focus may not necessarily be explicitly discussed in a strategy document where hoops need to be jumped through to gain the necessary support and resources from those in positions of influence. A certain degree of lip service must be paid to national strategy and government policy to ensure those on the ground are able to do their jobs with whatever resources they are able to acquire. However, the approach that the organisation takes to strategy (as discussed in the Introduction) as well as the decisions made at a local level (as covered in Chapter 4) should be more in line with the hearts and minds of the workforce expected to carry out the stated goals of the strategy.

POLICY MODELS, PROCESSES AND CHALLENGES

Coalter (2007) offers an insightful look into how sport policy is often conceived and implemented without any evidential basis for such decisions. He and others argue that evidence-based policy making is often replaced by a practice which sees policy based on hypotheses or theories rather than on knowledge of best practice. This means that those in influential positions, be they politicians or former sport stars whose popularity is tapped into, can often be guilty of promoting sport policy that is either a repackaged version of previous initiatives or impulsive policy based on subjective opinion. Frustratingly, for sport development professionals, once these policies have been made they are obliged to implement them to the best of their ability, whether or not they actually agree with them. As discussed earlier, central governmental policy is predominantly ideologically-driven so policy shifts are almost inevitable once a change of government takes place.

This too can be exasperating for sport development professionals when they have invested so much time and other resources into making something successful, only for it to be halted due to the need for an incoming government to stamp its authority and identity on sport policy. Houlihan and White (2002) detail how policy is also impacted upon by the environment in which it exists. They consider how certain policies and structures are susceptible to change in the short term due to their vulnerability (offering as an example, New Labour's jettisoning of the Department of National Heritage for the DCMS following its success at the 1997 elections). Others are more stable but may be prone to change over the medium term (they cite a shift in policy paradigm through the writing of *A Sporting Future for All* which replaced the Conservatives' *Sport: Raising the Game*), whilst certain policies/values become deeply entrenched in the prevailing political climate, such as the acknowledgement of equity within the sport discourse.

The final issue to acknowledge around sport policy is that despite what most politicians portray as a rigorous and logical approach to policy, it is often "irrational, pragmatic and incremental, driven forward or subverted by powerful vested interests" (Bramham 2008:11). Bramham goes on to give examples of how policy and political decisions were made, with often little evidence or forecasting to support the actual policy outcomes. This is often due to the short term gains that can be accrued through policy that win favour with powerful individuals and groups and also to the need to address immediate rather than long term problems to capture the votes of the electorate. It is crucial for sport development professionals to keep one eye on these political and policy shifts whilst continuing their every day roles. A key aspect of the role of a sport development professional is therefore to be flexible and able to adapt to the changes imposed on them within this political context.

This does not mean that sport development professionals should passively accede to such policy and political decisions. There is a need for them to voice their opinions in pursuit of policy change. Despite the historical problems of the political and philosophical differences between organisations such as National Association for Sport Development (NASD), Institute of Sport and Recreation Management (ISRM) and Institute of Leisure and Amenities Management (ILAM), etc., professional bodies such as the Chartered Institute for the Management of Sport and Physical Activity (CIMSPA) provide environments in which sport development professionals can congregate to discuss such issues and formulate plans to influence change. Many may scoff at this suggestion but we must stop viewing such organisations as anthropomorphic entities, as if they cannot be changed and will never empathise with the real world issues of sport development colleagues. Organisations' culture and philosophy are made by the people within them and it behoves sport development professionals to take steps to mould the culture of such organisations rather than condemning them from a distance.

INTRA- AND INTER-ORGANISATIONAL POLITICS

Following on from this another political dimension of sport development is the complex relationships and partnerships within and between sport development individuals and teams. The intricacies of partnerships are dealt with in Chapter 7 but it seems apt to look at the political aspects here. As discussed in Chapter 2 the personal politics of individuals within organisations will have an obvious influence on the culture of the workplace and their working practice. Understanding and empathising with a team mate's politics is crucial if you are to contribute to creating a cohesive unit of colleagues that are able to work together in a trustful manner. This may also present an opportunity for others to learn from each other and therefore create not only a professional culture but also an educational one. Discussing the ramifications of political decisions from above and how these can be successfully navigated as a team, rather than being subjected to directives from an autocratic manager can develop the team.

Individuals' political beliefs and therefore world view may also impact upon the ability of discrete organisations to work together. Strange partnerships are often created within sport development. There have been many collaborations between sporting organisations and various fast food restaurants, confectionary manufacturers and soft drink

188

companies, all of which can be regarded as contributing to unhealthy consumption and ultimately the causes of obesity, tooth decay, etc. This confronts sporting organisations with uncomfortable ethical quandaries related to this chapter's key themes of capitalism and sport's fight for scant resources. Those making these difficult decisions have to weigh up the benefits of the resources provided by such companies (and their contribution to the scale of activity they can pursue) against the promotion of products that can be seen as anti-sport in terms of the health claims often made for sport. There are no easy answers to these problems but sport development professionals should endeavour to resource their activities as ethically as they can, which means thinking on a global scale beyond the potential impact at local level. Scouting for alternative funding, sharing resources with other, like-minded groups and creating imaginative programmes that reduce the need for substantial funding are some of the ways in which this can be achieved. It will not always be easy and at times the moral principles that a team may hold may have to be compromised for a greater good. The key consideration is that these decisions are not made lightly and members of the team / organisation need to be able to justify to themselves that the right way forward has been taken, with all the variables and potential solutions considered.

SPORTING MACHINATIONS

An additional use of hegemonic analysis to evaluate sport development is the application of a critical lens to the various schemes and initiatives that have been marketed over the years with the apparent intention of tackling inequalities within sports participation. I have promoted and heralded such schemes in my own working life and yet the constant need to 'repackage and reinvigorate' old schemes to tackle the same problems starts to become wearying at best. For thirty years outreach programmes ranging from Action Sport to the more recent Sportivate (Sport England 2012) have tried to find solutions but I conclude that sport development professionals will not make any long term impact whilst capitalism is the adopted system of the West. This is not to say that sport development professionals claim to be able to change the world through such programmes, but the claims of short term improvements in crime reduction, participation rates, etc. need to be set in the context of the negligible outcomes achieved in the long term.

This is why this chapter questions the need for the politicisation of sport development, and why the bottom-up approach encouraged throughout this book should perhaps be at the forefront of any role undertaken by sport development professionals who desire and advocate social justice. This is not intended to disrespect the purposeful and energetic way in which sport development professionals do their jobs; in my view, relative to those in comparable professions they are undervalued, underpaid and not empathised with. Most of us though do not enter this field for the financial gains available elsewhere, yet we continue to swim against impossible currents without ever having the capability to reach the utopian land of equality and justice. Even if there was a concerted effort within the UK to achieve such radical change its impact would be blighted if this endeavour was not replicated internationally. As Eagleton (2011:16–17) suggests:

> If a socialist nation failed to win international support in a world where production was specialized and divided among different nations, it would be unable to draw upon the global resources needed to abolish scarcity.

STRATEGIC INTERNATIONALISATION OF SPORT DEVELOPMENT

A more strategic network involving information swapping, shared practice, shared resources and shared experiences therefore needs to be pursued. This will help to create a commonality across borders that strengthen the ability of sport development professionals to bring about significant change. Although this may appear unrealistic to many there are pockets of activity already happening across Europe, using sport as a tool to get messages across in society. Tucker (2011) and Totten (2011) have written about how football clubs across Europe have been united in their fight against racism, sexism, homophobia and capitalism. Sport development professionals would benefit from using such networks as a starting point to alternative practice. This bottom-up approach is crucial in creating the necessary ownership and empowerment that those at grass roots level need to make positive changes within their communities and beyond.

190

SUMMARY

This chapter may sometimes come across like one left wing radical's opportunistic rant at the political system. Yet this is often the problem faced with such views. Ralph Miliband (1969), the late father of New Labour's Miliband brothers made an insightful observation of how this works in Britain to ensure the protection of the established elite. His example within the context of the media, although written over 40 years ago still has resonance. He states how the media accept views of left and right wing persuasions within certain parameters as it is good for the readership to see that the media represents views from all aspects and ideologies, and even occasionally criticises the powerful. However, Miliband goes on to explain that once any individual or group steps outside of those parameters then they are automatically stripped of their credibility by being labelled as the 'loony left or the dangerous right'.

Noam Chomsky also highlights how this system works from an early age in terms of the filtering which takes place to ensure that only those who are willing to contribute (or at least not destabilise) the established order gain positions of power and influence. In an interview with Andrew Marr (1996), the BBC political correspondent, Chomsky outlines how school reports, employment references, etc. have subtle messages for prospective employers that point out 'troublemakers'. Herman and Chomsky (1994) go further and discuss the 'propaganda model' that again alludes to the media, etc. and how those in power are able to manufacture consent from citizens.

Applying this to sport and sport development professionals, it is crucial that we play our part in evolving the next generation of politicised communities if we are serious about having any long term impact on inequality and producing a more just society. Undoubtedly there are those who love working in sport purely for the thrill of helping develop the next gold medal winner and have no interest in contributing to any kind of political reform (or revolution) that involves them thinking about politics. Their role is important but those same people should not claim to be contributing to wider social agendas, for instance helping to reduce crime by 'keeping kids off the street'. This is an overused argument which lacks rigour. We must not forget about the beauty of sport and its potential to bring excitement, fitness, achievement and social cohesion into our lives, but we must also be aware of the distraction it can produce. If we really care about the people with whom we work then we need to deal with the challenging questions that increase awareness of the power actually possessed by those who perceive themselves as powerless.

We need to work hard to create communities of practice that share experience and knowledge in order to help build provision and community links from grassroots and not from the top down. We need to have the courage and conviction to challenge the existing policy and practice that papers over the cracks and has no real long term benefits for those it espouses to cater for. We need to create opportunities for people to develop the skills and networks that will help them to organise and unite with others to tackle social ills such as sexism, racism, homophobia and so on, but at the same time not become so fragmented that we become isolated in pursuit of single causes.

This needs to be done in the classroom on sport development degree courses in raising the profile of authentic community sport development; in the dressing rooms of sport teams where we can challenge prejudicial attitudes through providing information on some of the falsities we are fed from sources such as the media and politicians; in the community centres where we can engage community groups in problematising issues faced and their root causes, therefore creating a better understanding of what needs to be done to solve them; we need to pressure local councillors and politicians in Westminster to challenge austerity measures that deny the resources communities need to help make the changes needed. We must also think beyond our local boundaries and acknowledge that we cannot solve a lot of these problems by thinking inwardly. Instead we need to think more globally about what is happening to millions of people around the world and that we need to fight back to wrest control from those who hoard an inordinate amount of resources and power for their own selfish accumulation of wealth.

Quite clearly this chapter has not always been about working within existing political and policy frameworks, which for some may be a problem. For those people this may not seem helpful in terms of useful advice for their day to day working lives. No apology is made for this. Sport is a fertile context within which to engage young people in particular with the political processes that impact upon their everyday lives. This should not be done in a manner that deters them from asking about and engaging with the difficult issues they face. It needs to be done gradually and thoughtfully, but it must be done. If not, a new

192

scheme will be introduced in a few years time to replace the current one that has seen its shelf life expire. The poverty and other social issues that we continually seek to tackle through sport will still be present. If this means that we need to politicise ourselves more by reading widely and engaging in political debates at conferences, team meetings, etc. then so be it. If we do not do this then we are accepting a fate of remedial change that shifts problems around without ever making the significant changes of which we are truly capable.

LEARNING ACTIVITIES

Developing skills

See below some of the factors stated in the National Occupational Standards (Skills Active 2010) that impact upon sport development and of which professionals in the field should have knowledge:

- International, national and local political ideology and policy that influences sporting policy and processes e.g. Lottery funding and free-swimming initiative.

Thinking about your own organisation, who are the key policy makers and strategists that impact upon your working lives and what are their personal ideologies? How does this complement or clash with your working culture and philosophy and what steps can you take to influence this? What lobbying groups are active around your area with whom you can make alliances (this may require some digging around)? Who is the best person or people to act as gatekeepers to the information you need to gain access to these groups? How can you ensure your strategic goals harmonise with the political influences of these future stakeholders?

Role play

If you have a team whose members are comfortable around each other then try to create a role play situation that allows you to engage with some prevalent social issues within the community you serve. See below the different factors suggested within the National Occupational Standards that can impact upon sport development:

- Equality issues e.g. age, disability, gender, race, religion and belief, sexual orientation, gender re-assignment, social class and sporting ability.

Can you create a back story for individuals to adopt and then get one of the team to take the role of the sport development professional? The 'professional' should then seek to create dialogue with the group or individual to allow a discussion to take place about the circumstances that affect their participation and lives in general. Thinking about and suggesting solutions to the problems faced, as well as how to carry out the conversation may help to uncover ways and means of engaging more meaningfully with participants in the field, leading to longer and deeper relationships with impact. This is something that can be utilised by students either in study groups or via modules.

Developing knowledge

The political compass

Visit www.politicalcompass.org and complete the task along with others in your team/student study group. Discuss the findings from each of your results and discuss the implications for your working practice and/or relationships. Think about how you can draw upon these discussions to influence your future practice and knowledge of political issues that may permeate the lives of the participants you work with.

Networks

Despite the often pretentious way in which this term can be used I can think of no better way to describe the need for contact to be made with a range of contacts beyond your local boundaries. The internet is an excellent means of finding out about and making contact with a diverse range of groups and organisations that can help to share experiences and solutions to common social problems. How this is resourced is a challenge, but in keeping with the message of the chapter it is important that the parochial nature of how we work is broken down to allow an exploration into a better future. Raising awareness within your organisation of good practice happening elsewhere, from which you can

194

learn as well as offering advice to others is an outcome that can hopefully be gained here. This is also vital for students to gain an appreciation of the different organisations working within sport across national boundaries (maybe even doing case studies on them whilst at university). Hopefully this will lead them to becoming more enlightened graduates entering the workplace.

REFERENCES

Adamson, W. (1980) *Hegemony and Revolution: Antonio Gramsci's Political and Cultural Theory*. Berkeley, University of California Press.

Bramham, P. (2001) 'Sports Policy'. In Hylton, K., Bramham, P., Jackson, D. and Nesti, M. *Sport Development: Policy, Process and Practice*. London, Routledge, pp. 7–18.

Bramham, P. (2008) 'Sports Policy'. In Hylton, K. and Bramham, P. *Sport Development: Policy, Process and Practice*, 2nd ed. London, Routledge, pp. 10–24.

Chomsky, N. (2011) 'Noam Chomsky: is state capitalism making life better?' Available at http://www.youtube.com/watch?v=HFxYyXGMfZM.

Coalter, F. (2007) *A Wider Social Role For Sport: Who's Keeping the Score?* London, Routledge.

Credit Suisse Research Institute (2011) 'Global Wealth Report, October 2010'. In 'Inequality.org: Connecting the dots on a growing divide'. *Inequality Data & Statistics*. Available at http://www.Inequality.org/inequality-data-statistics/.

Davies, W. (2000) 'Understanding Strategy'. *Strategy & Leadership* 28/5 pp.25–30.

DCMS (2011) 'Young People's Sport. What We Do'. Available at http://www.culture.gov.uk/what_we_do/sport/7440.aspx.

Eagleton, T. (2011) *Why Marx was Right*. New Haven, Yale University Press.

Freire, P. (1972) *Pedagogy of the Oppressed*. Harmondsworth, Penguin.

Goulding, R. (2011) 'Big Society? Big Deal'. *Red Pepper*. Available at http://www.redpepper.org.uk/big-society-big-deal/.

Hargreaves, J. (1986) *Sport, Power and Culture: A Social and Historical Analysis of Popular Sports in Britain*. London, Polity Press.

Hall, M. (2011) 'The age of the deserving and undeserving poor is back, only this time the leader of the British Labour Party has joined the Tories and Lib-Dems in propagating such wicked nonsense'. *Organized Rage*. 15 June 2011. Available at http://www.organizedrage.com/2011/06/age-of-deserving-and-undeserving-poor.html.

Herman, E. and Chomsky, N. (1994) *Manufacturing Consent: The Political Economy of the Mass Media*. New York, Vintage.

Houlihan, B. and White, A. (2002) *The Politics of Sports Development*. London, Routledge.

Leach, R. (2002) *Political Ideology in Britain.* London, Palgrave.

Ledwith, M. and Springett, J. (2010) *Participatory Practice: Community-Based Action for Transformative Change.* Bristol, The Policy Press.

Miliband, R. (1969) *The State In Capitalist Society: The Analysis of the Western System of Power.* London, Quartet books.

Prynn, J. (2008) '"Millionaire bankers" blamed for credit crisis'. *London Evening Standard.* 24th April. Available from http://www.thisislondon.co.uk/ standard/article-23480081-millionaire-bankers-blamed-for-credit-crisis.do.

Richards, S. (2011) 'Can the Big Society Work?' *The Independent.* 8th February. Available at http://www.independent.co.uk/news/uk/politics/can-the-big-society-work-2207352.html.

Shaxson, N. (2011) *Treasure Islands:Tax Havens and the Men Who Stole the World.* London: The Bodley Head.

SkillsActive (2010) 'National Occupational Standards for Sports Development (Level 3)'. London, SkillsActive.

Socialist Worker (2011) 'Don't Let Torries Play Race Card'. *Socialist Worker.* 12th February 2011, p. 1 and 2, London, Larkham P&P.

Sport England (2012) *Sportivate.* Available at http://www.sportengland.org/ about_us/places_people_play/sportivate.aspx.

Schwarzmantel, J. (2008) *Ideology and Politics.* London, Sage.

The Big Idea (1996) *Noam Chomsky.* London, BBC [video: VHS].

The Political Compass (2001–02) 'The Political Compass'. Available at http:// www.politicalcompass.org.

Totten, M. (2011) 'Freedom through Football; A tale of football, community, activism and resistance'. *Community and Inclusion in Leisure Research and Sport Development.* LSA Publication No. 114.

Treanor, J. and Wearden, G. (2011) 'Anger as JP Morgan bankers get $10bn pay and bonus pot', *The Guardian.* 14th January. Available at http://www. guardian.co.uk/business/2011/jan/14/jp-morgan-bankers-share-10bn.

Tucker, L. (2011) 'Forza Forza Republica: a case study of politics and socialist culture in a Sunday league football club'. *Community and Inclusion in Leisure Research and Sport Development.* LSA Publication No. 114

Veal, A. (2010) *Leisure, Sport and Tourism, Politics, Policy and Planning.* 3rd ed. Oxfordshire, CABI Tourism Texts.

Whannel, G. (1983) *Blowing the Whistle: the Politics of* Sport. London, Pluto.

Whannel, G. (2008) *Culture, Politics and Sport: Blowing the Whistle, Revisited.* London, Routledge.

Williams, R. (1977) *Marxism and Literature.* Oxford, Oxford University Press.

Wright, A. (1986) *Socialisms: Theories and Practice.* Oxford, Oxford University Press.

Youth Sport Trust (2011) 'New Funding Provides Lifeline for School Sport'. Loughborough, Youth Sport Trust. Available at http://ssx.youthsporttrust. org/page/business-honours-club-news-detail/sport-funding/index.html.

CHAPTER 9

STRATEGIC LEADERSHIP

LEE TUCKER

INTRODUCTION

> Collaborative leadership is an influence relationship among
> leaders and collaborators who intend significant changes that
> reflect their mutual interests.
>
> (Rost 2008:57)

The purpose of beginning the chapter with the above quote is to try and
encapsulate the philosophical and practical essence of what strategic
leadership should involve. Strategic leadership as described in this
chapter is not just for those people in recognised leadership positions; it
is not for 'leaders' per se. The intention of this is to acknowledge that
anybody and everybody in a sport development team, unit or organisation
should be given the responsibility to contribute to the strategic leadership
goals that 'the organisation' works to and therefore where appropriate,
the messages conveyed are aimed at all those with an interest in this
process. However, it is also acknowledged that there are those with the
official responsibility to write and permeate the strategic vision of an
organisation, and thus some of the chapter's themes need to be absorbed
and acted upon by those with the 'authority' to do so. At times, these
individuals have the additional responsibility of ensuring all
stakeholders are included and empowered within the strategic process,
which is a central tenet of this chapter.

The strategic leadership of any organisation should be aiming to reach a
better place in the future, to improve and develop. Sport development is

about contributing to the common good. It is fundamentally about creating opportunities and building relationships. It is about knocking down barriers, helping to rid society of prejudice and discrimination and to develop community cohesion and spirit through sport. I believe that sport development professionals at all levels have a leadership role to play in contributing to these goals. The intention is not to devalue the role of elite sport, but this is not where my focus lies in terms of sport development for this chapter, therefore my interest is in development through sport and not of sport.

Trying to break down or avoid any barriers that create a 'them and us' situation should be a key concern for any leader involved in the formulation, implementation and measurement of the organisation's strategy. By being empathetic and inclusive, strategic leaders can ensure that those people whose work is impacted upon by a strategy can feel a sense of ownership throughout the process. It is common sense that people want to be valued and appreciated for the work that they do, and therefore it is the responsibility of those leaders to create an appropriate environment that encourages a meaningful engagement by all concerned with the strategic process. As discussed later in this chapter it should be the aim of every strategic leader to adopt the authentic transformational leadership role discussed by Bass and Steidlmeier (1998). This is a role that positively and genuinely supports/encourages others to be the best that they can be (incorporating their leadership development), and simultaneously helps to ensure the success of the strategic process.

It is appreciated that there may be calls for 'more pragmatism' but it is suggested that during such busy periods in modern working conditions that offer little escape from the day-to-day operational aspects of the job, there is a need for sport development professionals to take time out to do some blue-sky thinking that may re-energise those involved into looking at different ways of doing things. This just might create better working environments for all – this is what I hope to achieve within this chapter.

PURPOSE OF CHAPTER

This chapter will focus upon how the strategic process should be led from vision to implementation focusing upon the bottom-up consultation process, which is crucial to community sport development (Hylton and

Lee Tucker

Totten 2008). It will draw upon the experiences of those practitioners who have led the strategic process and therefore provide a 'real world' picture of the opportunities as well as pitfalls of this process. Students will gain an insight into the practicalities of strategic leadership as well as a critical awareness of leadership theory and its importance in motivating others. Practitioners will gain an insight into 'other ways of leading' that they may use to inform their future 'inclusive' leadership practice.

LEADERSHIP

Before getting into the detail of how the above can be achieved it is worth providing a brief overview of the different ways in which leadership can be viewed. Grint (2005) offers an excellent and interesting analysis of leadership from four different perspectives. The first examines the person (is leadership about characteristics and attributes of an individual?); next, position is considered (is leadership about the status that comes with being at the top of a hierarchical structure within an organisation?); followed by process (is leadership about process, including learning how to become a leader and the behaviours expected and desired in a specific leadership role?); and finally, results (is good leadership evident through success?). Although not specifically based around sport development, other sporting leadership experts have produced models such as basketball coach John Wooden's Pyramid of Success (in Wooden and Jamison, 2005), which proposes 15 different factors that contribute to successful leadership. Chelladurai (1999) discusses his multi-dimensional model of leadership and how it has a close relationship to coaching. These may be useful models to draw upon and contextualise for sport development professionals. There are also many other academic and business models and interpretations of leadership by such authors as John Adair and Warren Bennis who provide their own toolkits for leaders.

Many other leadership styles, skills and behaviours, etc. that have been written about cannot be covered here, therefore we shall move on with the understanding that leadership is a contested concept that can mean many different things and be interpreted in many different ways by many different people. However, the focus of this chapter is on strategic leadership within the sport development sector so a useful starting point would be to determine what is meant by strategic leadership.

STRATEGIC LEADERSHIP

Notions of strategy have been discussed in earlier chapters and consequently are not further developed here. However, drawing on the earlier definition of strategy can be useful in helping us to distinguish the nature of strategic leadership. Strategic leadership is about the visioning, communicating, inspiring and empowering of the strategy to all stakeholders. The person or people responsible for these activities are the strategic leaders, and they must ensure that the strategy has an impact on the organisation in the hearts and minds of those who influence its success (Gill 2001). As can already be ascertained from the introduction is the importance placed on ALL of those with a vested interest in the success of a strategy and not just those with the designated status/title of 'leaders'. An example of this is that those at Sport England headquarters might have had total belief in their strategy 'Grow, Sustain, Excel' but if they did not engage and convince those working within the eight regional offices then it is unlikely that the strategy will have been communicated in the necessary way to achieve its potential. Therefore, it is important to acknowledge the important relationship between leaders and followers (collaborators).

THE LEADERSHIP-FOLLOWERSHIP DYNAMIC

Grint (2007) discusses the concept of phronesis, which explains how lived experience informs current and future leadership behaviour. Implicit within this notion is that leaders learn whilst following, by observing others (in terms of strategic leadership as discussed by Duggan (2002)) and forming/developing their own leadership style and skills. Most leadership/followership research focuses on leaders, with less attention given to the follower's experience (Collinson 2005). This is despite there being a lot more followers than leaders, added to which it is often the skills of the followers that determine the success of a strategy.

However, there is a burgeoning body of work on followership by authors such as Riggio, Chaleff and Lipman-Blumen (2008) that is beginning to acknowledge the importance of followers within this often over-hierarchical relationship. Chaleff (1995) has written a meditation of followership that can be used as a set of ethical guidelines for followers to utilise in their role. Kelley (2008) has created a set of followership

200

styles that helps to distinguish between those 'star followers' who are capable of standing up to poor or unethical leadership, down to the 'sheep followers' who blindly accept decisions and orders from leaders irrespective of the intent or consequences. Hopefully, the outcome of this is that leaders start to pay attention to the indispensable contribution that 'followers' make and start to see them as empowered collaborators, rather than passive foot soldiers taking orders from those above them in hierarchical structures.

LEADERSHIP IN SPORT DEVELOPMENT AND THE NATIONAL OCCUPATIONAL STANDARDS

A range of issues provide challenges for those responsible for strategic leadership in a sport development context. Compared to other professions sport development does not have a plethora of well-paid jobs, which means that something else has to be on offer to maintain an effective and motivated workforce. However, despite the best efforts of those in positions of influence there is an inevitable turnover of staff, which creates situations of transition to be dealt with. One of the mechanisms introduced to aid the development of SDPs to deal with these issues is the National Occupational Standards for Sports Development.

The National Occupational Standards, published by SkillsActive (2010) have introduced benchmark leadership behaviours, knowledge and understanding for sport development professionals to compare against. Key aspects permeating the Standards are the visioning, communicating and empowering factors of leadership central to this chapter. It is expected that the National Occupational Standards will provide the necessary framework for the continuing professional development of those within the sector.

LEADERSHIP V MANAGEMENT

Although these two concepts have often been used interchangeably there are distinct differences, which can be drawn upon to inform us of how to distinguish one from the other. Kotter (1999:11) explains how

...the fundamental purpose of management is to keep the current system functioning. The fundamental purpose of leadership is to produce change, especially nonincremental change.

From this we can gain a sense of the different skills needed for each and Daft (1999:39) draws upon Kotter's work in creating the following model that categorises them into six different areas.

Table 9.1 should not be used for a summative assessment of whether you are a leader or a manager. Leadership is something that can be developed, and although the opportunity to develop leadership is often influenced by various societal factors, it is a learned process and not a birthright.

Table 9.1   Distinguishing between leadership and management

	Management	*Leadership*
Direction	■ Planning and budgeting ■ Keeping an eye on the bottom line	■ Creating vision and strategy ■ Keeping an eye on the horizon
Alignment	■ Organising and staffing ■ Directing and controlling ■ Creating boundaries	■ Creating shared culture and values ■ Helping others grow ■ Reducing boundaries
Relationships	■ Focusing on objects – producing/selling goods and services ■ Based on a position of power ■ Acting as boss	■ Focusing on people – inspiring and motivating followers ■ Based on personal power ■ Acting as coach, facilitator, servant
Personal qualities	■ Emotional distance ■ Expert mind ■ Talking ■ Conformity ■ Insight into organisation	■ Emotional connections (heart) ■ Open Mind (mindfulness) ■ Listening (communication) ■ Non-conformity (courage) ■ Insight into self (integrity)
Outcomes	■ Maintains stability	■ Creates change, often radical change

202

BARRIERS AND OPPORTUNITIES IN LEADING THE STRATEGIC PROCESS

As alluded to above, one of the key barriers for leaders is their mindset. Bennis (1998) discusses how socialisation at an early age through various institutional and structural factors such as family, school, etc. shapes us but we do not become leaders until we decide for ourselves how to be. Therefore, the way in which you perceive the world, your organisation and the people you work with is crucial in determining the values and behaviours you will possess and demonstrate as a leader. Without a positive outlook that is authentic in its desire to develop the organisation and people you work with, you become your own worst barrier to success. This will inevitably impact upon your relationships and ultimately the successful implementation of your strategy.

A wider and more problematic barrier within sport development (as well as most other professions) is created by societal structures and discrimination that accompany them, meaning that significant sections of the population do not get the opportunity to lead the strategic process. Most leaders in most industries have traditionally been white, middle-class men and although this situation has improved in recent years due to targeted legislation and policy, some barriers still remain. The education of future leaders is something that is now widely recognised by training centres and various institutions. A good example of this is UK Sport's Women and Leadership Development Programme (WLDP). Recruiting and training leaders at the strategic level of sport development, particularly from traditionally under-represented groups, will hopefully breed new ideas, enhance the quality of leaders and engender better sport development outcomes. This is hopefully a step in the right direction towards creating more opportunities for more people to take on leadership challenges.

There are also many opportunities for leaders in the strategic process. There is a great opportunity through the strategic process to really get the workforce on board with the vision that the organisation is trying to create. This can only be done successfully with the buy-in of the workforce, and therefore how you communicate with, enthuse, inspire and empower stakeholders is crucial. The launch of a strategy is a key time in any organisation's life cycle as it is an opportunity to improve performance or change direction; hence it has that 'fresh start' appeal. However, enshrined within the strategic process there needs to be an authentic, meaningful engagement to improve all concerned. It should serve as much more than a gimmick to buy time for poor performance and leadership.

A LEADERFUL WORKFORCE

Getting people onside with a strategy will be much easier if they believe that they are being listened to and have the opportunity to input into the strategic process, as opposed to being seen as followers who wait for instructions from senior management. A way of creating this environment is through the use of the concept that Grint (2005) calls 'leaderful teams'. Similar to the notion of 'flat organisational structures', Grint discusses the advantages of working in a heterarchy rather than a hierarchy. The key merit of this is that with an open mind you can tap into the many different talents that exist within the workforce: followers are substituted by collaborators. Kelly Simmons led a consultative approach for the Football Association (FA) in compiling The National Game Strategy. Giving stakeholders the opportunity to input opinions and ideas regarding the FA's strategy was a fundamental aspect of the strategy formulation.

The various skills that those in sport development should possess are comprehensively covered in the National Occupational Standards. The development of such skills will obviously take time and resources but one of the benefits is that more ownership can be taken of more tasks by more people without the need of a top-down management approach to work allocation. Success with this approach is heavily predicated upon teamwork. Heterarchies are dependent on effective teamwork, and any individual who has an alternative agenda that seeks glory or power can bring the team and the concept of heterarchal organisations crashing down. The Table 9.2 highlights some examples of positive and negative teams.

As can be seen from Table 9.2 there is still room for debate, disagreement and tension within teams but the key concern is that it is done for the right reasons in terms of developing the team and achieving the task. As a strategic leader within sport development it is up to you to create the necessary frameworks and systems to allow this to happen and encourage all to contribute. If you are able to do this then you are creating an environment that fosters inclusivity and the empowerment of collaborators (the workforce).

204

Table 9.2 Examples of positive and negative team work

Positive examples and aspects of team work	Negative examples and aspects of team work
Shared responsibility	Blame culture
Honesty	Deception
Team orientated	Self-interest
Communicative (open channel)	Non-communicative (selected/closed channel)
Hard working (effect: creates trust)	Scheming/minimal input (effect: creates distrust)
Creative tension (progressive, open debate)	Team conflict (arguing, fall out)
Pool resources (ideas, experience, etc.); effect: karma	Covet knowledge (effect: no-one to share success with, team will be less effective)
Opinionated	Narrow minded (parochial)
PHILOSOPHY	
What did we do? – shared value	What did I do? – individual goal
OUTCOME	
Maximise potential – no regrets	Unfulfilled potential – regrets

INCLUSION AND EMPOWERMENT

A quote from an ancient philosopher named Lao Tzu (600 BC) encapsulates a lot of what is meant by the terms inclusion and empowerment from the perspective of strategic leadership. It has been quoted in many texts with slight variations, but this adapted version sums it up quite effectively:

> A leader is best when people rarely know she exists
>
> Not so good when people serve and acclaim her
>
> Worst when they despise her
>
> Fail to honour people, they fail to honour you
>
> But of a good leader, who talks little, when her work is done, her aim fulfilled,
>
> They will all say, "We did this ourselves".

The sentiment behind this is empowering people to believe that they can achieve without necessarily being cajoled, forced or told what to do. The message for leaders here is to know when and how to lead from behind rather than always being the dominant figure (this is expanded upon in the last section of this chapter). If people are to believe in themselves then first they need their leaders to believe and trust in them. Only by including people in the decision-making process, giving them the responsibility to act independently and allowing them the opportunity (and confidence) to make mistakes (as well as to learn from them and put things right) will they then have the opportunity and experience of achieving great things for themselves and their organisation.

Two of the key words that should be part of the strategic leader's armoury in this respect are trust and motivation. Trusting others to take responsibility via delegation not just of menial tasks but also of important ones will enhance the motivation of the recipients of these opportunities. A key objective for the strategic leader should be to create an environment where people want to come to work each day. This may be a useful exercise for you to do today. Look around you: how many people can you honestly say want to be in work today? Forget about the fact that most people would rather be on holiday etc., and think about whether it was a grind for those people around you to come in today or not. The next piece of honest reflection is to look at yourself and ask 'Is it because of me or despite me that these people do or do not want to be in work today?' Once you have the answers to those questions you can then put into action your plans to either change the situation (if necessary) or build upon it further to improve the environment you and others work in.

One of the key factors in determining whether people feel included and empowered within the organisation is the extent to which they buy into the vision of the organisation. Is it something that is central to their working philosophy or is it just words printed on a strategy document that needed to be done to show that the management they were actually doing something? It is to this that our attention now turns.

THE IMPORTANCE OF VISIONING

I spend time trying to convince people that the vision is right, to get people to agree with me, so we're all [working] together,' he

Lee Tucker

said, but 'there comes a time at the end of the day that you find out some people just aren't buying it. They don't buy your values and they don't buy your vision. They're the frowners. And they bring everybody else down. Shoot the frowner. It makes you feel good…They're the ones who are actually the obstacles, and at a certain point you have to just say, "you're out of here. Time for you to go."

(Diamond 2009)

Although quite a blunt summation of what happens to those not buying into the vision, this quote from Harris Diamond (CEO of public relations firm Weber Shandwick) highlights the importance and investment that strategic leaders place on the vision of their organisation. However, something that needs to be addressed before discussing the importance of visioning is how important it is for people within the organisation to believe in those that espouse the vision. This is to say that in most organisations some kind of hierarchy will probably be in place, with those at the top of the hierarchy seen as the leader(s). John C. Maxwell (2007:171), a successful CEO and leadership author states how often during leadership seminars he fields questions about vision and answers it is initially more important for people to believe in the leader. He explains how:

…many people who approach the area of vision in leadership have it all backward. They believe that if the cause is good enough, people will automatically buy into it and follow (*does this sound familiar?* – my emphasis). But that's not how leadership really works. People don't at first follow worthy causes. They follow worthy leaders who promote causes they can believe in. People buy into the leader first, then the leader's vision. Having an understanding of that changes your whole approach to leading people.

So the message here, as the chapter thus far has intimated, is for leaders to be the type of person that other people will believe in first before thinking about getting others to subscribe to organisational visions. However, once this interpersonal credibility has been achieved it is then important to get others to buy into the vision. As with a lot of these key concepts such as leadership, management, strategy, etc., vision is another term that needs to be defined before discussing it further.

WHAT IS A 'VISION'?

Adair defines vision as "foresight together with an unusual discernment of the right way forwards" (2002:110). This means that whoever is responsible for creating the vision must have the ability to judge many different factors that impact upon an organisation (internal and external environments) as well as being able to 'predict the future', to see where the opportunities lie ahead and tailor the vision to be adaptable enough to exploit the opportunities that will be created.

The vision of an organisation is something that is often described in a strategic document with the aim of giving people an indication of the organisation's overriding philosophy in terms of a desired future state. The vision also needs to articulate something new or a change to the organisation in terms of its positioning, philosophy, goals, etc., otherwise what is it being done for? Mintzberg, Ahlstrand and Lampel (1998) offer what may be a slightly more romantic and perhaps purer sense of what a vision should be. Drawing upon the work of Bennis and Nanus (1985) they state that a vision should not necessarily have to be written down for it to be effective. However, it does need to tap into the emotions and motivations of those at every level of the organisation.

OWNERSHIP OF VISION

Bennis and Nanus (1985) discuss how a clear sense of direction shared by individuals within an organisation helps to clarify their roles and empower them. The vision within a sport development context is critical in articulating the contribution it will make to its surrounding community. If this vision is shared, it embodies a consensus at all levels and the likelihood is that it will succeed in energising everyone and instilling worthiness about the work that people are carrying out; they will believe that they are making a difference. It is this ownership of the vision that will ensure they want to come to work.

PERMEATING THE VISION

The value of conversation and interaction between those working within an organisation should not be underestimated. This is the message that

208

Lewis, Passmore and Cantore (2008) stress in their excellent book *Appreciative Inquiry for Change Management*. The message of this book is that by participating in a series of activities where people share their stories and dreams, people can get on board with the values and aims of an organisation. The positive emotions drawn on through this process could be useful to you and your team, revealing stories about what is good about your organisation which could be used to design the vision for the future. Seeing conversation as an end in itself, rather than leaders being resolutely devoted to outputs, is part of the appreciative inquiry process.

COMMITMENT AND CONSISTENCY

Once a vision has been established then it is important that the behaviour of those signed up is consistent with their pledge. Ensuring that your actions are in line with the values and expected behaviours to which you have committed is one of the ways in which leaders can lead by example. This is something that Kouzes and Posner (2002) consider to be important and what they call 'modelling the way'. Bennis believes it is crucial if you are to inspire others you must act in a similar way to them. However, as Cialdini (2007) suggests the 'consistency rule' can also have its disadvantages as often people become tied to a commitment and therefore do not show the flexibility to adapt to factors that may challenge these initial pledges. An example where this may occur in sport development is where initial commitments to certain partnerships or projects set out in strategies are not revisited, despite a change of circumstances in the external environment (Chapter 3 examines the various factors that could influence these changes). Adaptable leadership is necessary within sport development, but conviction to your core values and beliefs should not be so prone to regular adaptation.

AUTHENTIC TRANSFORMATIONAL LEADERSHIP

In order for you to become an authentic transformational leader your values and core beliefs should include empathy towards the needs of others. But what does it mean to be an authentic transformational leader? To understand the term it is useful to compare it to other styles of leadership. Bass and Steidlmeier (1998) do this by analysing transactional leadership and pseudo transformational leadership. According to Bass and Steidlmeier, transactional leadership involves contingent reinforcement. Followers are either motivated by rewards and praise that a leader gives them or they change their behaviour if given negative feedback, threats, disciplinary actions, etc.

Therefore, transactional leadership is about doing something to get something back. Authentic transformational leadership, however, contains four components: idealised influence, inspirational motivation, intellectual stimulation and individualised consideration. As can be gathered from these 'attributes', transformational leadership is about creating a challenging, supportive and stimulating environment in which people can grow and prosper. This does not mean that the two different styles cannot be combined (after all, transactions still need to be made), but monetary and positional rewards should not be the only drivers for people to want to do well within an organisation. This relates to the earlier point of engaging not only the minds but also the hearts of the people who work within the organisation. It should be apparent that there is a shared culture of wanting each other to do well and ensuring that the support mechanisms are in place to achieve this.

The danger that emerges from this theory is that of the pseudo transformational leader. This is the type of leader who appears supportive on the outside but this is part of their deception. Again, Bass and Steidlmeier (1998) give us a valuable insight into the behaviour of the pseudo transformational leader:

> They may have the public image of a saint but privately are deceptive devils. They may appear to their followers to behave as a transformational leader but the appearance is deceptive for inwardly they remain more interested in themselves than their followers. They knowingly focus their followers on fantasies instead of attainable visions.

This is the type of leader who may say that they are fighting your cause at the managers meeting, who laughs and jokes with you in the office but who is primarily full of self-interest and would sooner let you go than take a hit in the wage packet. This is the type of leader who talks the talk but certainly fails to walk the walk.

210

To ensure that the appropriate leadership style is present within your team and organisation an open channel of communication must be in operation to allow honest feedback without fear of reprisal. It may be worth conducting a confidential test/questionnaire to see if this is the case for you and your team, giving people the opportunity to really say what they think. Staff feedback should not be taken lightly and even when things appear largely positive it is still worth taking the time to deal with individual concerns. Any negative feelings should be seen as a problem for the team to remedy and not for any individual to 'get over it'. One of the ways to work towards this 'utopian culture' is to ensure people have the opportunity to develop the type of leadership skills that can give them the confidence to handle such situations.

LEADERSHIP TRAINING

Part of the authentic transformational leader's role is to develop the leadership skills of others around them. Getting others to job shadow through the various stages of strategy is a useful way of taking potential leaders through the process of formulating and leading the strategic process. Actual leadership mentoring (rather than generic, appraisal-style mentoring) is another way in which to develop the understanding of what it means to lead a team and organisation through the various issues that emerge (the use of the National Occupational Standards may be beneficial here). There is also external support for 'future leaders', which can be tapped into, but this needs to be researched and planned to ensure it meets the desired outcomes for both the individual and the team. A good example of this type of training is that which has been offered by UK Sport, the CCPR and the British Olympic Foundation aimed at getting more women into leadership positions through training and mentoring schemes. This Women and Leadership Development programme may only initially be for a minority of women but it is hoped that the outcomes of training of this sort will cascade and benefit others (Langley 2006). Although quite specific it is this type of programme that may be required to meet specialised needs for particular individuals within your organisation. The message is that leadership should be something you proactively seek to develop and not just something that you do.

SUMMARY

Effective strategic leadership involves creating an empowering culture, which draws upon the talents of all team members as well providing support for their future as strategic leaders. Leading the strategic process is cyclical as we are always in one phase or another, whether this is formulating strategy, implementing it, measuring its success or looking at future strategic aims. Therefore, the ability to remain true to the values and beliefs that underpin the organisation is vital in ensuring all those within the organisation feel appreciated, listened to and empowered to contribute in a meaningful way to the strategic process.

The National Occupational Standards offer a framework against which sport development professionals can plot and measure their development, and this should be a positive step forward for the industry. The NOS regarding leadership is a useful tool for those aspiring to assume the responsibility of leading the strategic future within all strands of sport development. Ensuring that the Standards permeate influential fields within sport development such as national governing bodies, sport development courses at further and higher education institutions and sport development units, so that they are recognised more widely, is a challenge for all those hoping to bring more recognition to sport development as a profession.

There are many barriers that exist within sport development organisations as well as within the communities that sport development seeks to support. Accepting that these barriers exist, whilst proactively looking to encourage more diversity within leadership positions provides a challenge to all those in positions of power within sport development, and should be a compulsory part of the ongoing strategic process within organisations.

Teamwork within sport development should be prioritised over individuality. Having an appreciation of others' skills and strengths as well as their allowable weaknesses is essential in developing team intelligence that can be used as a foundation for goal setting. There is a need to ensure that open channel communication networks are utilised so that people can talk openly and frequently. Fostering this environment of trust and reciprocity is essential to developing team morale and creating a spirit of togetherness.

Getting all stakeholders to buy into a vision can be a time consuming yet empowering and rewarding activity. Ensuring that people buy into you

212

as a leader before trying to sell them a vision is of critical importance. However, once this is achieved it is important to create a sense of ownership of the vision by seeking the opinions of others who will ultimately be given the responsibility of turning the vision into something more tangible. Allowing the time and space for conversations is a simple yet productive technique in giving people the opportunity to make their voices heard.

Finally, all those in positions of power (or with the ambition to be in such a position) should aim to be an authentic transformational leader if they are serious about being people centred, developing others and creating the appropriate environment for their organisation to flourish. Having a selfless attitude that entrusts others with responsibility and having the conviction to 'walk the talk' are necessary qualities if you are to make a difference in sport development. Supporting actions, such as making resources available for people to get training to develop their own leadership skills is one such way of demonstrating your investment in the talent of others.

LEARNING ACTIVITIES

Developing skills

The vision

Two of the National Occupational Standards outcomes in Standard A322 'Provide leadership in sport and active leisure' are:

1 Enable colleagues and/or stakeholders to contribute towards setting a clear direction.
2 Encourage a commitment to shared aims and objectives, within existing constraints (SkillsActive 2010).

Obviously these outcomes are concerned with the visioning process that organisations undergo. An exercise for this outcome is for readers to first of all articulate to themselves what they believe to be the vision of their organisation and then decide whether this vision is inclusive. An alternative is for the reader to practise writing up a set of aims and objectives (particularly useful for students), clearly articulating the differences between the two and how they link to an overall vision. This can be for anything that the reader feels appropriate, i.e. the vision for the sporting team that they are involved with, the organisation that they work in, etc.

Johari window

We all have our own perceptions of ourselves and of others which if not challenged, can sometimes lead to self-deception, a mindset that can lead to negativity within an organisation. Others will form their own perceptions that can lead to conflict, etc. The Johari window is a useful tool in developing self-awareness and providing useful evidence for personal development plans. Follow this link to the exercise, http://www.businessballs.com/johariwindowmodel.htm, and do the exercise with a specific focus on your leadership styles and skills.

Developing knowledge

Leadership analysis

This is an exercise that can be done in a variety of ways. Select four or five great leaders from throughout history. In your opinion, what are the attributes that made or make them great? What influence can these leaders have in your daily life as a leader? Ways in which this can be adapted include using it as an exercise with the rest of your team, and through the problem-solving process of synectics (Parker and Stone 2003) you may be able to adapt the findings of your discussion to solve real leadership issues/problems occurring in your own area of work.

REFERENCES

Adair, J. (2002) *Inspiring Leadership*. London, Thorogood.
Bass, B. and Steidlmeier, P. (1998) 'Ethics, Character and Authentic Transformational Leadership'. *The Leadership Quarterly*. (1999) 10(2) Summer, pp. 181–217.
Bennis, W. (1998) *On Becoming a Leader*. London, Arrow Books.
Bennis, W. and Nanus, B. (1985) *Leaders: The Strategies for Taking Charge*. New York, Harper & Row.

214

Business Balls (2010) 'The Johari Window'. Available at http://www. businessballs.com/johariwindowmodel.htm.

Chaleff, I. (1995) *The Courageous Follower; Standing Up to and for our Leaders.* San-Francisco, Berrett-Koehler Publishers.

Chelladurai, P. (1999) *Human Resource Management in Sport and Recreation.* Leeds, Human Kinetics.

Cialdini, R. (2007*) Influence: the Psychology of Persuasion.* New York, Collins.

Collinson, D. (2005) 'Rethinking Followership: a post-structuarlist analysis of follower identities'. *The Leadership Quarterly.* (2006) 17(2) April, pp. 179–189.

Daft, R. (1999) *Leadership: Theory and Practice.* Texas, Dryden Press.

Diamond, H. (2009) 'Negative Perceptions Can Trump Positive Messages: interview with Knowledge@Wharton'. Available at http://knowledge.whar ton.upenn.edu/article.cfm?articleid=2207.

Duggan, W. (2002*) Napoleon's Glance: The Secret of Strategy.* New York, Nation Books.

Gill, R. (2001) 'Beyond Transformational Leadership: developing vision, values and strategy'. In Bernard M. Bass Festschrift conference. Binghamton, New York, May 31–June 2.

Grint, K. (2005) *Leadership: Limits and Possibilities.* Basingstoke, Palgrave Macmillan.

Grint, K. (2007) 'Learning to Lead: can Aristotle help us find the road to wisdom'. *Leadership* 3(2) May, pp. 231–246.

Hylton, K. and Totten, M. (2008) 'Community Sports Development'. In Hylton, K. and Bramham, P. eds*. Sports Development: Policy, Process and Practice.* 2nd ed. Abingdon, Routledge, pp. 77–117.

Kelley, R. (2008) 'Rethinking Followership'. In Riggio, R., Chaleff, I. and Lipman-Blumen, J. eds. *The Art Of Followership: How Great Followers Create Great Leaders and Organizations.* San-Francisco, Jossey-Bass, pp. 5–16.

Kotter, J. (1999) *What Leaders Really Do.* Boston, Harvard Business School.

Kouzes, J. and Posner, B. (2002) *The Leadership Challenge.* 3rd ed. San Francisco, Jossey-Bass.

Langley, R. (2006) 'Women in Leadership Programme launched'. Available at http://www.uksport.gov.uk/news/women_in_leadership_programme_ launched/.

Lewis, S., Passmore, J. and Cantore, S. (2008) *Appreciative Inquiry for Change Management: Using AI to Facilitate Organizational Development.* London, Kogan Page.

Maxwell, J. (2007) *The 21 Irrefutable Laws of Leadership: Follow Them and People Will Follow You.* Nashville, Thomas Nelson.

Mintzberg, H., Ahlstrand, B. and Lampel, J. (1998) *Strategy Safari: The Guided Tour Through the Wilds of Strategic Management.* New York, Free Press.

Parker, C. and Stone, B. (2003) *Developing Management Skills for Leadership.* Essex, Pearson Education.

Riggio, R., Chaleff, I. and Lipman-Blumen, J. eds. (2008) *The Art of Followership: How Great Followers Create Great Leaders and Organizations.* San-Francisco, Jossey-Bass.

Rost, J. (2008) Followership: An Outmoded Concept. In Riggio, R., Chaleff, I. and Lipman-Blumen, J. eds. (2008) *The Art Of Followership How Great Followers Create Great Leaders and Organizations.* San-Francisco, Jossey-Bass, pp. 53–66.

SkillsActive (2010) 'National Occupational Standards for Sports Development'. Available at http://www.skillsactive.com/our-sectors/sport/national-occupational-standards/item/3260.

Wooden, J. and Jamison, S. (2005) *Wooden on Leadership.* New York, McGraw-Hill.

Lee Tucker

CHAPTER 10

A DIFFERENT BALL GAME? IN PURSUIT OF GREATER STRATEGIC COLLABORATION BETWEEN SPORT-SPECIFIC AND COMMUNITY SPORT DEVELOPMENT

JANINE PARTINGTON AND STEPHEN ROBSON

INTRODUCTION

This book's stated commitment to inclusive sport development is consummated in this and the following chapter as we consider the strategic implications of developing truly inclusive sport. What, if anything, is intrinsically different about the strategic development *of* sport compared to development *through* sport? How does this impact upon strategic decision-making and implementation? This chapter argues that assumptions of an irreconcilable division between community sport development (CSD) and sport-specific development (SSD) are conceptually flawed, and that attempting to work in either of these settings in isolation from the other impairs progress. We will examine the common weaknesses of the two approaches and consider how greater collaboration may lead to improved strategic outcomes.

Before attempting to address these questions it is helpful to briefly consider the unique characteristics of national governing bodies (NGBs) (as the largest stakeholders in SSD) and their sports as well as the nature of CSD. The bulk of SSD occurs within what is now commonly referred to as the third sector, traditionally known as the voluntary sector. Historically, the codification and organisation of sport in the UK largely has its origins in the eighteenth and nineteenth centuries. Initially the establishment of governance arrangements for sport would reflect the structure of society, with those in positions of wealth and authority assuming control over bodies such as that which would become the Royal and Ancient Golf Club (Houlihan 1997). Resistance to this ruling class domination of sport eventually emerged, one famous example of which being working class rugby league's breakaway in 1895, as the Northern Rugby Football Union, from the RFU (see Collins 1998). Throughout the twentieth century NGBs became a significant part of a growing movement of leisure-related voluntarism, which became increasingly enshrined in legislation. This suggests that for a long time there has been evidence of bottom-up movements within sport not only in specific sports, but also in community settings.

Outside of physical education and school sport the overwhelming majority of sporting opportunities in the UK are offered by third sector sports clubs, usually as part of the NGB system. It is difficult to envisage a NGB not wishing to ensure that the delivery and development of its sport is inclusive. Despite this, a number of NGBs are routinely criticised for the apparently unrepresentative nature of participation and performance in their sports. For instance, recent Active People research (Sport England 2011a) indicates that just over 1% of the 16+ population of England participate in tennis at least once a week. The highest participation rate was in London at 1.42% whilst in the North East of England, a less economically prosperous region the rate was 0.55%. Elsewhere in the development continuum it is well known that British tennis has struggled to produce players capable of competing at the highest levels, and those who have reached the upper echelons of the sport were privately funded and coached or born elsewhere (*The Guardian* 2011). Whilst it would be irresponsible and intellectually lazy to attempt to assign responsibility for these disparities in participation and elite performance to any single organisation or phenomenon, it is plainly the preserve of the NGB, in this case the Lawn Tennis Association (LTA) to lead the process of addressing it. An array of organisational and individual stakeholders across all sectors and walks of life interact in pursuit of a supposedly common goal: to enable athletes with the requisite levels of talent and motivation to progress and prosper in their chosen sport, but significant opportunities are missed without an acknowledgement of the potential strategic contribution of CSD.

CSD as a practice can be identified as originating in the late 1970s in response to concerns about urban unrest and the health of the nation, in addition to a recognition that the users of sports centres and other facilities tended to be middle class white males (Hylton and Totten 2008). It was viewed as a form of practice that challenged traditional ways of providing access to sport and recreation. As a result the 1980s

Janine Partington and Stephen Robson

saw the emergence of National Demonstration Projects which were designed to target under-represented groups, and Action Sport which was designed to combat rising levels of tension in inner-city areas (Houlihan and White 2002; Hylton and Totten 2008; Collins 2010). Later, increasing levels of financial support via a raft of Sport England programmes such as the Active Communities Development Fund led to the employment of a new batch of CSD practitioners focused on increasing access and tackling social exclusion. The majority of these CSDOs were employed by local authorities, with a remit to work in partnership with community groups and utilise community development principles in their work. Further recognition of the value of CSD work came with the emergence of the StreetGames charity, which has promoted the value of 'doorstep sport' and lobbied, with some success, for an increase in resources for this type of approach (StreetGames 2011).

Shortly after Houlihan (1997) highlighted the accusation that many NGBs practised isolationism, outmoded managerial practices and paternalism, sport in the UK under New Labour experienced a period of heightened governmental interest accompanied by unprecedented levels of investment. New Labour's 'strategy', 'A Sporting Future for All' (DCMS 2000) implied that community sport and SSD were part of the same development system. Unfortunately this was not borne out in practice as a division steadily emerged between practitioners who developed sport(s) and those who developed communities (Green 2006). This has ultimately resulted in an ineffective, fractured development system, which has comprehensively failed to substantially increase participation levels (DCMS/Cabinet Office 2002; Sport England 2011a), or make sustainable changes within disadvantaged communities (Long and Sanderson 2001; Coalter 2007).

Attempts have been made to remedy this situation, reinforced by a culture of performance management, resulting in Sport England's (2008) landmark refocusing of National Lottery resources towards selected NGBs and their Whole Sport Plans. We can query whether this is due in part to renewed confidence in NGBs as result of modernisation of their strategic practice, or if it is merely a reflection of the failure of countless alternative approaches to increase mass participation. Do the 'chosen few' NGBs who receive Lottery funding display exemplary, inclusive strategic management influencing all levels of their sports? What about the numerous sports outside of the funding mainstream or local authorities? The 2010 change in government from New Labour to the Conservative-Liberal Democrat coalition once again impacted upon sports development with a series of budget cuts particularly affecting grassroots provision delivered by local authorities. Whilst the 2012 Olympic and Paralympic Games afforded protection to NGBs and their Whole Sport Plans, they still felt the force of these cuts due to the reduction in resources experienced by key partners at local levels. Changes of this sort accentuate the need for a co-ordinated approach to both the development of sport and the development through sport. This will firstly require a change in mindset to view what has previously been seen as separate, even dichotomous activities as part of the same practice, and secondly the recognition of poor strategic practice that has blighted both approaches in the past.

DIFFERENT APPROACHES?

This section critiques many of the commonly assumed differences between sport specific development and community sport development and questions whether the two approaches are as different as often perceived. One approach targets wider societal outcomes, and the other is focused on developing clear pathways to support athletes through to elite levels of performance: superficially, these could appear to be mutually incompatible goals, but is this actually the case? Let's look more closely at some of assumptions made about the two approaches:

CSD works in communities; SSD is focused upon a sport

In sport development settings the use of the term 'community' is often applied selectively, and seen as the preserve of community sport development practitioners who are perceived as working at the cutting edge of inclusive practice within marginalised, disadvantaged and disenfranchised, geographically bounded communities. However, definitions of 'community' accommodate a far broader range of activity. Hylton and Totten (2008) argue that community encapsulates a notion of collectivity, commonality, a sense of belonging or something shared. This shifts the focus beyond geographical confines and recognises communities based around interest and shared experiences, a definition which would incorporate those traditionally served by NGBs and their

220

constituent clubs, in addition to sport specific activity that occurs outside of the formalised structures of NGBs. The Conservative-Liberal Democrat coalition government spelled out a localism agenda and plans for a 'Big Society' underpinned by a perceived need to:

> ...reform public services, mend our broken society, and rebuild trust in politics...these plans involve redistributing power from the state to society; from the centre to local communities, giving people the opportunity to take more control over their lives. (Conservatives 2010:5)

This was followed by the severe budget cuts to local authorities that impacted significantly on leisure departments and sport development teams, and to QUANGOs such as Sport England, which saw a 30% reduction in its funding from central government (Conn 2010). This exacerbates the need for greater collaboration to make the best use of limited resources, the majority of which are channelled through NGBs at present (see below), in order to ensure that local groups and communities are supported to realise their sporting goals.

CSD is more focused on grassroots than SSD

Whilst CSD is undeniably a grassroots-based practice, the work of SSD at grassroots is often overlooked. This may be due to the misleading assumption that sport specific work undertaken by NGBs mainly impacts at a national level. It could also be argued that the media focus on international success and the attribution of this success or otherwise to NGBs again plots them as makers of national pride, less concerned than their CSD counterparts with more localised, grassroots development. However, the core business of NGBs could be argued to be supporting their members: sports clubs, volunteers and participants who not only belong to a sporting community but who frequently ply their trade at a grassroots level. It is now estimated that two million adult sport volunteers contribute at least one hour a week (Sport England 2011a) as part of a network of many thousands of sports clubs, mostly volunteer-led and mostly under the auspices of a 'parent' NGB. In recent times the expectations and burdens placed by the public sector establishment upon the shoulders of sport volunteers have increased significantly. Whilst it is undoubtedly the case these days that the benefits of volunteering are more clearly recognised and articulated (e.g. Cuskelly, Hoye and Auld 2006) with extrinsic rewards offered, volunteers are also expected to acknowledge an array of legislative demands. It is relevant to enquire of both SSD and CSD whether their work is genuinely bottom-up, involving their communities in decision-making regarding strategic developments and the development of initiatives and activities. Whilst they both function at grassroots level, the challenge is to ensure grassroots representation when making strategic decisions.

SSD is better resourced than CSD, particularly in the 46 focus sports

A key motivation for the shift in National Lottery priorities towards the NGBs was the aspiration, integral to London's bid to host the 2012 Olympic and Paralympic Games, to become the first host nation to achieve a tangible mass participation and volunteering legacy (DCMS 2008). As a consequence of this shift, 46 sports were awarded Lottery investment via Sport England totalling over £480 million, a condition of which was that a four-year Whole Sport Plan should be produced covering, for example, the period 2009–13 (Sport England 2011b). The strategic leaders of each of the chosen sports agreed headline targets in the accordance with the themes of the Sport England (2008) Grow, Sustain, Excel strategy. For instance the English Table Tennis Association (ETTA) was charged with growing participation from a 2009 baseline figure of 75,700 to 92,200 in 2013 (Sport England 2009). This has far-reaching implications for the voluntary workforce: this target would need to be achieved through a collective effort on the part of almost 3000 affiliated clubs (English Table Tennis Association 2011).

CSD, in comparison, does not have a stable source of funding, frequently relying on local authorities investing in this type of work and providing often limited resources for its delivery. This is supplemented by external, time-limited sources such as Sport England grants, or funding via initiatives such as those managed by StreetGames. As a result of the 2010 budget cuts the core support (offered via local authorities) for CSD was vastly reduced, with the amount of potential external funding also negatively affected as sport development agencies were forced to tighten their belts (Conn 2010; Elder 2010). Cuts at a local authority level have been made easier by the disparate nature of CSD provision and a lack of focus at governmental level by the Conservative-Liberal Democrat

222

coalition. In essence, the strength of a CSD approach with its tailored, flexible methods focused on meeting individual community needs has in fact become a convenient excuse for a lack of significant resourcing and ultimately significant cuts in funding, as CSD has failed to provide a set of standardised, measurable outcomes across the UK which can be compared to more conventional sport development approaches. This has resulted in an uncertain future for CSD, and once again stresses that if we are serious about the role of sport (and individual sports) as an agent for meaningful social change there is a need for greater collaboration between SSD and CSD. This is not purely to secure a future for CSD work but also because enhanced co-operation will result in better strategic outcomes all around. There remains a need for improved co-ordination throughout the entire sport development system from grassroots to elite level. Since no comparable funding stream to WSP monies exists for CSD, a significant departure is required from the 'silo mentality', examined in Chapter 7, exhibited by some NGBs (which, sadly is encouraged to an extent by the WSP regime). NGBs, as the custodians of the greater share of central resourcing need to demonstrate advanced leadership and openness in order for the strategic outcomes desired by sporting stakeholders to be realised.

CSD is and should be more politicised than SSD

The origins of CSD lie in state-sponsored activity; however, more recent writing on CSD has strongly supported its role as a mechanism through which power relations can be challenged (Frisby and Millar 2002; Hylton and Totten 2008; Partington and Totten 2012). The assumption follows, therefore, that people who practise CSD are intrinsically politically motivated by the desire to combat social inequality and tackle the hegemonic structures which perpetuate it. The work of SSD practitioners, meanwhile, is heavily influenced by mainstream political processes, but it could be argued that their focus has been on navigating their way through these political waters instead of directly confronting them. As a result of this, most sport specific development programmes are not transformative, having to seek state authorisation for their work via controlling mechanisms such as Whole Sport Plans, which act to subordinate NGBs within the boundaries of the state. This has served to stagnate the services offered by NGBs. Clearly, there has been a failure to generate a significant increase in participation levels or increase the engagement of under-represented groups in sport. Although it should be recognised that it is not only NGBs that fail to achieve sustainable change, there is a significant need for sport specific development officers to become more politically aware and develop a critical consciousness of how power structures within their sport and also broader society contribute to social inequalities, which in turn influence people's abilities and motivations to participate in sport. Ironically, this is essential if the sport development profession is to achieve ambitious increases in participation levels such as those in the Game Plan document (DCMS/Cabinet Office 2002) or anticipated in the aftermath of the 2012 Olympic and Paralympic Games (DCMS 2008). As discussed throughout the book it is also necessary for strategy documents to reflect greater attention to flexibility in order to survive the inevitable and ongoing changes to which NGBs are subjected as a result of the political cycle.

SSD is well planned and professional, whilst CSD is more ad hoc and spontaneous/informal

The dominant policy discourse, despite notions of sport for good, remains shaped by the requirement to construct talent pathways: this is witnessed in much more stable governmental support for NGBs which has allowed them to undertake strategic planning, relatively safe in the knowledge that they have a reasonable period of time accompanied by more regular funding with which to achieve their strategic goals. In comparison, CSD has been characterised as lacking clear policy direction and subjected to fragmented funding regimes, which have emphasised the "sustainable vulnerabilities of small scale projects with funding dependencies in delivering broader sustainable change" (Partington and Totten 2012:29). The Audit Commission (2006:58 quoted in in Green 2006:235) warns that "if councils fail to adopt clear comprehensive approaches to strategic decisions they will fail to meet participation targets and community needs." Yet Green acknowledges that there has been little guidance to local authorities on their role as deliverers of sport and recreation activities. In a report entitled More Than a Game (2011) The Centre for Social Justice (CSJ) argues that all of this has undermined the ability of CSD to achieve social objectives and resulted in fractured, isolationist delivery which has been criticised as ineffective in generating long-term change (see also Long *et al.* 2002; Coalter 2007). Ultimately, the lack of structured resources for CSD, both nationally and subsequently locally, prevents CSD practitioners from undertaking meaningful strategic planning. The Centre for Social Justice (2011) argues that this situation must change as 'sports for sports' sake' is not a sustainable policy stance, and the only justifiable stance is to advocate and support development through sport. It calls for improved funding arrangements and clear policy directives from central government for CSD.

There is evidence to suggest that these arrangements would provide much needed stability and direction for CSD. This is supported by the improvement witnessed within elite athlete development, where changes to development structures over a sustained period transformed what Green (2006:218) describes as changing a "fragmented, makeshift and unplanned state of affairs" into a clear, legitimised and well-structured system that begun to bear fruit. For instance, England Hockey (n/d:8), when discussing the achievement of its strategic vision and objectives, recognised that its "ambitious proposals will require an 8–10 year plan for implementation." Support of this duration is presently a pipe dream for CSD. Similar support for CSD would offer opportunities for a more strategic collaboration between CSD and SSD to develop, and make what is at present a sporadic link between talent pathways and grassroots development an achievable reality.

SSD is more output driven than CSD and has better evidence of impact

Whilst we are arguing for recognition of the importance and value of community sport as an end in itself, we acknowledge that increasing pressure to provide robust monitoring and evaluation data to evidence impact against a range of targets has, in essence, marginalised its importance to those in positions of power. There is significant pressure for work in SSD and CSD to make a contribution to either social policy goals, in particular challenging health inequalities, or to develop talent pathways and improve the performance of national teams. Whole Sport Plans placed increasing emphasis on adopting a target-driven culture to develop sport, requiring NGBs to report annually on their progress against participation and excellence targets, and against their financial status biannually. This effectively removes an element of flexibility, with jobs depending on the attainment of the targets set out in these plans.

In comparison, CSD has been heavily criticised for taking a ramshackle approach to performance management, hiding behind a façade of social benefit, but frequently failing to provide real evidence of impact (Long and Sanderson 2001; Long and Bramham 2006; Coalter 2007). The tightening of monitoring procedures in local government as a result of the Comprehensive Performance Assessment and more recently the Comprehensive Area Assessment required CSD practitioners operating at that level to gather much more robust evidence and data relating to the impacts of their work. The increasing focus towards tackling health inequalities and subsequent increase of partnerships between local authorities and health authorities once more placed a requirement on CSD practitioners to provide clear evidence of their work. Despite this, there are still strong arguments that evaluation often ignores the real benefits and outcomes of CSD work such as community empowerment and the development of social capital, in favour of providing outputs to satisfy the needs of the state, rather than the real change that is occurring at grassroots level (Partington and Totten 2012).

As these discussions indicate, both SSD and CSD are required to evidence their work, although there is a lack of standardisation to the approaches taken which limits practitioners' ability to compare, contrast and collaborate.

There's no role for SSD in tackling community issues or social concerns

Bloyce et al.'s (2008) research into sport development officers within local authorities found that the majority of officers felt that there was a link between increasing opportunities for people to play sport and improvements in elite level performance. They saw a clear link between the work they were involved in at grassroots level and that of elite development, despite feeling pressured to evidence their work in terms of social outcomes rather than sporting ones. This again demonstrates the confusion that exists within the sports policy arena: if those responsible for the development of sport are unclear as to their remit, it is no surprise that sport development is ineffective and regularly fails to meet ambitious national targets. Bloyce et al. (2008:36) argue further that:

Janine Partington and Stephen Robson

Given the relatively powerful position of Sport England and their greater capacity to set the government's policy agenda for local authorities, it was not surprising to see that the current policy focus on health issues was cited widely as a justification for re-orienteering sport development activity away from the development of sport *per se*, towards using sport and physical activities as vehicles of social policy.

However, are these not one and the same? If more people are supported to become active, then participation levels in sport and physical activity increase which will contribute to both policy objectives of improved health and increased participation. The emphasis on health outcomes effectively masks what is still a Sport for All agenda. We still need to engage under-represented groups who, in the main, still live in the same communities, with the same issues and barriers that were targeted in the 1980s! The difference between then and now is the need to wrap up this type of work as meeting social policy goals, with the result that it is seen as different to the work undertaken by NGBs who have been 'authorised' to focus on increasing participation levels in their sports in order to meet medal targets rather than social outcomes. This slight difference in rationale has created an ideological gap between SSD and CSD practitioners, which has effectively constrained them from working together.

The need for greater collaboration was recognised by government and Sport England when, during the New Labour administration, a conceptual model of 'Single System for Sport' (later referred to as the 'Delivery System') was extensively promoted by Sport England (2007). This mechanism included the creation of Community Sport Networks (CSNs), each of which was intended to serve as a decision-making body and clearing house for the delivery of *all* sport in a given geographical area. Many of these have survived the withdrawal of direct funding and operate under a variety of guises (e.g. Brent Community Sport and Physical Activity Network; St Helen's Sport and Physical Activity Alliance), usually co-ordinated by the County Sports Partnership or local authority, neither of which is a direct recipient of core, WSP funding. They do provide a ready framework for the greater integration of SSD into deprived and disadvantaged communities, potentially beyond a focus on purely club-based activities. Vail (2007) points out the significant parallels between SD and community development: both wish to help groups of people to improve their life conditions and both are concerned with facilitating a process of change. However, the difference between SD and community development is that the latter is frequently self-determined by the targeted community (Pedlar 1996 in Vail 2007:572). In other words, community development is bottom-up rather than predetermined by SD professionals, either at national level or in local authority sport development teams, acting in the 'best interests' of communities.

COMMON WEAKNESSES

The preceding section aimed to dismiss a number of assumptions held about differences between SSD and CSD that we feel prevent effective collaboration between the two approaches. To further progress the discussion, this section aims to identify common characteristics between SSD and CSD, specifically in relation to poor practice and weaknesses shared by both approaches in terms of working with their communities. Butcher and Robertson (2007) identify a number of problems and weaknesses related to the organisational management of community practice that are applicable and relevant to both SSD and CSD. These are shown in Table 10.1.

By recognising that practice in both SSD and CSD is affected by the challenges outlined above, we hope that this chapter will enable readers to use the ideas presented to critically reflect upon their own practice and understanding of SSD-CSD, in order to develop the 'critical consciousness' discussed in Chapter 7 (Ledwith 2005). The development of this will result in more effective sport development programmes, as an improved conceptual understanding of SSD and CSD will lead to better strategic outcomes.

WEAKNESSES IN STRATEGIC APPROACH

Hylton and Totten (2008:80) define community sport development as "a form of intervention in sport and recreation, which in some way addresses inequalities inherent in more established, mainstream sports provision." Whilst an accurate description of CSD activity, the term 'intervention' could be interpreted as a paternalistic input from 'we

228

Table 10.1 Problems and weaknesses of the management of CSD and SSD (adapted from Butcher and Robertson (2007:104)

	Challenges, Problems and Weaknesses
1	'Short-termism' and a reactive approach to planning and delivery
2	Ah-hoc project and programme-based approaches.
3	Bureaucratic models of service provision: policies and plans are devised in a 'top down' manner and practitioners fail to involve or consult with communities.
4	An insular and inward-looking organisational stance: 'silo mentality'.
5	A one-solution-fits-all approach that ignores differences between communities.
6	Deeply entrenched ways of delivery: 'this is how we do things around here'.
7	A focus on operational issues and contingencies, and a lack of flexibility in planning or delivery of services.
8	Initiative overload: too many programmes, policies and demands being juggled at the same time, resulting in ineffective delivery.
9	Staffing of interventions and programmes often lacks consistency due to reliance on casual and part time staff. These staff can also lack the necessary skills to work in communities.
10	Poor quality monitoring and evaluation of interventions and programmes, resulting in a lack of evidence of impact, and a lack of consistency in approaches to monitoring and evaluation between CSD and SSD.

know best' practitioners, rather than a true bottom-up approach involving the target community in the design, delivery and management of activities. Taking this a step further, we might also infer from the existence of a body of literature that focuses on CSD as a separate practice that there is a schism between sport for sport's sake and development through sport. As Vail (2007) argues, often it is the traditional SDOs (brought up on a diet of mainstream SD) who do not appreciate the importance of community champions and the benefits of their involvement in the delivery of sports programmes. She argues that there is a 'philosophical chasm' between the development of sport and development through sport. Development of sport and traditional approaches to this appear inflexible, rooted in short-termism and focused on promoting the sport above all else, whereas collaborative ventures in communities, built around addressing the needs of communities through common goals will sustain themselves (if strategically) planned over time.

We therefore now turn to the key, theoretical principles presented earlier in this book to assess the strengths and weaknesses of CSD and SSD practitioners' strategic practice. Strategic plans and documents are ubiquitous in sport development and often produced as a requirement in order to access funding, as is the case with Whole Sport Plans. This leads us to consider who are these plans written for? In discussing strategies written for regeneration programmes such as the Single Regeneration Budget, Turner (2009:232) argues that plans such as these present an "alternative agenda, defined centrally, by government" and by people from outside of the community and social context for which the strategy is targeted. It also provides a partial explanation for the lack of strategic innovation or significant change in levels of sports participation despite millions of pounds of investment. The dynamic nature of the organisational environment led writers such as Herbert Simon and Charles Lindblom to advocate for a less pseudo-rational, more flexible approach to strategy and strategic management (see for instance Clegg et al. 2011). The application of emergent approaches to strategic thinking, discussed in Chapter 2, would surely provide communities and promoters of specific sports with a more context-sensitive approach. We acknowledge that the terms and conditions of Exchequer or Lottery funding often mitigate against this, with national key performance indicators to be met and regular monitoring of progress via the Active People Survey (Sport England 2011a), but if anything, the presence of these constraints exacerbates the need for innovative strategic thinking.

As we have shown in earlier chapters, strategic innovation is under-pinned by a keen appreciation for the organisation's internal and external environments. In an internal sense Butcher (2003) discusses organisational management in relation to community practice arguing that frequently, the organisational and management systems are not suited to the task and do not facilitate quality work outputs. Certainly there has become a trend of setting up sport development units in local authorities in a highly structured manner with staff responsible for specific job roles such as coach development or club development. In effect, this compartmentalises aspects of work and reduces the likelihood of joined-up work within the team, let alone in a community. In role

Janine Partington and Stephen Robson

cultures (Handy 1993) a higher sense of organisational purpose can be diminished as practitioners pursue their personal targets. Externally the political cycle often militates against effective long-term planning, and nowhere is this more apparent than in SSD. In keeping with its predecessors, the Conservative-Liberal Democrat coalition adopted differing priorities for sport to those of the outgoing New Labour regime. In the wake of the global financial crisis of the preceding two years the coalition chose to make wide-scale cuts across the UK public sector (HM Treasury 2010), including the discontinuation of funding support to the Youth Sport Trust and by implication the School Sport Partnerships (SSPs) programme (Elder 2010; Hart 2010). Many links forged between schools and sports clubs were initiated and maintained as a consequence of the SSPs (Loughborough Partnership 2005), leading to concerns that clubs would lose this ready supply of new members. To many NGBs it seemed that, not for the first time, politicians were asking for them for an ever-greater contribution to public health and 'national pride' agendas whilst withdrawing the material support which might enable them to achieve this. CSD's ongoing struggle for resources was worsened by the cuts with the savings required of local authorities having an especially strong impact, for example, forcing the closure of local sports facilities that provided training spaces for sports teams and recreational sports for local communities (False Economy 2011). The need could hardly have ever been greater for CSD and SSD practitioners to make strategic choices, which would insulate against these sorts of environmental shocks and lead to sustainable outcomes.

Despite both CSD and SSD being focused ostensibly on the sustainability of long-term change it is often the last thing considered in the planning of a programme. Thus there has been much criticism of the short-term nature of sport development programmes and interventions (Long and Bramham 2006; Coalter 2007; Partington and Totten 2012). For many, sustainability is seen as an end product, not something that requires planning from the outset. The financial pressure on local government has led recreation departments to make the 'strategic' choice to focus much of their work on income generation, in the process denying access to services to those unable to contribute to revenue streams (Reid, Frisby and Ponic 2002 cited in Frisby and Millar 2002:226). Ironically, many CSD and SSD strategies discuss tackling social exclusion without the recognition that they are subconsciously perpetuating it. Frisby and Millar (2002) highlight that for excluded people who may have to demonstrate their poverty in order to access reduced rates, well-intended gestures such as leisure cards can prove tokenistic rather than inclusive. Choice of strategic partners, a major determinant of a sport organisation's success, is also compromised when funding becomes the principal driver. Robson (2008) and Bloyce *et al.* (2008) discuss how partnership arrangements become less consensual and how control is lost by the SD practitioner when, for instance, local authority SDOs increase their networks of partners to include more financially secure local organisations such as NHS primary care providers. Bloyce *et al.* question whether this shift has actually damaged the ability of sport development to meet participation targets, as much time is spent developing partnerships, adapting activity to meet the goals of both organisations to the extent that its impact can become blunted.

Finally, for this section we consider the delivery and evaluation of CSD and SSD through strategic implementation and performance measurement. Vail (2007), when discussing sport policy and development in Canada, which has many parallels to the UK, describes how SD has often taken the form of top-down, national or regional initiatives delivered in uniformly for a fixed period. Communities are exposed to such initiatives in a 'shotgun' manner for a period of time with the hope they will deliver sustainable change. These approaches have frequently failed to deliver increases in participation or tackle social exclusion, an example of which is the national Sport Unlimited programme. Sport England (2011c) claimed that this was an innovative programme, intended to cascade funding for sport to local communities. In reality, whilst the scheme often involved local sports clubs, the performance measurement arrangements (mainly quantitative key performance indicators (KPIs) such as ethnicity, attendance levels and participant retention (Coventry, Solihull and Warwickshire Sport 2011)), in addition to the pressure to deliver the scheme in the tight time frame meant that attempts to engage excluded young people were limited. It was also very ambitious to think that ten-week programmes of taster sessions such as these would result in long term, sustainable changes in participation.

Ledwith (2005) describes this practice as 'thoughtless action', when plans are implemented without critical thought, often resulting in ineffective programmes. 'Thoughtful action', conversely, is based on the development of critical consciousness where practitioners develop an understanding of how structures in society continue to privilege certain

Janine Partington and Stephen Robson

groups and disadvantage others. We can readily apply this to a CSD context with its focus on tackling inequality but it is also applicable to SSD, especially in terms of the representation of disadvantaged and minority groups on talent pathways and in senior management positions. The monitoring and evaluation regimes of programmes such as Sport Unlimited make it even more difficult for CSD and SSD to avoid accusations of tokenism. The pressure on deliverers to 'prove' sustainability diverts the focus from achieving an appropriate mode of delivery with a genuine legacy towards delivering outputs in the time frame provided. This inevitably results in minimal long-term impact on participation levels or exclusion.

TOWARDS GREATER COLLABORATION

Whilst not wishing to argue for collaboration between all SSD and CSD activity, this chapter urges a greater relationship between the two practices when it is mutually beneficial. We are arguing for a more inclusive approach to SSD, achieved by its practitioners working collaboratively with CSD colleagues to increase the diversity of people accessing pathways and playing recreational sport. For meaningful change to occur SSD practitioners must also be open to authentic, bottom-up decision-making processes in collaboration with excluded communities. In addition, we are also campaigning for a less isolationist approach to CSD, with benefits from this of accessing longer-term resources and providing clearer exit routes for participants. Green (2006) returns to the findings of the Impact of Sport for All Policy 1966–84 report by McIntosh and Charlton (1985:193), which concluded that:

> ...sport as a means and sport as an end are not mutually exclusive. There is a continuum of emphasis from extrinsic to intrinsic rewards and from sport as a useless enjoyment to sport as social machinery.

In addition, Green (2006:224) describes sport for good and sport as an end in itself as "increasingly distinct storylines". He argues that the Sport for All policy has been neglected due to the focus on elite performance and sport for good, which are seen as policy directives with little connection. Despite CSD's and SSD's stated commonality of purpose of facilitating long-term sustainable change to both participation levels and social exclusion, there have been numerous arguments over their compatibility in relation to aims versus rationales and outputs versus outcomes to the extent that they have frequently been viewed as separate professions. Whilst it may be the case that tackling social issues using sport as a tool is a different activity from developing talent pathways and elite performers, both approaches should utilise similar methods to address the needs of target communities.

To illustrate the benefits to be gained, England Hockey (n/d) in its document, 'A single system for hockey', argues for a long-term view of player development, and sets three main goals: bring more young people into hockey; develop a thriving club infrastructure; and achieve international success at the highest level. Good practice needs to be supported by "systems of competition, calendar planning, talent identification and coaching provision" (England Hockey n/d:2). The main structures used to support the plan are school-club links and club development. However, this does not recognise that many young people are not engaged by sport at school (particularly those from lower income backgrounds and BME groups (Smith *et al.* 2007)) and therefore 'slip through the net'; they are however often engaged by CSD programmes that take place within their own communities. NGBs are missing out on potential talent by not engaging with community sport activity.

Bloyce *et al.* (2008:373) remind us that there is competition amongst sport organisations for scarce resources, effectively turning sport development into a market place rather than an arena where co-operation between organisations thrives, and:

> Even if the requisite resources have been secured and distributed appropriately, policy effectiveness is still dependent upon the understanding, skills and abilities of those who administer it as well as those charged with implementation.

The 'Big Society' agenda (Conservatives 2010) placed even more emphasis on the identification of local solutions to local issues. With reductions in funding to local authorities it behoves NGBs to 'step up to the plate' and support local groups and communities to realise their sporting needs (and consequently meet some of their social needs through sport). Despite the perpetual scramble for resources described by Bloyce *et al.* (2008) and regardless of the prevailing funding

234

conditions, collaboration is surely the way to maximise the impact of limited resources.

Just as it would be inappropriate to label all SSD work as excluding disadvantaged communities and individuals, we should not blithely assume that all participants in 'community sport' are realising the life-changing potential of sport. Professionals need to understand the communities they work in: this involves undertaking research and consultation. Crucially it also means acting upon the results, not simply ignoring them if they are not what were expected or if they offer an alternative view to that of policy makers. Ironically, the intended beneficiaries of sport development schemes are often not involved in developing the strategic plans that will impact on their communities (be it geographical communities such as a deprived housing estate or an interest-based community such as tennis clubs in a town) (Partington and Totten 2012). Collaborative action is at the heart of community development, and thus should also be at the heart of sport development practice targeting communities. As Frisby and Millar (2002) argue, social action is more likely to occur when knowledge based on the lived experiences of community members is combined with the instrumental and technical knowledge of professional staff.

SUMMARY

With apologies for stating the obvious, the only way to increase participation is to engage non-participants. To do this, politicians, policy-makers and practitioners need to recognise that for many of these people, participating in sport is low on their agenda. For it to be placed higher, work needs to be undertaken to combat the social issues and barriers that impact on their lives. It is not enough to just provide *opportunities* for participation; these opportunities need to be appropriate and supportive for long-term participation. This inevitably requires practitioners to tackle the causes of exclusion, not just the symptoms (Ledwith 2005; Long and Bramham 2006) and to take a more integrated approach to the provision of sport. This is referred to by the Centre for Social Justice (2011:51) as developing a "united front."

Clearly this is easier said than done! However, it has become increasingly common to see community development terminology bandied around within SD policy and practice to the extent that it has become the norm for SDPs to use buzzwords such as 'sustainability', 'empowerment' and 'community engagement' without it necessarily following that they understand the true meanings of those terms. In effect, these terms endorse change: changing the position, experience or influence of a community or social group in some way. There are clear similarities and synergy with the aims of CSD, whether it be supporting a disempowered group to be able to exert influence over or within a sporting structure that previously marginalised it, or using sport as a mechanism to impact on the long-term behaviour of an individual. Worryingly, the warnings of academics of the dangers of simply repackaging mainstream SD as CSD and hoping for a positive impact have been largely ignored and we still frequently see examples of poorly planned, confused initiatives (Butcher *et al.* 2007, Coalter 2007, Hylton and Totten 2008). One of the aspirations of this book is to encourage practitioners in both community and sport-specific settings to embrace truly empowering, bottom-up approaches to their work. This would potentially extend the reach of SSD into larger and more diverse talent pools whilst enabling pressured resources such as Lottery funding for NGB 'Grow' and 'Sustain' targets to be distributed more fairly.

Despite Butcher (1994) arguing two decades ago that top-down, enforced schemes rarely result in any sustainable change, there has been little change in the way that sport development initiatives have been developed and delivered. His advocating of a *community-practice* approach (see also Banks *et al.* 2003), where decision-making and planning is shared between statutory agencies and community groups, has been all but ignored. Instead, a plethora of schemes initiated by agencies such as Sport England, designed to increase participation in sport by under-represented groups, has been imposed on communities with little impact. The massive network of third-sector sports clubs, many of which exist in the same deprived communities targeted for CSD interventions, provides a rich environment within which these possibilities can be explored. It is necessary to recognise that following a community development approach takes time, and as such, will require a long-term commitment from partners and an acknowledgement of this approach from funding agencies. The provision of multiple, short-term funding streams from government agencies and others has not worked. The four-year cycle of Whole Sport Plan funding does not accommodate the reality that meaningful change can take a generation to accomplish (Centre for Social Justice 2011), but even here a platform

236

can be built and a tangible contribution demonstrated if CSD and S practitioners work together to stimulate interest and participation in specific sports in new constituencies. The practical implications of this call for enhanced collaboration will be considered in the next chapter.

LEARNING ACTIVITIES

Developing knowledge

1   Gather information on a community sport development project of your choosing. Critically evaluate its existing development strategy with reference to partnerships with sport-specific development. Make a list of at least five benefits to be gained from increasing its strategic partnership working with sport-specific development organisations.
2   Gather information on a sport-specific development organisation of your choosing (possibly, but not necessarily a national governing body). Critically evaluate its existing development strategy with reference to inclusive, grass roots work in communities. Make a list of at least five benefits to be gained from increasing its strategic partnership working with community sport development organisations.
3   Create a set of shared aims for a strategic partnership between the two organisations you looked at in exercises 1 and 2.

REFERENCES

Audit Commission (2006) 'Public Sports and Recreation Services'. London, Audit Commission. In Green, M. (2006) 'From 'Sport for All' to not about 'Sport for All'?: interrogating policy interventions in the United Kingdom'. *European Sport Management Quarterly.* 6 (3) September, pp. 217–238.

Banks, S., Butcher, H., Henderson, P. and Robertson, J. eds. (2003) *Managing Community Practice: Principles, Policies and Programmes.* Bristol, The Policy Press.

Bloyce, D., Smith, A., Mead, R. and Morris, J. (2008) ''Playing the Game (Plan)': a figurational analysis of organizational change in sports development in England.' *European Sport Management Quarterly.* 8 (4) December, pp. 359–373.

Butcher, H. (1994) 'The Concept of Community Practice'. In Haywood, L. ed. *Community Leisure: Theory and Practice*. Oxford, Butterworth-Heinemann, pp. 3–25.

Butcher, H. (2003) 'Organisational Management for Community Practice'. In Banks, S., Butcher, H., Henderson, P. and Robertson, J. eds. *Managing Community Practice: Principles, Policies and Programmes*. Bristol, The Policy Press, pp. 57–82.

Butcher, H. and Robertson, J. (2007) 'Critical Community Practice: organisational leadership and management'. In Butcher, H., Banks, S., Henderson, P. and Robertson, J. eds. *Critical Community Practice*. Bristol, The Policy Press, pp. 97–115.

Centre for Social Justice (2011) 'More than a game: Harnessing the power of sport to transform the lives of young people'. London, CSJ.

Clegg, S., Carter, C., Kornberger, M. and Schweitzer, J. (2011) *Strategy: Theory and Practice*. London, Sage.

Coalter, F. (2007) *A Wider Role for Sport. Who's Keeping the Score?* Abingdon, Routledge.

Collins, M. (2010) *The Development of Sports Development*. In Collins, M. (ed) *Examining Sports Development*. Abingdon, Routledge, pp. 14–42.

Collins, T. (1998) *Rugby's Great Split*. London, Frank Cass.

Conn, D. (2010) 'Spending review: Where the axe will fall on our sporting infrastructure'. *The Guardian*. 20 October.

Conservatives (2010) 'Building a Big Society'. London, The Conservative Party.

Coventry, Solihull and Warwickshire Sport (2011) 'Sport Unlimited'. Available at http://www.cswsport.org.uk/sportunlimited.

Cuskelly, G., Hoye, R. and Auld, C. (2006) *Working with Volunteers in Sport*. Abingdon, Routledge.

DCMS (2000) 'A Sporting Future for All'. London, DCMS.

DCMS (2008) 'Before, During and After: making the most of the London 2012 Games'. London, The Strategy Unit.

DCMS/Cabinet Office (2002) 'Game Plan: A strategy for delivering Government's Sport and physical activity objectives'. London, The Strategy Unit.

Elder, A. (2010) 'How will the coalition budget cuts affect British sport?' Available at http://www.sport.co.uk/features/Sportcouk/1348/How_will_the_coalition_budget_cuts_affect_British_sport.aspx.

England Hockey (n/d) 'A Single System for Hockey'. Milton Keynes, EHA.

English Table Tennis Association (2011) 'Structure of the ETTA'. Available at http://etta.co.uk/our-sport-modules/about-us/structure-of-the-etta/.

False Economy (2011) 'Lochwinnach Sports Annexe'. Available from: http://falseeconomy.org.uk/cuts/item/lochwinnoch-sports-annexe.

Frisby, W. and Millar, S. (2002) 'The actualities of doing community development to promote the inclusion of low income populations in local sport and recreation'. *European Sport Management Quarterly*. 2 (3), pp. 209–233.

Green, M. (2006) 'From 'Sport for All' to not about 'Sport for All'?: interrogating policy interventions in the United Kingdom'. *European Sport Management Quarterly*. 6 (3) September, pp. 217–238.

Handy, C. (1993) *Understanding Organisations*. 4th ed. London, Penguin.

Hart, S. (2010) 'London 2012 Olympics: Government accused of 'devastating' legacy with school spending cuts'. Available at http://www.telegraph.co.uk/sport/othersports/schoolsports/8076966/London-2012-Olympics-Government-accused-of-devastating-legacy-with-school-spending-cuts.html.

HM Treasury (2010) 'Spending Review 2010'. London, HM Treasury.

Houlihan, B. (1997) *Sport, Policy and Politics.* London, Routledge.

Houlihan, B. and White, A. (2002) *The Politics of Sports Development: Development of Sport or Development Through Sport?* London, Routledge.

Hylton, K. and Totten, M. (2008) 'Community Sports Development'. In Hylton, K. and Bramham, P. eds. *Sports Development: Policy, Process and Practice.* 2nd ed. Abingdon, Routledge, pp. 77–117.

Ledwith, M. (2005) *Community Development: A Critical Approach.* Bristol, The Policy Press.

Long, J. and Bramham, P. (2006) 'Joining Up Policy Discourses and Fragmented Practices: the precarious contribution of cultural projects to social inclusion?' *Policy and Politics.* 34 (1), pp. 133–151.

Long, J. and Sanderson, I. (2001) 'The Social Benefits of Sport – Where's the Proof?' In: Gratton, C. and Henry, I. eds. *Sport in the City: The Role of Sport in Economic and Social Regeneration.* London, Routledge, pp. 187–203.

Long, J., Welch, M., Bramham, P., Butterfield, J., Hylton, K. and Lloyd, E. (2002) 'Count Me In: the dimensions of social inclusion through culture, media and sport'. London, DCMS.

Loughborough Partnership (2005) 'School Sports Partnerships: annual monitoring and evaluation report'. Loughborough, Institute of Youth Sport/ Loughborough University.

McIntosh, P. and Charlton, V. (1985) 'The Impact of Sport For All Policy'. London, Sports Council.

Partington, J. and Totten, M. (2012) 'Community Sports Projects and Effective Community Empowerment: a case study in Rochdale'. *Managing Leisure.* 17, January 2012, pp. 29–46.

Pedlar, A. (1996). 'Community development: What does it mean for recreation and leisure?' *Journal of Applied Recreation Research,* 21, 5–23. In Vail, S. (2007) Community Development and Sport Participation. *Journal of Sport Management.* 21, pp. 571–596.

Reid, C., Frisby, W. and Ponic, P. (2002). 'Confronting Two-tiered Community Recreation and Poor Women's Exclusion: promoting inclusion, health, and social justice. *Canadian Women's Studies, Special Issue "Women and Sport",* 21(3), pp. 88–94. Cited in: Frisby, W. and Millar, S. (2002) 'The actualities of doing community development to promote the inclusion of low income populations in local sport and recreation'. *European Sport Management Quarterly.* 2 (3), pp. 209–233.

Robson, S. (2008) 'Partnerships in Sport'. In Hylton, K. and Bramham, P. eds. *Sports Development: Policy, Process and Practice.* 2nd ed. Abingdon, Routledge, pp. 118–142.

Smith, A., Thurston, M., Green, K. and Lamb, K. (2007) 'Young People's Participation in Extra-curricular Physical Education: a study of 15–16 year olds in North-West England and North-East Wales'. *European Physical Education Review*. 13 (3), pp. 339–368.

Sport England (2007) 'Sport England Policy Statement: the delivery system for sport in England'. London, Sport England.

Sport England (2008) 'Sport England Strategy 2008–2011'. London, Sport England.

Sport England (2009) 'English Table Tennis Association'. Whole Sport Plan briefing note. Available at http://www.sportengland.org/funding/ngb_investment/ngb_whole_sport_plans.aspx.

Sport England (2011a) 'Active People Survey 5'. Available at http://www.sportengland.org/research/active_people_survey/active_people_survey_5/aps5_quarter_two.aspx.

Sport England (2011b) 'Investing in National Governing Bodies'. Available at http://www.sportengland.org/funding/ngb_investment.aspx.

Sport England (2011c) Sport Unlimited. Available at http://www.sportengland.org/support_advice/children_and_young_people/sport_unlimited.aspx.

StreetGames (2011) 'About Us'. Available at http://www.streetgames.org/www/aboutus.

The Guardian (2011) 'Guardian Focus Podcast: Wimbledon and the state of British tennis'. Available at http://www.guardian.co.uk/world/blog/audio/2011/jun/15/focus-podcast-wimbledon-british-tennis.

Turner, A. (2009) 'Bottom-up Community Development: reality or rhetoric? the example of the Kingsmead Kabin in East London'. *Community Development Journal*. 44 (2) April, pp. 230–247.

Vail, S. (2007) 'Community Development and Sport Participation'. *Journal of Sport Management*. 21, pp. 571–596.

CHAPTER 11

TOWARDS A 'COMMUNITY PRACTICE' APPROACH

STEPHEN ROBSON AND JANINE PARTINGTON WITH
ROSEMARY LEACH, LEE TUCKER AND KIRSTIE SIMPSON

INTRODUCTION

The preceding chapter argued for a more critical approach to bridging the CSD/SSD 'divide'. We have suggested that enforced separation is a conceptually and strategically weak approach that does little to help serve the needs of communities and/or sports. This seems particularly pertinent in view of the widely-held scepticism toward NGBs' capacity to engage in community agendas. The Centre for Social Justice (CSJ) voiced the concern held by many that the rationale behind the Whole Sport Plan (WSP) programme was flawed:

> Instead of highlighting under-performance by individual NGBs, Sport England and the Government would do well to consider the overall value of the strategy adopted in 2009, and to question whether they made the right decision. It may be simply that NGBs are not the best possible partners to deliver a mass participation agenda.
>
> (CSJ 2011:45)

Regardless of any subsequent changes to the funding regime it remains the case in perpetuity that NGBs are responsible for driving up participation in their own sports, even if a scenario were returned to in which meaningful central funding was made available to those closer to under-represented communities. The previous chapter therefore concluded with a call for CSD and SSD professionals to collaborate more often and more effectively: this chapter utilises material presented throughout the book to consider how this may be achieved in practice.

A prime opportunity for greater integration of CSD and SSD exists at what might be termed the participation-performance nexus, the stage at which talented performers move from recreational participation into performance programmes. This transition point is therefore a very significant site for any discussion of NGBs' inclusive, strategic management with reference to strategic CSD practice. Most NGBs, Lottery-supported or otherwise, attempt to model their development pathways to illustrate the progression of talented athletes and sometimes to show how resources will be deployed at each stage. The Gymnastics England 'Gymnast Pathway' (Gymnastics England 2009) is an example of this. The accompanying notes offer a refreshing acknowledgement of the need to function strategically and align resources to the needs of the participant:

> The Model reflects a step change in the strategic and operational thinking of the sport. It places the participant at the heart of the planning and delivery process with all interventions – coaching, clubs, competition, volunteering designed to ensure that the requirements to support a participant at any given stage in the pathway are met.
>
> (Gymnastics England 2009:nn)

The Gymnast Pathway illustrates the multiplicity of possibilities for transition from participant to performer and the above quote begins to hint at the diversity of stakeholders (clubs, coaches etc.) with a role to play. English Lacrosse, meanwhile, identified in its Whole Sport Plan a 'Club Development Pathway' (English Lacrosse 2009) where, in broad-brush terms the progression of a club to 'Performance' status is mapped and the support to be offered by the NGB is specified. As ever, the devil is in the detail (or lack thereof) such that it is not immediately clear how statements such as 'Create system to manage increased club volunteer workforce' (English Lacrosse 2009:13) would be operationalised. However, it gives us a foothold from which to base our assessment of NGBs' strategic intentions and suggests that athletes' progressions from participation to performance are being mapped with more sophistication than was often previously the case. The participation-performance nexus can only be effective if the strategic intentions, resources and

242

capabilities of all stakeholders can be unified and co-ordinated for the advancement of the sport.

CSD, meanwhile, incorporates two main strands of work. The first is concerned with increasing participation in sport and physical activity amongst social groups who are traditionally non-participants. This has been described as 'developing sport in the community' compared to the second approach, 'developing communities through sport' (Coalter 2002; Houlihan and White 2002). This approach sees sport being used in community settings as a tool to achieve broader social policy goals such as social inclusion. It may also incorporate more radical objectives, where sport is used to further the interests of, and divert power to disadvantaged or minority groups in society (Hylton and Totten 2008). As the previous chapter outlined there is no convincing reason why young people participating in CSD activities should not and could not be able to progress in their chosen sport(s). Any separation between CSD and SSD is socially constructed and should be challenged by those with a commitment to inclusive sport development. With relatively minor modifications to the sporting infrastructure, coupled with more significant ideological shifts on the part of those who control the resources it is eminently possible for participants from more diverse backgrounds to access long-term participation opportunities and talent pathways.

As such, this chapter advocates a combined community development-strategic management approach to CSD and SSD, building upon the work of Banks *et al.* (2003) around the management and leadership of 'community practice'. This approach encompasses a range of professions and situations where community work methods are utilised, but where practice is broader than just community development or community work, and sets out a range of principles to follow when managing this type of work. This chapter now turns its attention to the strategic practicalities of implementing a community practice approach, drawing upon the book's key themes for guidance.

STRATEGIC THINKING/APPROACHES TO STRATEGY

Previously, we have questioned the relevance of the 'glossy document' to meaningful sport development be it in disadvantaged communities, specific sports or any other setting. Vail (2007) and others would no doubt argue that inherent to such weighty strategy documents is an assumption by those in managerial positions that they have the expertise and experience to make effective and efficient decisions. This approach would not be condoned as a method in community development with its emphasis on involvement and empowerment. Agile strategic thinking does not manifest itself in the production of long-term plans with limited shelf lives that, in the context of inclusive sport development, only serve to reinforce the dominant, hegemonic structures which sport development is supposed to be challenging. Sport development professionals' commitment to inclusivity will be captured in their praxis. Praxis is generated through thoughtful action, such that practice is informed by a critical awareness of the social context in which it takes place (understanding how and why things happen): it is the combination of outlook and action with the underlying goal of transforming society for the better and achieving social justice. Long and Bramham (2006:136) argue that policies relating to social exclusion often tackle the symptoms and not the causes and a "simple inversion will not promote inclusion if it fails to tackle the process of exclusion". A community practice approach recognises the need to tackle the underlying issues that cause inequalities in society. This should be instinctive for CSD practitioners and an important aspiration for sport-specific practitioners and others working in sport development. A commitment to inclusive approaches will result in more flexible and responsive strategic thinking.

Greater strategic flexibility means being more sensitised not only to the needs of those we are paid to serve but to the emergent nature of the work being undertaken. A community practice approach would advocate that contextually-appropriate ways of agreeing and articulating strategic priorities are sought (although this is manifestly not always the case), in comparison to the assumption that development work should be tied to long-term goals expressed in detailed plans. For Vail (2007), a sense of control and self-determination on the part of all service users and other stakeholders is crucial. All of the above requires a commitment on the part of the practitioner to a more logically incremental approach to strategic thinking (Mintzberg and Quinn 1998) which neither expects nor requires stakeholders to align to fixed, esoteric, unrealistic plans over the long term. Instead, shared learning through experience and experimentation can lead to more appropriate outcomes. The following Volleyball England case study illustrates how this ambition can be accomplished in practice.

244

Case study: Volleyball England

The Volleyball England Strategic Plan 2009–2013 was developed on strong foundations in that the national governing body had proven its ability to deliver, having exceeded all targets in the 2008 Whole Sport Plan, and that members expressed satisfaction with all 23 services provided in survey conducted at the end of the previous strategy period. The existing strategy was reviewed and evaluated mid-term, something that Volleyball England (VE) continuously carried out throughout its lifespan so a new strategy (2013–2017) was in the process of being developed long before the end of the preceding cycle. It is evident that VE fully recognises and accepts the need to meet the requirement of funding organisations, and the chosen approach has been to work within Sport England-prescribed cycles. The appointment of a new Chief Executive Officer and the recruitment of a forward thinking Board of Directors led to a new approach and made the organisation adaptable and receptive. A new organisation with a new direction materialised and this was influenced by strong, knowledgeable characters on the Board and by visionaries and strategists within the team.

It would appear that the adopted strategy approach had both deliberate and emergent tendencies. The strategy was 'planned' in that it set explicit objectives and that the central leadership of VE controlled the method of strategy formulation, however the 'process' can be considered emergent in that the content was determined at the discretion of those making it. For example, the development of the Higher Education Volleyball Programme (HEVO) was needs-led and relied heavily on the full engagement of identified individuals with the higher education sector. This helped 'EV' to maximise and develop the natural voluntary workforce and provide students with opportunities to gain valuable experience in coaching, officiating and event organisation.

As VE is in effect a membership-led organisation it was fundamental requirement of the strategic approach that a full and detailed consultation with members took place. The VE strategy also fully engaged and directly involved specific landscape partners (Sport England, Department for Culture Media and Sport, UK Sport, Youth Sport Trust and the Volleyball Federation) and any other external organisation that would impact or influence their proposals. VE also fully utilised any available market intelligence, in particular the Active People Survey (Sport England 2012a) and Market Segmentation data (Sport England 2012b). VE strategists state that this was extremely helpful to them in that it provided solid evidence on which to justify and channel new activity, an example of which is the Go Spike programme that grew from research linked to the successful Sky Ride initiative.

The 2013–2017 strategy required a range of new interventions and initiatives based on robust evidence if increased funding was to be accessed following the 2012 Olympic and Paralympic Games. VE would no doubt seek to adapt to meet any new requirements but it would appear certain that it will retain its dual approach to strategy in order to continue to be flexible enough to respond to new circumstances and challenges. This would include engaging everyone involved in the sport in the strategic process and utilising the recognised expertise of the Board of Directors. In summing up VE's strategic approach the Development Director states "...we will always look to bring the membership with us and will constantly be looking for new ways of thinking. It is extremely important to all of us that we retain and further develop the strategic agility of the organisation."

INTERNAL ANALYSIS

As discussed in Chapter 2 it can be a thankless task in sport development to try and pin down precisely what is the organisation we are attempting to analyse, particularly if we are committed to bottom-up strategy. Strategic leaders of NGBs oversee an especially complex network of internal stakeholders and we should refrain from glibly demanding that cultural, capability and resource analysis should be undertaken in impossible levels of detail. However, it is not unreasonable to aspire towards a more thoroughgoing approach to internal analysis in both SSD and CSD with the focus on making better use of scarce resources. Despite the multiple changes in government priorities for sport, or relative lack of success in achieving participation targets, the structures of sport development units and NGBs have not significantly changed. Butcher and Robertson (2007) argue strongly that constant 'white-water change' (such as that experienced within the sport development policy arena) has left practitioners with a thankless task when trying to oversee the organisation, management and leadership of interventions. Restricted by the bureaucratic, hierarchical structures in which they work, they are often pushed into ad hoc and partial changes instead of being able to develop fit for purpose organisational strategies. The ability to free oneself from historical ways of working is a challenge for all sport development practitioners, particularly if following a community practice approach.

Vail (2007) discusses asset-based planning, which involves community leaders playing a role in identifying assets in the community and helping to structure a strategic plan around these assets in order to address an issue or opportunity. A comprehensive needs assessment involving the organisation(s) and community is required at the start of this process to help identify the assets and gaps from both perspectives (Frisby *et al.* 1997 in Vail 2007:578). The applicable National Occupational Standard, "Support the efficient use of resources" (SkillsActive 2010) emphasises, amongst many other things, the need for practitioners to "enable people to identify and communicate the resources they need" and to "develop and argue an effective case for changes in the management of resources". The adoption of a community practice approach necessitates the practitioner engaging with, and advocating for relevant members of the volunteer workforce. As Chapter 2 stresses, this requires sensitivity to organisational culture but in this case, in the spirit of consultative, bottom-up planning the definition of 'organisation' needs to accommodate layers of stakeholders beyond the paid workforce. Once again this may require a shift in mindset on the part of traditionalist sport development practitioners who see themselves as service providers and communities as customers as opposed to potential collaborators. This complexity is exacerbated by the governance arrangements for NGBs that usually involve a non-executive elected Council, Board of Governors or equivalent, and even without the mass of additional stakeholders in any given sport this seems potentially troublesome. The following Football Association case study demonstrates how a considered analysis of human, financial and material resources and capabilities can be used to achieve better outcomes.

Case study: The Football Association (The FA)

Macmillan and Tampoe (2000:232) argue that "the success of any strategy depends on the vigour with which those entrusted with its implementation carry it out." As such, the development and management of strategy requires strong leaders, and those leaders need to have a thorough appreciation of the internal environment in which that strategy will be implemented. Kelly Simmons is the Football Association's National Game Manager and responsible for leading the implementation of the The FA's National Game Strategy 2008–12. She is a firm believer in the concept of 'grip self' which refers to the need

---

for leaders to understand themselves and the situations that they face to successfully manage the internal environment.

The FA National Game Strategy covers a large number of internal and external stakeholders and clearly, consultation with all these interested parties (an approach suggested as aspirational within a community practice approach) was a real challenge when formulating the strategy. It also presented the possibility that if managed poorly, the strategy could actually be resisted by internal and external stakeholders. As Townsend (2004) discusses leaders are responsible for establishing a culture as part of an overall control framework within which employees (and stakeholders) can either provide their consent and co-operation or can engage in activities that resist managerial controls. The latter situation would clearly impact on the ability of The FA to successfully implement its National Game strategy. However, as Kelly recognised, leadership is about having a clear vision and establishing an appropriate organisation culture to enable delivery of the strategy. She also recognised the importance of getting staff 'buy-in' to the strategy so that they could feel passionate about what the 'vision' was trying to achieve. One of the ways The FA did this was to use a 'consultative approach' involving both internal and external stakeholders. For example, stakeholders such as County FAs were involved early on in the strategy formulation process to discuss the potential focus and content of the strategy, as opposed to simply being handed a draft version of the strategy to comment upon. Not only has this served to 'localise' the strategy, but it has tied in these stakeholders to a proactive culture and motivated them towards the implementation of the strategy, as opposed to the resistance of it.

This inclusive approach to strategic leadership proves that the notions of inclusivity, consultation and empowerment are achievable in strategic management, and should be aspired to for achievement of strategic objectives. Although at times decisions do have to be made which may not always have consensual support, the culture and philosophy of an organisation should espouse a genuine and authentic engagement which has at its heart the best interests of the organisation and everyone within it. Research by Colyer (2000), on a number of sports organisations, suggests that organisational culture is a huge factor in an organisation's ability to perform, deal with change and provide a good working environment for staff and volunteers.

Stephen Robson and Janine Partington

EXTERNAL ANALYSIS

Confirming the need to consider one's own praxis prior to analysing the internal and external environments, Hudson (2004) states that the three main influences on community development schemes (and as such, sport development schemes) are the practitioner factors, organisational factors and *environmental* factors. National Occupational Standard A12, "Contribute to strategic development in sport and active leisure" requires practitioners to "Monitor the external environment to identify potential opportunities and threats relevant to strategic management in your organisation" (SkillsActive 2010). By now we are well versed in the chaotic nature of the social, political, economic and related domains which seem to change on a daily basis, always with implications for NGBs and other providers of sporting opportunities. We have not said this was easy! The complexity of inclusive strategic management in sport development is aggravated by the burdens placed upon stakeholders from the external environment, for example, in the form of national targets. As we have discussed throughout the book sport is of unique interest to central government, although this attention is supported with an at best modest response in terms of resources. This means that specific demands are made, often based on a superficial understanding of the potential of sport, whilst at the same time sport is highly susceptible to the caprices of the political class and fluctuations in the economy. At least in the case of Lottery-funded NGBs, published WSP targets provide some measure of certainty as other external drivers shift perpetually.

Chapter 3 applied the STEEPLE tool for environmental scanning and throughout the book the need for flexible strategic management has been emphasised along with tools to aid strategic leaders to practise it. Strategic leaders of sport organisations cannot be expected to anticipate and respond to every nuance of external phenomena such as a world championship win, but if their strategic management is supple enough that they can observe, interpret and react quickly to unexpected events, opportunities can be seized upon and threats staved off. Can SSD practitioners borrow from CSD practice in terms of monitoring the external environment? As would be expected there is plentiful evidence of many CSD programmes being particularly responsive to *local* political, economic and social factors: for instance Partington and Totten (2012) identify the use of community representatives from social housing estates who were able to provide insights into factors affecting participation in sport and physical activity in that geographical area. Conversely, there is reason to suppose that CSD programmes, with their focus on localism, lack penetrative impact due to their lack of awareness of the external environment at national and regional level. For sustainable change to occur, it is imperative that localised programmes have an awareness of the external environment in order to anticipate and respond to changes and insulate their work from any negative repercussions at regional and national level. WSPs and other NGB strategic documents, however, are more likely to encompass an awareness of national-level drivers, reflecting the location of their authors at the apex of the governance pyramid. For example, British Rowing developed a vision that incorporates references to both the 2012 Olympics and physical activity levels; both key national drivers for sport development (British Rowing 2009). At the participation-performance nexus, the point at which the work of CSD and SSD is most likely to intersect, there would seem to be the greatest opportunity for CSD's local political 'savvy' and SSD's grasp of the bigger picture to be utilised together, leading to better informed stakeholders and clearer strategic thinking. The following Sport Leeds case study is particularly revealing in terms of the benefits of using STEEPLE in a structured manner.

Case study: Sport Leeds

Sport Leeds is the strategic partnership for people and organisations with an interest in the provision and development of sport and active recreation within Leeds (Sport Leeds 2006). Various individuals representing organisations such as West Yorkshire Sport, Leeds City Council and Leeds Metropolitan University are members of the board with each organisation being tasked with actions linked to their own organisational interest, expertise or goals. As part of a wider strategic framework Sport Leeds is part of a cultural partnership which, in turn, sits under two city-wide groups (Going up a League and Narrowing the Gap) who are responsible for leading the Vision for Leeds: a "long-term strategy for the economic, social and environmental development of the city" (Leeds Initiative 2010:nn). This complex structure, which has been based around the development and delivery of a sustainable community strategy, was a requirement of the New Labour government and demonstrates how the work of sport development professionals is inherently political (whether or not they acknowledge it) and constantly affected by changes in the external environment. In

---

250

this case, Sport Leeds must ensure it meets the demands of wider governmental strategies in order to draw down funding which supports delivery against government targets such as increasing participation. The integration of national and regional strategies is evident in the business plans of both Sport Leeds and Leeds City Council Sports Development Unit, which both reference key national drivers such as the 2012 Olympics and Active People Survey.

Despite demonstrating an awareness of national and regional drivers across a policy area broader than sport alone, the Chair of Sport Leeds (who represents the partnership on the Cultural Partnership) has no presence on the two city-wide groups who have overall responsibility for the City's community strategy. This may well hit home with lots of sport development professionals who become rightly frustrated with sport not being given the voice it deserves at the higher echelons of power despite the frequent endorsement of sport being a force for good across multiple policy areas. To overcome this issue, Sport Leeds encourages co-operation between strategic partners and through this process has been able to create a more visible and vocal presence within the City. It may not have representation at the top table, but the impact of its work has made a lasting impression on those sat around the table.

One of the most interesting aspects of the social and political influences that have developed through the Sport Leeds initiative is the emergence of five sub-groups or Local Sport Alliances (each based around a geographical 'wedge' of the city), which between them represent the whole city. Community sport officers are briefed to engage with the various communities without their 'wedge' and report back to Sport Leeds on the needs and issues within those communities. This appears to reflect the Castleford example given earlier in Chapter 3 where local people have a real voice within their community. However, despite adhering to one of the principles of a community practice approach, this has not been without issues. It requires local needs to be addressed by those on the board of Sport Leeds (even though for some of the organisations represented, this responsibility may not have been a consideration when signing up to the partnership), and is further complicated by the variety of needs expressed by Local Sport Alliances, representative of the diversity of social contexts across the city. Yet the flexibility within Sport Leeds and the emphasis on co-operative working means that a multitude of issues can be covered by the expertise of board members, and results in genuine consideration of community need at a strategic level, with subsequent strategic planning to address those needs.

Technology is becoming an area of increased interest for sport development, particularly the Internet and social networking tools due to their ability to get messages out to current and potential participants. Within Leeds, the Sports Development Unit is looking to take ownership of its own website and circumvent some of the strict guidelines imposed around the City Council's website which have restricted its ability to make the most out of this technology. Other technological advances were based around the replacement of old membership card systems that generate purely quantitative information such as attendance at centres, to more sophisticated management systems that are able to capture more detailed data and support strategic decision-making within both Leeds Sports Development Unit and Sport Leeds.

Part of the strategic decision-making aspect of Sport Leeds centres around funding. Whilst the partnership does not directly attempt to gain funding for itself, an important aspect of its work is to act as an advisory panel for organisations such as Sport England (with what was Community Investment Funding) by recommending bids, and acting as consultants to community groups to support them with the writing and development of bids. One of the interesting dilemmas facing Sport Leeds and its constituent members is that without tangible outcomes that demonstrate the usefulness of being a board member, it is difficult for members to return to their organisations and request funding to support the work of stakeholders or to establish new programmes to meet community need. Once again this highlights the resource-driven mechanisms that impact upon sport development, and which ultimately determine whether sport development work is undertaken or forgotten.

The STEEPLE analysis also encourages practitioners to consider the impact of the environment, and although it was acknowledged that energy saving takes place in leisure centres and recycling is an accepted practice within Leeds Sport Development Unit it was noted that the environmental concerns that are so prevalent in today's society are not a big factor in the decision-making processes within Sport Leeds. It was felt that the work of other officers within Leeds City Council who already have this as their full time brief would negate the need for environmental concerns to be considered directly by the partnership. Despite the current lack of emphasis on environmental concerns, there is increasing awareness within Active Leisure and Physical Activity departments of the need to consider 'green' issues, albeit not as a priority.

Legal issues such as the CRB process were acknowledged as being extremely important but also recognised as being problematic. There

Stephen Robson and Janine Partington

is a need when undertaking planning whether it is for a summer camp or for a citywide strategy to consider the legal aspect of employing staff. For example, a delay in receiving a CRB check could render a staff member being unable to start work on time thus impacting on the organisation's ability to achieve certain strategic goals. Although there are cost and time implications accompanying adherence to legal guidelines such as safeguarding and CRB processes, Leeds Sports Development Unit acknowledges both the benefit and need for such safety mechanisms to ensure the safety and well being of customers and staff. This also relates to ethical influences that permeate the working practice of sport development practitioners through various means such as Leeds City Council Corporate Guidelines, Equal Opportunities Policy, child protection acts, equity policies and codes of conduct for staff.

STRATEGIC CHOICES

The internal and external environments having been analysed, Chapter 4 discussed how strategic choices can be made which are more robust and appropriate to the needs and shared values of stakeholders. A rigorous review of the internal state of the organisation, coupled with current data on trends and issues in the external environment can lead to the production of a range of future scenarios which Lapide (2008) believes can help to navigate through an uncertain future. Korte and Chermack (2007:653) discuss the possibility of changing organisational culture through scenario planning, stating that it "facilitates self analysis and challenges an organisation's shared assumptions, beliefs and values". Plausible scenarios affecting collaborative CSD-SSD work include familiar themes such as economic recovery versus further economic downturn, political changes at state and local authority level, withdrawal of WSP funding and so on. Strategic choices need to account for those scenarios considered to rank highly in terms of likelihood and potential impact, strengthening the case for collaboration between the worlds of 'development through sport' and 'development of sport'.

What form might these shared strategic choices take? Andrews, Boyne and Walker (2006) discuss the possible actions following strategic analysis from a commercial standpoint, but such actions can be readily adapted to fit a community practice approach. The first of these is *change the target environment*, which to a CSD practitioner could mean refocusing resources in a new area of need, also a possibility for a NGB seeking to move into new markets for more representative participation. The second possible action is *change the relationship with the existing environment*. This involves an alteration to a service or the resourcing of a service within an existing setting. The third action is to *change the organisation itself* through internal restructure to meet demands of external environment. In reality some combination of these options will be arrived at with different solutions devised to meet the many challenges faced by the sport organisation. The second and third options in particular hint at the divestment of power in which NGBs (and some CSD practitioners) would need to engage in order to bring the benefits of sport to the most disadvantaged and marginalised communities (Partington and Totten 2012). This enables communities not only to influence the decisions of those dominant groups but also to act independently of them.

There is little doubt, though, that bottom-up working and actively involving the community in decision-making and planning (Frisby and Millar 2002) offers new possibilities to NGBs, local authorities and others who desire a breakthrough in mass participation and the accompanying boost to talent identification programmes. In the NGB context, for instance, it is necessary to ask to what extent were volunteers consulted and involved in agreeing the numerous, exacting Grow, Sustain, Excel targets for their sports? Paid staff need to adopt facilitator or enabler roles, shifting power relations between professionals and citizens. The Huddersfield Giants Netball Club case study will illustrate how more imaginative approaches to community collaboration can begin to yield encouraging outcomes.

Case study: Huddersfield Giants Netball Club

Strategic realignment in favour of better outcomes for communities is neatly illustrated by the case of Huddersfield Giants Netball Club. Huddersfield is the principal town of Kirklees, a metropolitan borough in West Yorkshire. In the early 2000s a netball team known as FMA (Former Members' Association) had been running for over 40 years. This provided regular, competitive play for its experienced members but offered no training. With no school-club links and no members under the age of 20 it could not be said to be contributing to either CSD or SSD and there was a distinct lack of diversity amongst the playing membership. The absence of a developmental site for the sport was recognised as a strategic priority by the Kirklees Netball

---

254

Development Officer (NDO) (hosted by the County Sport Partnership and funded through the now-defunct Active Sports programme), who therefore exercised the strategic choice to *change the target environment* (Andrews, Boyne and Walker 2006) and began to set up inner-city clubs up around Kirklees to promote community access. For FMA this necessitated a move to Kirklees Active Leisure's Huddersfield Sports Centre (KALHSC). FMA was supported by the NDO and developed sufficiently that it attained Clubmark status (a quality indicator that rewards sports clubs who "encourage young people to take-up sport, improve their talents, possibly play a leadership role and give them the option to initiate and maintain life-long participation in sport" (Clubmark 2012:nn)). This was achieved without direct NGB support from England Netball and shows that the strategic option to *change the organisation itself* was also enacted over time. An opportunity to further develop the club's strategic partnership with KALHSC was prevented due to the club needing more court time and KALHSC being unable to provide it. FMA therefore relocated to Colne Valley High School Sports Centre.

Having been unable to elicit sufficient assistance from a resource-strapped NGB for the marketing of what was now a well-established and diverse club, the radical decision was taken to pursue a strategic partnership with Super League rugby league club Huddersfield Giants in 2006. This followed an analysis of the external environment to identify opportunities and threats influencing the future development of the club. This, by implication necessitated a strategic choice to *change the relationship with the existing environment*, illustrating that all three of the strategic possibilities outlined by Andrews, Boyne and Walker (2006) were in evidence at different stages in the club's evolution. A formal agreement between the netball and rugby league Giants was created on paper but by no means does it constitute a dreaded 'glossy document'. Giants netball is now part of the rugby league Giants' 'community development' programme (whether this really is authentic community development is another discussion for another day!). The rugby league community programme (delivered by *paid* coaches) leads the way in paving relationships with schools but netball is offered and promoted (and when requested by schools, delivered by *unpaid* coaches). Giants netball is able to tap into the very strong association with the Giants name in working class communities.

As the netball club has developed, so has its strategic appreciation of the communities it seeks to engage. For instance a 'pay and play' option is included in a sympathetic pricing policy. Geographical information systems (GIS) mapping has been used to help identify key areas of deprivation to be targeted and the club has an Access Support Fund. 'Back to Netball' sessions, aimed at attracting lapsed former players are run as a way of extending access and contributing to the recreational needs of communities. The club now has over 100 members and future plans include a move back to the newly rebuilt Huddersfield Sports Centre, closer to heart of the town. One of the identified benefits of this is the opportunity to works towards higher participation amongst Huddersfield's black and minority ethnic residents. The fact that the Regional Netball Board is served entirely by volunteers illustrates the scale of the challenge to minority sports such as this, but the Huddersfield Giants story demonstrates that even with limited professional support, imaginative strategic choices can lead to positive outcomes for both the CSD and SSD agendas.

IMPLEMENTATION

As covered in Chapter 5, we have now reached the potentially daunting stage of turning ideas into actions (of course, for the purposes of clarity we are dealing with these matters sequentially but, as has been pointed out elsewhere, a flexible strategic management process involves a continuous cycle of analysis-choice-action-evaluation). Regardless of how inclusive and rigorous the above stages have been, they are rendered meaningless if not enacted successfully. Implementation in itself can be a convoluted enough task, with Getz, Jones and Loewe (2009:18) asserting that it is "both deterministic and emergent". In other words strategic leaders must strike a fine balance between programming tasks and committing resources in a decisive fashion whilst allowing for the inevitable and frequent shocks in the environment. In CSD settings a further layer of complexity is added in order to satisfy Turner's (2009) call to avoid false promises and a lack of actual action or change.

The need for close collaboration may be great during the analysis and decision-making processes but this pales against the requirement for professionals, volunteers and associated stakeholders to work together intensively during implementation. It is essential that this collaborative, bottom-up process avoids tokenistic gestures of power such as those described by Partington and Totten (2012). They warn that empowerment can be little more than an 'ideological myth' but with appropriate support communities can generate their own, alternative provision. In particular they stress the need to avoid using empowerment and capacity building as strategies to justify the withdrawal of support to communities.

Stephen Robson and Janine Partington

Whilst they may result in shifts of power (for example, community management of a leisure facility) it is important that resources such as funding are not withdrawn, for example, as a knee-jerk response to cuts. Vail (2007) argues that successful implementation requires a figurehead to be drawn from the community to oversee the initiative/scheme and bring together other community leaders to help support developments. The credibility of the strategic initiative, and hence its successful rollout, may rest upon such individuals' involvement. Although it is important to recognise the limitations of gatekeepers where a dominant hegemony can emerge within communities, there is also danger of staff-led initiatives where *a* way of doing it becomes *the* way of doing it, leading to the stagnation of services (Partington and Totten 2012).

Perhaps we have not done a great job of selling this proposition to SSD professionals, but this is no easy sell! However, there are plentiful examples of good intentions falling by the wayside, so this call for an authentic bottom-up approach to the development of sport is not for the faint-hearted. Frisby and Millar (2002) state that managerial challenges are accentuated when a community development approach is used and this is due to shared power relations, incompatible values or goals, unclear authority and communication channels and use of jargon. The difficulties of doing this work are often underestimated, resulting in conflict between statutory agencies and community partners. Practical measures to address some of these concerns include the use of job descriptions for community representatives, the establishment of a steering group, the issuing of meeting schedules and so on. Turner's (2009) study found that a community group embraced an emergent approach to achieve objectives as they were identified. The group did not subscribe to a detailed business plan but identified a set of initial goals and worked towards their own timescales, not a set imposed on them by an external partner. Vail (2007) points out that even with these ingredients in place, key individuals or organisations can be resistant to change and 'set in their ways' (e.g. club officials). It is still important for agents of community practice to involve them in analysis-choice-action-evaluation activities (even if this increases the length of time to secure a consensus). The following case study illustrates some of these principles in practice.

Case study: Leeds North East SSP Community Cricket Project

This time-limited (April 2010–July 2011) project sought to provide opportunities for young people from under-represented groups to access cricket and in so doing briefly unite the worlds of CSD and SSD. An approach was adopted "which had not been taken previously" (Leeds North East SSP 2011:1). The project's key aims were to enable more children within the Leeds North East School Sport Partnership (LNE SSP) to access cricket and, more broadly, to stimulate extra-curricular activity in community facilities. Interestingly, community development was the principal driver for this sport-specific intervention and the regional governing body (Yorkshire Cricket Board) became involved at a relatively late stage once activities were well established. Woodhouse CC, a local cricket club, which was perceived as needing help with engaging young people, was chosen as the community venue for the project. The club is located in an area of Leeds exhibiting socio-economic deprivation, but despite having a less 'leafy' image than many others it was seen as remote and unattainable to many in the surrounding community.

Implementation took place on a phased basis and took the form of a gradual handover from the project's instigators within the LNE SSP. The implementing workforce evolved in line with the progress of the project, something which needed to be anticipated at the outset and managed flexibly in line with Collier, Fishwick and Johnson's (2001) assertion that implementation and development go hand-in-hand. An initial programme of "community clubs" was established at three LNE SSP schools. One of these yielded a poor response and was subsequently cancelled. Rather than abandon the young people at this school resources were diverted towards after-school clubs that were successful in engaging young people. Eventually Woodhouse CC was able to host Saturday morning sessions to convert the interest of young people into participation at a recognised facility. The project was implemented by a diverse workforce which included the paid project leader, paid and volunteer coaches and volunteer personnel at Woodhouse CC. Throughout this process it was necessary for the project's leaders to be cognisant of the wider strategic agenda for cricket, although in effect this was retro-fitted to allow the community in the form of the young participants to set initial direction as the project rolled out.

Whilst a major part of the delivery mechanism (statutorily-funded School Sport Partnerships) was lost as a consequence of the 2010 cuts, the total expenditure for this project of £3,500 shows that such interventions need not be expensive: an amount such as this falls well within the limits of many funding pots. The call of Vail (2007), Turner

258

(2009) and others to grow community projects in a bottom-up fashion may not have been met in full by this project but live examples of the more radical aspects of CSD discussed in this and the preceding chapter are currently few and far between! Communities that are as yet unaware of the possibilities of and for sport might initially require an external stimulus. We should still derive encouragement from the project's success that work of this nature can be relatively straightforwardly replicated as a precursor to more daring CSD-SSD collaboration.

PERFORMANCE MEASUREMENT

Chapter 6 highlighted the deficiencies of many existing approaches to performance measurement and offered more rigorous and valid alternatives. In particular, practitioners attempting to apply strategic thinking to all aspects of their work, as opposed to mechanistic, cyclical, planning methodologies need to consider the meaning of 'success'. The WSP target-setting regime forces NGBs to pursue an output-driven, 'tick-box' style of evaluation which skews the focus from long-term change towards individual results which can contribute to a positive evaluation from the funder. In authentically integrated CSD/SSD settings, how can this external demand be reconciled against the pursuit of 'softer', less headline-making outcomes which may take many years to be fully realised? As Coalter (2007) puts it, what constitutes a valuable outcome? How serious are we about making a difference? If we continue to judge 'value' on the basis of numbers through the door, are we really judging whether we have made a sustainable change? Coalter argues that there are few outcomes recognised by government that are compatible with a community development approach. Partington and Totten (2012) contend that evaluation often ignores outcomes such as the development of social capital and the strengthening of community groups, both of which are crucial elements in empowering local communities and fostering participatory democracy and social justice. In his study Turner (2009) adopted a *reflective practitioner* approach due to his inability to detach himself from research on his own place of work. This involves reframing and reconstructing experiences and adapting earlier understandings of problems. We have spoken previously of praxis and critical consciousness, and here lies one of the greatest challenges to the

NGB practitioner who wishes make a real contribution to tackling social inequalities through the medium of their sport. In particular, in the first few years of a truly integrated CSD-SSD approach there may be little to report in terms of significant numbers of previously under-represented people moving from recreational participation into talent pathways, so practitioners need to hold their nerve and be smart about the performance measurement methodologies they employ.

In practical terms, Turner (2009) discusses the importance of gathering information both informally (such as conversations with local residents and shopkeepers) and formally though methods such as questionnaires and open meetings. We often hear professionals use excuses for failing initiatives along the lines of "Well, they didn't attend, so they obviously aren't interested", instead of an inquiry-based approach asking why did they not attend, what needs to change and so on? The irony of this is that these communities do not need fewer services, but often they require a different type of service that actually meets their needs. This illustrates that the only way to achieve the outcomes supposedly sought by policy-makers and practitioners at all levels of sport is to involve communities at all stages of analysis-choice-action-evaluation processes. We need to ask the right questions, in the right ways, of the right people. The following case study illustrates how, given strategic direction by a Community Sport Partnership, practitioners can engage in more meaningful approaches to programme evaluation.

Case study: County Sport Partnerships

County Sport Partnerships (CSPs) are charged with reporting data to organisations such as Sport England on a regular basis. A useful example of how individual CSPs have been able to consider the most effective way of collecting and analysing data is the data collection method for Sport Unlimited. Cheshire and Warrington County Sport Partnership (C&WCSP). C&WCSP viewed this process as one of learning given that when they started collecting data, benchmarking identified them as number 46 (out of 49) in a league table of CSPs: deliverers were being paid up front and basic monitoring identified that, from a value for money perspective most Sport Unlimited initiatives were deemed to have failed or be failing. C&WCSP decided that a more effective process was required in order to give applicants clear guidance about the monitoring and evaluation data needed to gain and maintain funding, i.e. numbers attending (targets self-set by

---

those organisations planning initiatives) should meet the target of 80%. During week three, every deliverer would be contacted to ascertain the extent to which self-set targets had been achieved. In this way C&WCSP instigated a process of 'check and challenge' against criteria agreed in the Service Level Agreement with each provider. Initiatives appeared more successful (on a value for money basis) after a three week check was implemented; this may well be due to that fact that funding was withdrawn if the self-imposed targets were not achieved – a carrot or a stick? This approach highlights the comments made by Coalter (2007) regarding how serious sport organisations are about making a difference: the focus most definitely here is on 'value' and numbers through the door.

One of the main challenges encountered by C&WCSP was the importance of numbers and the subsequent significance of value for money in relation to the public purse. Colleagues were not given time or encouragement to really evaluate the evidence that this basic monitoring process was providing. Sport Unlimited has a self-reporting mechanism whereby funding is secured on the basis of a register and associated emails of participants being provided. Money is awarded for retention, a little like performance-related pay. Longer-term evaluation was conducted by the Sport Industry Research Centre who asked questions about 'longer-term' outcomes, the feedback from which was returned to the CSP. The CSP would collate a (school) term's worth of data, in line with Sport England's requirements and then a league table of sorts developed. As stated above C&WCSP started at number 46 (out of 49) on this table but ended up reaching the number one position over three years, with targets being exceeded by 160%. The irony of this situation is that C&WCSP still does not really know the extent to which the funded initiatives have actually created sustainable change: the system does not demand that this is ascertained therefore it is not.

The CSP Network (CSPN) has a strategic overview of each CSP, of which there are 49 nationally, each of which performs and is structured slightly differently. CSPN acts as a one-stop-shop for government and organisations like Sport England and acts as the collective negotiator for all forty nine CSPs. At a county-level, business plans tend to be written by the CEO (of the CSP) and this is contract-led which ultimately impacts on the CSP's aims and objectives. This is moving closer towards a commercial sector model of operation and takes the CSP a step further away from the community. Monitoring and evaluation of the business plan is based on user satisfaction and has a very strong service focus; ironic given how the business plan is developed in the first place (i.e. without the real input of the community). Wherever colleagues can, inputs, outputs and outcomes as related to each piece of work should be identified and these aspects should be defined in the Service Level Agreement. Outcomes and impacts tend to be described much less convincingly. There appears to be a stronger focus on monitoring within the work of CSPs. There is a clear focus on outputs in relation to value for money and this is reinforced through the contract-led nature of the business plan. The contract environment is a more competitive environment with much tighter controls and CSPs now find themselves in competition with the commercial sector. The idea of procurement and commissioning is often alien to public sector colleagues and will be a new and different skill set required for future practitioners.

SUMMARY

As with the book as a whole, this chapter has encouraged practitioners and students alike to open their minds to new possibilities. The focus of this and the preceding chapter has been on approaches to inclusive sport that join up the domains of sport-specific and community sport development to a far greater extent than is currently practised. In particular this chapter has examined the ways in which better value can be extracted from resources without undermining the *raison d'être* of either SSD or CSD. You are now urged to put our ideas to the test and consider more radical, imaginative solutions to familiar issues in sport development practice. More broadly, throughout the book we have shown how generic principles of strategic management, in the literature so often applied solely to commercial settings, can be used to shed new light on the thorny problems of inclusive sport development. We have also contested some of the commonly-held assumptions around strategy and strategic thinking which have held back sport development at all levels. Whatever your current or desired role in sport you are encouraged to throw off the shackles of unimaginative, mechanistic approaches to strategic sport development. Engaging with the ideas in this book is hopefully one important step towards a better sporting deal for our most marginalised communities.

Be aware that projects that start as bottom-up, often revert to top-down as they grow in size. The challenge for managers is to ensure this does not happen or the impact of these projects on tackling community needs

Stephen Robson and Janine Partington

is often lost "...as organisational capacity to listen and respond to... priorities articulated locally" is eroded (Turner 2009:242).

Ultimately, ask yourselves, are you willing to empower individuals and community groups? The answer to this question will determine how successful your community sport development work is likely to be.

LEARNING ACTIVITIES

Developing skills

(This exercise assumes you have read all of the preceding chapters and worked through the learning activities.) Return to the analysis of skills you conducted after reading Chapter 1 and answer the following questions:

1   How accurate was your analysis of the key skills required for strategic sport development? What was missing? What does your revised list now look like?
2   What has changed in terms of your personal development needs? What do you plan to do in the short and medium terms to further improve your ability to contribute to strategic sport development (express this as a SMART action plan)?

Developing knowledge

Review the answers you gave to the questions in the *Developing knowledge* section of Chapter 1. Has your thinking about strategic thinking in sport development changed significantly? To what extent have you challenged your existing practice? What do you need to do next to continue your development as a strategic thinker in sport development?

REFERENCES

Andrews, R., Boyne, G. and Walker, R. (2006) 'Strategy content and organizational performance: an empirical analysis'. *Public Administration Review.* 66 (1), pp. 52–63.

Banks, S., Butcher, H., Henderson, P. and Robertson, J. eds. (2003) *Managing Community Practice: Principles, Policies and Programmes.* Bristol, The Policy Press.

British Rowing (2009) 'Whole Sport Plan 2009–2013'. London, British Rowing Limited.

Butcher, H. and Robertson, J. (2007) 'Critical community practice: organisational leadership and management'. In Butcher, H. and Banks, S. and Henderson, P. and Robertson, J. eds. (2007) *Critical Community Practice.* Bristol, The Policy Press.

Centre for Social Justice (2011) 'More than a game: Harnessing the power of sport to transform the lives of young people'. London, CSJ.

Clubmark. (2012) 'About Clubmark'. Available at http://www.clubmark.org.uk/about/about-clubmark.

Coalter, F. (2002) 'Sport and Community Development: A Manual'. Research Report no. 86. Edinburgh, Sport Scotland.

Coalter, F. (2007) *A Wider Role for Sport. Who's Keeping the Score?* Abingdon, Routledge.

Collier, N., Fishwick, F. and Johnson, G. 'The Processes of Strategy Development in the Public Sector'. In Johnson, G. and Scholes, K. eds. (2001) *Exploring Public Sector Strategy.* Harlow, Pearson Education.

Colyer, S. (2000) 'Organizational Culture in Selected Western Australian Sport Organizations'. *Journal of Sport Management.* 14/4 October, pp. 321–341.

English Lacrosse (2009) 'Whole Sport Plan 2009–2013'. Manchester, ELA.

Frisby, W,. Crawford, S. & Dorer, T. (1997) Reflections on participatory action research: The case of low-income women accessing local physical activity services. *Journal of Sport Management. 11*, pp.8-28.

Frisby, W. and Millar, S. (2002) 'The Actualities of Doing Community Development to Promote the Inclusion of Low Income Populations in Local Sport and Recreation'. *European Sport Management Quarterly.* 2 (3), pp. 209–233.

Getz, G., Jones, C. and Loewe, P. (2009) 'Migration Management: an approach for improving strategy implementation'. *Strategy and Leadership.* 37 (6) pp. 18–24.

Gymnastics England (2009) 'Gymnast Pathway'. Available at http://www.gymnasticsengland.org/index.php?option=com_content&task=view&id=36&Itemid=124.

Houlihan, B. and White, A. (2002) *The Politics of Sports Development: Development of Sport or Development Through Sport?* London, Routledge.

Hudson, K. (2004) 'Behind the Rhetoric of Community Development: how is it perceived and practised?' *Australian Journal of Social Sciences.* 39 (3), pp. 249–65.

Hylton, K. and Totten, M. (2008) 'Community Sports Development'. In Hylton, K. and Bramham, P. (eds) *Sports Development: Policy, Process and Practice.* 2nd ed. Abingdon, Routledge.

Korte, R. and Chermack,T. (2007) 'Changing organizational culture with scenario planning'. *Futures.* 39 (6). pp. 645–656.

Stephen Robson and Janine Partington

Lapide, L. (2008) 'Insights: scenario planning for a successful future'. *Supply Chain Management Review*. October. pp. 8–9.

Leeds Initiative (2010) 'Leeds 2030...Our vision to be the best city in the UK: Vision for Leeds 2011–2030'. Available at http://www.leeds.gov.uk/files/Internet2007/2011/30/vision%20document%20final.pdf.

Leeds North East SSP (2011) *Leeds North East SSP Community Cricket Project Report and Feedback*. Leeds, Leeds North East SSP.

Long, J. and Bramham, P. (2006) 'Joining Up Policy Discourses and Fragmented Practices: the precarious contribution of cultural projects to social inclusion?' *Policy & Politics*. 34 (1), pp. 133–151.

MacMillan, H. and Tampoe, M. (2000) *Strategic Management: Process, Content, and Implementation*. Oxford University Press.

Mintzberg, H. and Quinn, J. (1998) *Readings in the Strategy Process*. 3rd ed. New Jersey, Prentice Hall International.

Partington, J. and Totten, M. (2012) 'Community sports projects and effective community empowerment: a case study in Rochdale'. *Managing Leisure.*

SkillsActive (2010) 'National Occupational Standards for Sports Development.' Available at http://www.skillsactive.com/training/standards/level_3/sports_development.

Sport England (2012a) Active People Survey 6. Available at: http://www.sportengland.org/research/active_people_survey/active_people_survey_6.aspx

Sport England (2012b) Market Segmentation. Available at: http://www.sportengland.org/research/market_segmentation.aspx

Sport Leeds (2006) 'Taking the Lead: a strategy for sport and active recreation in Leeds 2006–2012'. Leeds, Sport Leeds.

Townsend, K. (2004) 'Management Culture and Employee Resistance: investigating the management of leisure service employees'. *Managing Leisure*. 9/1, January, pp. 47–58.

Turner, A. (2009) Bottom-up Community Development: Reality or rhetoric? the example of the Kingsmead Kabin in East London. *Community Development Journal*. 44 (2) April, pp. 230–247.

Vail, S. (2007) Community Development and Sport Participation. *Journal of Sport Management*. 21, pp. 571–596.

INDEX

Page numbers in *italic* represent information contained in a figure and page numbers in **bold** represent information contained in a table.

266

267

268